Off the
Beaten Aisle

Off the Beaten Aisle

America's Quirky Spots to Tie the Knot

Lisa Primerano

A Citadel Press Book
Published by Carol Publishing Group

A Citadel Press Book
Published by Carol Publishing Group
Citadel Press is a registered trademark of Carol Communications, Inc.

Editorial, sales and distribution, rights and permissions inquiries should be addressed
to Carol Publishing Group, 120 Enterprise Avenue, Secaucus, N.J. 07094.

In Canada: Canadian Manda Group, One Atlantic Avenue, Suite 105, Toronto,
Ontario M6K 3E7

Carol Publishing Group books may be purchased in bulk at special discounts for
sales promotion, fund-raising, or educational purposes. Special editions can be
created to specifications. For details, contact Special Sales Department, Carol
Publishing Group, 120 Enterprise Avenue, Secaucus, N.J. 07094.

Manufactured in the United States of America

10   9   8   7   6   5   4   3   2   1

Library of Congress Cataloging-in-Publication Data

Primerano, Lisa.
Off the beaten aisle : America's quirky spots to tie the knot /
Lisa Primerano.
p.   cm.
"A Citadel Press book."
ISBN 0–8065–2003–5
1. United States—Guidebooks.   2. Weddings—United States.
I. Title
E158.P94   1998
917.304'929—dc21   98–7804
CIP

To my mother, my sisters,
and to Jessica and Sylvia, Jonas and Calvin.

And to Susan O'Nell,
a true friend on life's beaten path.
May your own words boldly go
where none have gone before.

Contents

Introduction:
Birds of a Feather

"There goes my wedding!" my sisters and I would yell whenever huge flocks of birds rose up out of the cornstalks in the fields behind our house in Pennsylvania. Swooping and diving overhead in graceful arches and turns, their movements like a giant dark sheet flapping in the sky, they'd caw and screech their way out of sight, up over the hill on their way south for the winter, their cacophonous cries echoing as they went.

We wanted our future weddings to be just as beautiful and just as raucous and just as big, so every autumn whenever we heard the swoosh of birds in flight, we strove to be the first to spot the largest flock and designate it as our wedding party. Weren't we supposed to want just such huge affairs, with lots of guests flitting about en masse, everyone looking vaguely similar, everyone twittering excitedly against a backdrop as vast and dramatic as the expanse of an autumn evening sky?

As children, the thought of having anything other than a traditional wedding never crossed our minds. Give us a white dress with a train long enough to hold the entire wedding party. Give us a towering multitiered cake covered with a blanket of icing roses. Give us a mile-long strand of rackety tin cans attached to a black limo and we'd be flying high.

But as Alfred Hitchcock's *The Birds* proves, beauty often has an ugly side. What starts out small and seemingly manageable can develop into a monstrosity of epic proportions. Often requiring over a year of intense and fretful planning with costs soaring into the stratosphere—according to a recent national survey by *Bride's* magazine, the average cost of a wedding is about $17,000 [and it's higher in large urban areas]—the traditional wedding promises a lot but often delivers little.

Ceremonies are predictable and generic—the same music, the same biblical readings, the same formalities. The wedding party is so harried making sure that everything is perfect that they barely have a chance to enjoy the event or appreciate its significance. At the end of the long-awaited day, all involved in the production breathe a sigh of relief, as performers do following opening night: only in this case there's no opportunity to change or polish the proceedings—unless, heaven forbid, there needs to be a cast change down the road. For this reason, feathers can be ruffled by the smallest breeze.

For instance, my sister gasped and fumed in the vestibule of the church just before her wedding when the florist gave her her bouquet. Several ribbons of lace trim on the bouquet were white. Her dress was off-white. This was clearly a disaster of epic proportions. I thought she was going to impale the florist with the bouquet or at the very least delay the wedding until a new bouquet could be created.

All I could think to say was, "Don't worry. No one will even notice." But she glared at the bouquet in disgust. Hadn't hundreds of dollars been spent on the flowers? Wasn't this event being photographed and videotaped for posterity by a photographer who cost over a thousand dollars?

She ended up tucking the offending ribbons into the flowers, but when she threw the bouquet at the reception, she did so with excessive vigor. It shot through the air, then pitched its way toward the squealing crowd like an angry bird of prey. Woe be to any unfortunate woman in its path!

My sister's wedding was a success despite the flower fiasco, and everyone involved still speaks to each other. But unfortunately, wedding horror stories far exceeding hers befall many families: inlaws who descend like vultures to pick away at their relatives-to-be; the bride and groom, nervous and stressed out, who nag each other until they can barely tolerate the other's presence; ill-fitting, garish, expensive, never-to-be-worn-again dresses that can make bridesmaids feel like ugly ducklings and unsettle stable friendships; tacky gifts—or, worse yet, gifts never given—which compel the bride and groom to mutter, "Cheap! Cheap!" and embitter them toward their friends and relatives; and seating arrangements that often result in brawls.

The elaborate staging of tradition can be a stressful, humorless affair. But things are changing. Although the traditional church wedding is alive and well, recent trends in the wedding industry indicate that the church aisle is too constricting for some couples. Whether for religious, social, or economic reasons, a growing number of couples now choose to leave the gilded cage that is the traditional church wedding and marry in a freer, more creative, and more relaxed fashion. One way they do this is by leaving the church behind—or at least the traditional church building.

Each year, thousands of couples travel to scenic or historic locales to tie the knot. Whether held on ocean beaches, in stately mansions, or at posh resorts, these "destination weddings" prove that the sacred and significant is not necessarily found only among the wooden pews, stained glass windows, and organ music of the neighborhood church.

For some couples, though, even these weddings are a bit too mainstream. They ask themselves, "If the sacred and significant can be found at sunset on a remote Pacific beach, why can't it also be found in caves, shopping malls, and roller coaster cars; in hot air balloons, pirate ships, or the 24-Hour Church of Elvis?"

Off the Beaten Aisle describes places where birds of a truly different feather flock together to marry. It looks at reasons why couples steered away from the traditional wedding and how they believe their chosen setting contributed to the significance of the day.

Although weddings of a wacky nature have taken place

everywhere from racetracks to aerobic studios, all the sites in *Off the Beaten Aisle* have a history of couples marrying there; they are not places unique to one particular couple.

But just because a wedding isn't held in a traditional setting doesn't mean that it lacks traditional elements or that it is simple—the price of a Magic Kingdom wedding at Disney World can look like the budget for a Disney film. It does mean that the couple has given serious consideration to how a particular place will reflect their personalities, their spiritual beliefs, and the love they feel for each other. It just so happens that a lot of places couples choose reflect the idiosyncratic nature of Americans when faced with one of the most important commitments in a person's life.

Who knows, maybe the next time I visit one of America's wedding caves and see several bats dip and swoop through their dank subterranean home, I'll quietly declare, "There goes my wedding!"

Off the
Beaten Aisle

1

Love in the Fast Lane

From the *Mayflower* to the Oregon Trail to Route 66 to the Information Superhighway, Americans have had a love affair with personal freedom and the open road. Refusing to believe that marriage ties people down, many couples tie the knot either while in motion or at a site related to travel and the quest for adventure.

Since dogs are man's best friend, some couples include them in the wedding plans and head to the Wyoming hill for a dogsled wedding arranged through Teton Mountain Weddings in Jackson, Wyoming. After mushing twenty-two miles alongside frozen streams in the Gros Ventre mountain range, couples change clothes in a tiny rustic cabin and marry alongside the steaming vapor of Granite Hot Springs.

Lovers of the open road get their kicks on Route 66, but lovers who wed at Read Ranch in Chandler, Oklahoma—just off the famous highway—hope the horses upon which they recite their vows won't be doing any kicking. Following a horseback wedding at this guest ranch's scenic Cowboy camp, couples ride to the Flying Spur Saloon for an evening of entertainment with staged gunfights and cowboy singers.

Couples eager to jump right into marriage head to Las Vegas for a Take the Plunge Bungee Jump Wedding arranged through Wedding Dreams. Up to twenty guests join the couple and the minister at the top of a 175-foot tower. Once married, the couple take the ultimate leap of faith as they fall and bounce and swing through the Vegas sky.

The Reverend C. Edward Linville of Portland, Oregon, was so spiritually in tune with his 1967 Chevy Bellaire that he turned it into a wedding chapel on wheels. Thus was born Mobile Unit #1 of Our Lady of Eternal Combustion. Also a refuge for once-worshiped toys and memorabilia, this outrageously decorated "art car" has been the site of Linville's "McMarriages." After eating their Little Debbie wedding cake, couples on the go are presented with their marriage certificate complete with "Time In" and "Time Out" sections.

Cynics would say that once a couple marries, it's all downhill. For couples who wed on skis in the mountains surrounding Taos, New Mexico, this is undeniably true. Marisha Breslow, owner of Marisha's Magic Carpet in Taos, gets a high from marrying couples on the snowy slopes of Taos Ski Valley resort at an altitude of nearly twelve thousand feet. Everything from the cake to the couple arrives via ski lift to the snow-capped wedding site. Couples who prefer water to snow can head to Taos in the summer and have Marisha lead a white-water-rafting wedding down the fabled Rio Grande.

As the following additional modes of locomotion show, love knows no limits when it comes to driving, flying, soaring, sailing, floating, or coasting to the state of wedded bliss.

Wedding Dreams' New Beginnings Skydive Wedding
LAS VEGAS, NEVADA

The woman who created Anita Schuler's bridal headpiece—a hair barrette with silk roses—secured the flowers with heavy-duty amounts of glue and tape. After all, it had to withstand speeds up to 170 miles per hour.

Anita, however, never got a chance to put the sturdy barrette to the test. When she and her husband, Mike, arrived at the airport in Boulder City, Nevada, for their wedding, she found

Anita Schuler and her jumpmaster in space

that the barrette would not fit under the standard-issue helmet and goggles. This was fine with her. After all, when you're jumping out of an airplane twelve thousand feet above the desert, wedding fashion takes a backseat to safety. And when you're jumping out of an airplane immediately after you pledged to live the rest of your life with someone, you want that life to be a long one.

While many people's hearts leap about nervously at the mere thought of jumping from an airplane, let alone doing so on their wedding day, it couldn't compare with the stress that Anita and Mike Schuler of Mesa, Arizona, felt when planning a traditional wedding with family and friends. They had planed to have a "normal" chapel wedding in Las Vegas. Anita had even bought a special dress for the affair, but several months before the ceremony she and Mike began to lose control of the guest list.

"All of a sudden the whole world was going to be there," says Anita, a stay-at-home mother who met Mike, an auto mechanic, at a neighbor's house. "We felt like we had to entertain everyone, even people who didn't get along."

Stressed out and insecure, Anita turned to Mike one evening and said, "I don't even know if you want to marry me."

"I do want to marry you," Mike said. "In fact, I want to marry you right now. Let's elope and get married this weekend." With that, they immediately dropped their plan for a chapel wedding, got on the Web, read about skydive weddings in Las Vegas, loved the idea, made plans in the middle of the night, and left the next day, all set to tie the knot in a twenty-seat passenger jet, then tie on a parachute and jump to the desert below.

"We both had always wanted to skydive," says Anita. "We like to try new things, so we were really excited about the idea. We weren't nervous at all."

"We could've eloped to Vegas and still gotten married in a chapel, something more traditional, but that's what everybody does," says Mike. "We thought a skydive wedding would be more fun and more memorable."

Mike and Anita's mothers were worried that the memory of Mike and Anita was all they would have after they took the plunge. "My mother was absolutely terrified about us skydiving," says Anita. "That's why we didn't invite her along. I could never have skydived in front of my mother and my children. They would've been scared for me. She was also mad that we were eloping, period."

"My mother thought a skydive wedding was crazy," says Mike. "She called up Anita and said, 'I thought you had more sense than he did.'"

Because Mike and Anita made their plans on such short notice, they didn't have time to dwell on their mothers' reactions, but Anita's children did cause her to think ever so briefly about their daring service. "My seven-year-old daughter looked at me and said, 'Mom, you could get hurt,' and I thought, Oh my God! What am I doing?"

Even though Mike and Anita weren't quite sure what to expect, wedding coordinator Jodi Varey was. Owner of Wedding Dreams, Varey arranges weddings in a variety of Las Vegas chapels and settings. When arranging a skydive wedding she works with Skydive Las Vegas in nearby Boulder City, which helps seven thousand people every year make first-time jumps.

"For a skydive wedding, all the jumps are tandem jumps, which means that each person jumps with a certified jump master," says Varey. "They're not out there jumping on their own. Of all the skydive weddings I've arranged, it's always been the couple's first jump. It's something they've always wanted to do."

A $1,650 New Beginnings Skydive Wedding includes a minister, two cameramen—one to photograph and videotape the bride as she floats through space, one to do so for the groom—jump masters, and use of a limousine for five hours. The only thing a couple has to bring is something comfortable to wear and tennis shoes.

The Schulers arrived in Las Vegas in the middle of the night. The next day the limousine picked them up at their hotel, and they were off to Boulder City. "Our driver was wonderful," says Anita. "He couldn't believe what we were doing. Even though Jodi called him on short notice, he said he washed his biggest and best limousine for us and bought us a bottle of champagne. He kept asking, 'Are you sure you want to do this? Aren't you scared?' He was nervous for us."

The first step for any couple about to take the plunge is to watch a video at the airport that shows what to expect on the jump. "At the end of the video, it says there is always the possibility that you'll be injured and even die," says Anita, "and we had to sign release forms saying they wouldn't be responsible in case of injury or death, so it does go through your mind that something could happen. But they really seemed to know what they were doing, so we weren't scared.

"The only thing they didn't show in the video was how you're supposed to land. I was kind of nervous about that. I kept asking my jump master about the landing, but he only said, 'I'll take care of it. All you have to do is enjoy the jump.'"

As for the wedding attire, the Schulers were given cotton jump suits to put on over their shorts. "Even before we planned the skydive wedding I kept joking with Anita that I was going to get married in a tank top and shorts," says Mike, "and she kept saying, 'There's no way you're going to get married to me in shorts and a tank top.'" He laughs. "But in the end, I basically got married in shorts and a tank top."

"I'm still in shock that I got married in shorts and tennis shoes," says Anita. "I'm glad the jumpsuit they gave me to wear was bright purple. I thought if I had to wear shorts for my wedding, I was at least going to wear a purple jumpsuit. And then there was the helmet and these goofy-looking eye goggles."

Once airborne in the small passenger jet, the minister began the ceremony. "He's a pilot himself," says Anita, "so he thought what we were doing was cool. He wore a shirt and tie. He was dressed up for all of us."

"There were two benches lining the sides of the airplane," says Mike. "We sat on one side and the minister sat on the other, but we were so close our knees were touching. It was also really noisy. He was talking really loud, but it was still hard to hear him."

"We were so excited," adds Anita. "I kept thinking, Oh my gosh, we're in this plane, about to get married. We heard what the minister was saying, but we weren't really paying attention. I just wanted to look out the window, and the minister kept going on and on, and Mike and I were going, 'Un-huh, un-huh.' It wasn't until we watched the video at home that we really got it all. He related the service to what we were doing. He said, 'When you jump out of this plane, you're making a big commitment. You're going to fall to the ground, but you're not going to fall to the ground in your marriage.'"

Anita and Mike did make one concession to their mothers' fears while in the air. "We're not really religious," says Anita, "but when the minister asked if we wanted him to say a prayer, we thought, Well, we are just about to jump out of an airplane. My mother would've killed me if we didn't say a prayer, so he prayed that we'd be kept safe while jumping."

Immediately after Mike and Anita were pronounced husband and wife they found themselves clinging not to each other but to their respective jump masters. Large metal hooks and tight straps keep the jump master securely attached behind the jumper and in control of every aspect of the jump. Once set to go, Mike, Anita, their jumpers, and cameramen made their way to the open door, braced themselves against the gushing wind as they soared through the air twelve thousand feet above the earth, and readied themselves for their lovers' leap.

"I looked at Mike and said, 'Okay, I just married you, now see you later.' My cameraman jumped, and then I jumped right after him. He took pictures of me as I floated, then he dropped quickly to the ground to videotape me as I came down."

"When Anita jumped out, she just went *woosh* and was gone," says Mike. "I thought, Holy moly, where did she go? You think you're going to float, but you go straight down in a free fall at around 170 miles per hour for about a mile before you release the parachute. I said to my jump master, 'If she dies you better just cut me and let me drop to the ground because her mother will kill me.'"

Once floating through the air, Mike and Anita were quite literally almost in heaven. "When you first jump out, it's hard to breathe," says Anita. "It's like gasping for air. I thought, Oh my God, I'm going to pass out and not enjoy this, but if you take slow deep breaths, you're fine. Then you release the parachute and just float. That part was wonderful. It was like being a bird just flying around. It was so quiet, and you could see Vegas, and Boulder City, and Lake Mead, and the mountains. You could see everything. I didn't want it to end."

"I felt the same way," agrees Mike, "but I was strapped so tight I felt my legs were starting to go numb. My jump master was a joker. He said, 'Good. You won't feel them when you fall to the ground and break them!'"

Despite Anita's initial concern with the landing, it went smoothly and easily; catchers are on the ground to steady jumpers when they land. "I was so excited," says Anita. "I went over and gave my cameraman a big hug and said, 'Let's do it again!' We also called our parents to let them know we survived."

Their limousine driver also couldn't control his excitement.

"He ran over and took pictures," says Anita. "He said, 'I can't believe you did that!' It was like he was our brother. Once we got back in the limo, we were tired. It was an emotional rush, and I was getting all black and blue from the straps, so we went to the grocery store and got some rum and coke and had our driver ride us around Vegas. He thought we were some kind of crazy people and asked if we wanted to go bungee jumping next."

The next day Mike and Anita walked around Vegas in shocking honeymoon attire—bright neon T-shirts that read Shut Up and Jump. "People were shocked enough when we told them we went skydiving," says Anita. "When we told them we got married right before, they were like, 'You did what??!!'"

When the couple returned safely to Arizona, their families were actually quite thrilled with what they had done. "My mother calls me her 'little skydiver,' and my kids love watching the video," Anita says. "It really was a wonderful and romantic experience. We were going to do this totally outrageous thing and we didn't know what to expect. Sometimes people think just because you're a mom you shouldn't try new things, but I can't wait to go again."

Falling in love has always been a heady adventure, a leap of faith into uncharted territory. Happily, Mike and Anita's wedding-day dive into the mapless sky landed them firmly on cloud nine.

Wedding Dreams / 800-2-WED-N-LV
www.weddingdreams.com

Vows' Drive-Through Wedding

DAVIE, FLORIDA

When Karen Emery converted a fast-food restaurant in Davie, Florida, into a tasteful wedding chapel called Vows: A Wedding Establishment, she didn't fold up the restaurant's drive-through window. Instead, Emery converted it into a drive-up wedding window catering to couples with a distinctly different taste in marriage.

While couples ordering off the menu choose a traditional ceremony in Vows' elegant indoor chapel, those preferring more daring fare pull up in their car to the sliding glass window to order their value wedding on wheels. It's truly love in the fast lane.

"Since we opened in March of 1997 we've had couples come through on Harleys, John Deere tractors, pick-up trucks, convertibles, bicycles, a horse and buggy, and a boat," says Emery. "One couple had their kids coming before them on bicycles as the ring bearer and flower girl. We also have a limousine available for couples who don't want to get married in their beat-up old car."

Like any other drive-through service in convenience-hungry America, a drive-through wedding is quick and easy. Couples pull up to the window, pay their seventy-five dollars, get married, receive their complimentary wedding cupcake, and head back into the traffic that courses up and down State Route 84 with its strip malls and shopping centers. Couples wishing to linger over the experience can go inside for a glass of champagne on the house.

With the famous twenty-four hour drive-up wedding window at the Little White Chapel in Las Vegas already there to satisfy a couple's craving for a marriage to go, what drives couples on Florida's east coast to leave tradition by the wayside, flip down their sun visor, and pull up for some noontime nuptials?

"Most of the couples who come to our drive-through window live in the area," says Emery. "We do about two to three wedding a week. They're people who don't want a big shindig, who don't want to be the center of attention. It's not always about the money. We've had couples pull up with huge diamond rings."

Pat and Dennis Melegari of Davie were one of the first couples to sample a drive-through wedding on Vows' opening day. Rather, the Melegaris had a trot-through wedding—they got married in an antique horse-drawn surrey.

"We have a Jeep Cherokee, but we wanted to get married in something more fun than that," says Pat, who met Dennis through their jobs with the city of Davie. "Davie is a western theme town, so we thought marrying in the horse and buggy would be a good idea."

Drive-through windows cater to spontaneous people on the go. Dennis and Pat were no exception. "We saw an article in the paper on Wednesday telling about the opening of the drive-up window that Saturday," explains Pat. "Our friends told us they thought we should get married there, and we decided to go for it. We thought it'd be unique and funny. We'd already been looking for someplace easy and simple to get married, and since weddings were free on opening day we couldn't go wrong with that."

"A drive-through wedding was right up my alley," says Dennis. "I'm kind of a nutball. Pat's more traditional than I am, so I'm surprised she did it. But both of us had already been through a traditional wedding. I don't think your second wedding should be traditional. You've already broken the tradition by being divorced. We're also not the traditional googly-eyed types who gaze into each other's eyes at a candlelit wedding ceremony. I'd be more embarrassed by something like that. If we had to stare into each other's eyes we'd bust out laughing."

On Vows'opening day, Dennis in his suit and tie and Pat in her white dress showed up for their big treat. Their children Brad, eleven, and Brianna, thirteen, also came along for the ride. They parked their Jeep, got into the horse-drawn black buggy that was waiting in the parking lot, and pulled around to the wedding window, down Vows' Tunnel of Love. Because it was opening day, they were met by a throng of photographers eager to sample the event.

"When we got to the window, a photographer's camera spooked the horse and it started bucking up," says Pat. "I could just see myself flipping over in back of the buggy. The driver had to settle the horse down, back up, and go through again. On the news, they said the horse was the nervous one."

But once the horse was calm, the wedding took place as

ordered. "They just slide open the window like you're ordering food and start saying the vows," explains Pat.

"About fifty of our family and friends gathered in the parking lot to watch," says Dennis. "They all cheered. A lot of cars out on the street also slowed down to watch."

Some of those passersby even stopped in at the opening-day reception. "This couple we didn't even know came up to us, threw their arms around us, and said, 'We're just passing through, but can you take our picture in case you're in any magazines?'" says Pat. "So we all just stood there grinning getting our picture taken with these strangers."

Some of Dennis and Pat's family members, however, were a little more concerned about the media coverage. "When my five-year-old granddaughter saw us on TV, she thought we were going to jail," remembers Dennis. "She was worried. She associated the news with being arrested."

Once the opening-day fanfare was past, drive-through weddings at Vows were decidedly more low key, which is exactly what Anna and Daniel Moynihan of Fort Lauderdale wanted. "You can't have a traditional wedding without things going wrong, without being told what to do by a bunch of people who don't know you," says Anna, who works for a mortgage broker. "I used to work in the printing business and I'd see couples fighting from the very beginning over the invitations and I'd wonder if they'd ever make it to the wedding. It's something I never wanted. Even my first wedding was just held before a notary."

"Our wedding was just an 'us' thing, not an 'everybody in the world' thing," says Daniel, who works in the marine industry and who met Anna through a friend. "The drive-through wedding was my idea. We're private people and didn't want all the fuss. It was different, but it was also quick and easy. It took us all of an hour to plan, arrange, execute, and be done with and move on."

"A drive-through wedding sounded fine to me," says Anna. "I'm real flexible. Since Daniel had never been married before, I kind of let him do what he wanted. I just didn't want it to turn into a 'wedding.'"

There was little chance of that happening. Anna and Daniel told only their families they were marrying. "My mom thought it was funny," says Anna. "But my family loves Daniel, so anywhere would've been fine."

With two cars to choose from, Anna and Daniel decided to marry in her 1995 Ford Ranger pickup. "I had a cooler truck than she did," explains Daniel, "but it's bigger, and longer, and harder to maneuver around corners."

Couples dressing for a drive-through wedding don't want seat belts crushing their corsages, so comfort is key. "I just wore a plain white dress," says Anna, "something real comfortable, something I could move in. Daniel wore jeans, boots, and a button-down shirt."

For lovers on the go, it's often hard to stick to a schedule. "We didn't know what time we were going to get married," says Anna. "The people at Vows just told us to give them a call before we left home." The Moynihans ended up giving Vows a call directly from the drive-up window. "They didn't see us pull in, so we called them from our cell phone to let them know we were waiting."

It turned out, however, that Anna and Daniel had to make a last-minute detour before the ceremony. "When we got to the window, we realized we didn't have any rings," says Daniel. "The ones we ordered from the jeweler weren't ready yet, so we pulled over to this party supply store and bought a package of plastic party favor rings, the kind five-year-old girls play with. They were these big old obnoxious chrome-plated plastic rings with big colorful fake jewels. We got a packet of six for only $1.89. Only in America! Anna picked a pink one to match her lipstick, and I picked a green one to match my eyes. Of course, they didn't fit, so I had to heat 'em up with a Bic lighter and stretch 'em out a bit. We resized them right there in the truck."

Armed with their $1.89 wedding bands, Anna and Daniel pulled around again to the window. "The ceremony was very nice," says Anna. "I had tears in my eyes. Afterward, they gave us our cupcake and a receipt that said 'Drive-Through Wedding,' and we drove off."

"It was romantic because it was just the two of us," says Daniel. "It was tight and compact."

"Maybe years down the road, we'll renew our vows in a church," says Anna. "We are religious, but since Daniel's Catholic and I'd been married before, a drive-through wedding was right for us right now. Doing it this way also says that I make my own choices. I don't care what people think. But all our friends were happy for us. We got nothing but positive responses."

Although a drive-through wedding might not be everyone's cup of tea, couples who relish experimenting with the standard wedding recipe find it a satisfying alternative.

Vows: A Wedding Establishment
9170 State Route 84, Davie, Fla. 33324
954-472-1186 / www.aweddingforyou.com

Reverend Cliffert Herring's Roller Coaster Weddings

During his years in seminary, the Reverend Cliffert Herring, Jr., pastor of St. John's United Church of Christ in Northampton, Pennsylvania, had to ponder some tough philosophical questions about the nature of God. There's one question the world's great theologians never raised, though, yet it's a question Herring's come to ponder in his ministerial career: Would God look favorably on a roller coaster wedding?

Despite his lack of formal study of the topic, Herring's formed his own heartfelt opinion. "There's great meaning in getting married on a roller coaster," he firmly says. "I don't think it trivializes the ceremony at all. It shows that the couple knows what they want and that they have a sense of fun. A wedding on a roller coaster combines the joyous aspect of life with the seriousness of commitment. I think God has an incredible sense of humor that the church often fails to recognize."

If God is not amused, he's done nothing to discourage Herring from marrying couples on coasters. Since officiating at

The Phoenix roller coaster at Knoebel's Amusement Resort in Elysburg, Pennsylvania

his first coaster wedding on the Thunder Road at Carowinds near Charlotte, North Carolina, in 1985, Herring has married couples on coasters throughout the United States. "I've married couples in everything from shorts and T-shirts to full traditional attire," says Herring. "The bride just needs to make sure she straps her veil on extra tight. I usually sit in the car in front of the couple. We stop at the top of a hill, and I turn around to perform the ceremony. Some parks don't like me to stand up, so I twist around or kneel on the seat. The trickiest part is the ring exchange. If you drop a ring, you drop a ring. It's a long way down."

Herring's even 'branched out' and performed weddings on other rides. When Six Flags Great America in Gurnee, Illinois, introduced its new Giant Drop freefall ride, it called upon Herring to officiate a group wedding of one hundred couples about to take the ultimate plunge. After marrying them in the show arena, Herring pronounced each couple husband and wife over the public address system as they rose twenty-two stories to the top of the drop, then fell toward earth at sixty-two mph.

Herring himself has ridden on about 250 different coasters and is a faithful member of American Coaster Enthusiasts (ACE), an organization devoted to the appreciation of the coaster. It's not hard to find other people seriously committed to the coaster and eager to extol its virtues—ACE boasts over five thousand members. These are people who make passionate pilgrimages to coasters, who reverently stand in line for hours on end, again and again, for the fleeting minute when fear is fun, when terror leads to transcendent revelations about the joy of existence.

Given coaster lovers' fervent, almost spiritual devotion to these graceful structures, it should come as no surprise that coaster-loving couples choose to wed on them. Lisa and Vernon Zweifel of Palmerton, Pennsylvania, could think only of the highs associated with a roller coaster wedding. "We were seventy-eight feet closer to God," says Vernon, an airport maintenance technician who wed Lisa on the Phoenix, a classic wood coaster at Knoebel's Grove Amusement Resort in Elysburg, Pennsylvania.

"Our wedding shows we're prepared to face all the ups and downs of life," explains Lisa, a buyer for a department store, who met Vernon through a dating service. "Joining our two families together from previous marriages was the biggest challenge. Getting married on a roller coaster shows that we have a good outlook on life and that we're not afraid to face this challenge."

"I've always liked the thrill and suspense and the speed of roller coasters," says Vernon. "I knew I wanted to do something exciting for our wedding, something the kids would love and remember. I suggested to Lisa that we get married either skydiving or on a roller coaster."

"It's kind of hard to wear a dress skydiving," Lisa points out, "so we decided on the roller coaster. I've always enjoyed coasters, and since we're members of Cliff's church, we knew he'd perform the ceremony. We decided on Knoebel's Grove because it's a lovely old park with a lot of rides for kids, and the Phoenix is rated one of the ten best wood coasters in the world."

According to Herring, one of the biggest challenges of a roller coaster wedding is convincing older family members that the wedding can still be meaningful even if it's not held in a church. "Lisa's grandmother was hesitant at first," says Vernon, "but after the wedding, she couldn't stop talking about it. My father also reacted kind of negatively at first. He's terrified of coasters, and he'll let everyone know it. But after the wedding when all the newspaper and TV reporters were interviewing him, he suddenly thought a wedding on a roller coaster was a great idea! He even hinted that it was his idea!"

But older family members weren't the only ones with the jitters. "During rehearsal, we took our older kids on the coaster," says Lisa. "We told them it was going to stop at the top of the hill, but when we got up there, my eight-year-old daughter, Amber, started screaming, 'Get me off of here!' I kept telling her, 'Honey, you can't get off now. You'd have to walk down the stairs.' She eventually calmed down, but our other kids loved it."

Come the big day, Lisa and Vernon didn't have to worry about waiting in line for the Phoenix, as they married several hours before the park opened to the public. Lisa wore an ivory-colored tea-length lace dress, and Vernon wore a 1940s-style suit. The proceedings began with a procession from the park entrance to the platform of the Phoenix. Their 150 guests gathered around the platform and sat on the many park benches.

After Lisa and Vernon presented flowers to their mothers and grandmothers on the platform, they climbed aboard the bright orange coaster emblazoned with the mythological phoenix rising from its flaming ashes. Even thought it was their wedding day, they did not get the cherished first car. This was reserved for the photographer and the cameraman. Reverend Herring took the second car, while Vernon and Lisa sat in the car behind him.

"Needless to say, Amber didn't ride with us the day of the

wedding," says Lisa. "After what happened with her, we had our best man and maid of honor split up and ride with the kids in the two cars behind us just in case the kids got scared. Then we had our attendants and other guests in the rest of the cars. Our parents were scared of the coaster so they didn't ride. It was hard to select who was going to ride with us, but we had a TV on the platform and one out among the guests, so everyone could still see the ceremony. The kids were so excited, they were ready to jump out of their pants."

Then, with the giddy expectancy of a thrilling roller coaster ride coupled with the nervous expectancy of the marriage ceremony, Lisa and Vernon were off to become riding partners for life. The Phoenix shot through a dark tunnel before making the lurching climb, inch by inch, up the steep wooden incline.

"I couldn't believe it," says Lisa. "The cameraman was leaning way out of the front car to get pictures. Meanwhile, another cameraman had climbed up the narrow wooden flight of stairs along the tracks to take pictures of us as we came up the hill. When we stopped at the top of the hill, Cliff took off his safety bar, stood up, and turned around to do the ceremony. All around you could see the Blue Mountains. It was a sunny day in May and it was just gorgeous."

"We had microphones on, so our vows were miked all over the park," remembers Vernon. "After the ceremony, everyone went wild. We were all yelling and screaming. Cliff said, 'Let's count to three and all wave down to everyone on the ground.' When we did that, they all screamed. And then we were off on the ride."

"When we pulled in after the first time through, we were all screaming, 'Keep going! Keep going!'" says Lisa. "They hardly even slowed it down; we just kept going. I was surprised the headpiece I wore stayed on after that second time around. When we got off the coaster, there were so many reporters there. It took us almost an hour to get back to our guests, but it was so much fun. Everyone was hugging and kissing us, and our kids just loved it. They still talk about it and take pictures to their teachers."

If joy is any indication of God's blessing, then the Zweifels were blessed in abundance on their wedding day, a sign, most assuredly, that God was greatly amused.

The Rev. Cliffert Herring
943 Lenape Circle, Catasauqua, Penn. 18032
(no set fee)

Balloon Adventures of New Bedford's Hot-Air Balloon Wedding

SOUTH DARTMOUTH, MASSACHUSETTS

David Gifford has flown his balloon over the Italian Alps. He's flown over the verdant vineyards of France and the snowy, imposing pinnacle that is Mont Blanc, but he believes that nothing can compare with flying over coastal Rhode Island and Massachusetts at the point where the hills of New England disappear into the vast Atlantic sea.

"The *New York Times* called this piece of coastline one of the most spectacular and unspoiled of the eastern seaboard," says Gifford, owner of Balloon Adventures of New Bedford, in South Dartmouth, Massachusetts. "Flying over it produces a feeling similar to flying over the dramatic cliff drops of the Alps. You get the sense of there being a brink, a point where the safety of the land disappears and the ocean begins. You can swoop down and pick flowers out of fields, then skim the waves of the ocean, but as you climb, you get this expansive, spectacular feeling as you're out over the water. And then there's the screaming silence. You can't get it out of your mind."

Apparently neither can the couples who cast their fate to the wind and allow Gifford to carry them five thousand feet heavenward to tie the knot. "Sometimes a couple gets so caught up in the scenery that I have to remind them what they're up there for," he says.

But it's not just the bird's-eye view of crashing Atlantic surf, white sand dunes, salt marshes, offshore islands, flowering

Diana and Sam Wiley about to launch

meadows, and grand country estates that enthralls couples. It's the singular experience of ballooning. In a fast-paced world where the insistent blips and beeps of technology command immediate attention, it's a humbling and serene experience to drift at five miles per hour above the earth in a straw basket subservient to the call of the winds in a world of airy and expansive silence.

"All your senses can be maxed out till they burst," says Gifford. "What actually is so hard to describe is the silence and the freedom of sensation. You don't feel yourself rising or falling. The earth just changes perspective below you. People tell me that the experience is indescribable, that everyone ought to be required to take a balloon flight at least once in their lifetime."

It's this once-in-a-lifetime feeling that compels couples to celebrate their wedding, a day of a lifetime, in a balloon. Ceding control to the elements, however, can be unsettling for some.

"One time the best man panicked and said, 'I'm not getting on that thing,'" says Gifford. "He did get on, and after the flight he was the most adamant in saying that he would definitely do it again."

A pilot can control where the balloon flies, but the winds have the final say as to whether the balloon can launch as planned. "There's always a good chance a flight won't take place," says Gifford, who charges $750 for the airy nuptials, "especially here on the coast where weather patterns aren't as stable as in some parts of the country. I tell couples that on the wedding day they need to be prepared to fly either at sunrise or sunset because that's when the weather is most predictable. I also let them know that they might not be able to go up that day at all. A lot of couples don't want to take the risk, but I usually end up doing several weddings a year. It's always a happy assignment for the minister."

Diana and Sam Wiley traveled from San Marcos, Texas, to take that risk. "We always wanted to see the fall colors of New England, so we planned to get married while vacationing there," says Sam, a mining engineer, who met Diana, a sales representative for Pitney Bows, while they were vacationing in Mexico. "We'd both been married before, so we wanted to do something different. Neither of us had ever been ballooning, so getting married in a balloon seemed exciting."

"Sam suggested it, and I thought it was a great idea," adds Diana. "We're both adventurous people. David was the most enthusiastic person we talked to, so we decided to marry in his balloon. Our friends and family were also excited, but they kept asking us, 'Aren't you scared?' My mother really worried about whether it was safe, but I think unless you're scared of heights, there's nothing to worry about."

When Sam and Diana arrived in Massachusetts in October, the one thing they did worry about was whether the breezy weather would allow them to wed on the day they had planned. The dark predawn hours are a crucial time for couples planning a balloon wedding. It's then that Gifford decides whether conditions are right for the balloon to launch at sunrise.

"David told us that if we didn't hear from him at four-thirty in the morning, we'd have to plan the wedding for sunset," says Diana. "He didn't call that morning, so we had to wait around all day to see whether conditions would be okay at sunset. I was getting a little worried because I had had Sam's wedding ring inscribed with the date, so I was really hoping it would work out. When David called later that day and said, 'Let's do it,' we were so excited. After we were married, he told us that he did have an alternate plan—the minister would've married us in a church steeple, some place as high up as possible."

Just getting to the launch site was an adventure. The minister, Gildon Stillings, picked Diana and Sam up at their bed and breakfast and drove them along country roads to a local sheep farm that had enough field space to lay out the balloon. "We were bouncing in his car over these hills," says Diana, laughing. "We had no idea where we were going."

"Most people going into a traditional wedding are worried about so many little things, like whether they're dressed right," says Sam. "We were so lost in the excitement of thinking about the balloon ride that we didn't worry about details."

There were many details to attend to, however, before they launched—namely, getting the balloon inflated. Diana in her off-white wool pantsuit and Sam in his suit and tie helped David unfold his multicolored striped balloon—named *Talani* after his two daughters Tala and Lani—and inflate it for their journey. Once David gave them some landing instructions—how to brace themselves and how to lean—there was no place to go but up.

At 5:30 P.M. on an October evening in New England, as the setting sun intensified the reds and golds of the autumn leaves, Diana and Sam stepped into Gifford's colorful balloon and started rising into the dusky blue sky.

"As we were taking off, people from nearby houses were calling to us, 'Don't get cold feet!' and "Where's the reception?'" says Diana. "We were hollering back to them. We were so giddy! The balloon ride was so smooth, it felt like we were floating. We almost didn't notice we took off. Once we got up we could see for eighty miles all around us. We could see Martha's Vineyard and Cape Cod and the sun shining off the buildings in Boston. It was so exciting. Everyone in the balloon was yelling, 'Look! Look!' at everything around us. We almost forgot for a minute what we were up there to do."

"We rose up for about a mile," adds Sam. "It was so quiet. When you're on the ground you can hear the wind, but when you're in the balloon you're moving with the wind so you don't hear it. Then we went right up through these clouds. Emerging out of the clouds was incredible. It was like we were sitting on bunches of cotton with orange and yellow and golden sunshine reflecting off the clouds. Everything was golden-hued. It was very heavenlike."

"The minister suggested we do the ceremony above the clouds," says Diana. "He was wonderful. He offered a prayer that the winds would be kind to us and that our spirit of love and adventure would take us far. It was a beautiful event. We were totally encompassed by clouds and beauty. We felt very near God up in heaven."

After the couple spent about an hour in the air, darkness set in and it was time to find a place to land. "The only time I worried was when it came time to land," says Sam. "You have to land in an open area. As it was getting darker we were floating over a sea of trees, and I kept hoping we'd see an open spot before it was completely dark. I didn't want to land in the water or in the middle of all those trees and get swatted in the face with limbs."

The wedding party didn't land in water or the woods, but they did swoop down over a river and land in someone's backyard. "The yard we landed in belonged to a man who often waved up to David and his balloon," says Diana. "We were calling from the balloon for him to come out and see us, but he wasn't home. I thought it was sad that he wasn't there to see us land in his yard, but we left him a bottle of champagne in his mailbox."

"It was dark by the time we landed," says Sam. "We had to use a flashlight to help David pack up. Then we went inside his van and drank champagne. We actually drank award-winning champagne from the winery we figured we were married over. We had so much adrenaline. It was wonderful."

"It was the most incredible thing I've ever done," agrees Diana.

When Diana and Sam returned to Texas, their families were relieved that they survived but also excited about what they had done. To celebrate their wedding "somewhere over the coast of New England" they treated them to a party with a balloon-shaped cake.

Diana and Sam still get carried away by balloons. "Now we collect things with hot air balloons," says Diana. "Every time we see one it takes on new meaning and we get so excited. We plan to spend our anniversary in Albuquerque. Every October they have the largest balloon rally in the world, with up to nine hundred balloons."

The first balloonists in eighteenth-century France carried bottles of champagne with them so that when they landed in a surprised farmer's field, they'd have something to show him that would prove they were "of this earth" and not some otherworldly creature dropped from the skies. Even though balloons are now a fairly common site across the world, they still invoke feelings of wonder, awe, and delight as they float through the skies like giant Christmas ornaments.

But no matter how well equipped with sophisticated communication devices, a modern balloon is still ultimately subject to the same winds that blew across those French fields more than two centuries ago. If the uncertainty of ballooning reminds couples of how little control they ultimately have over the forces that will shape their life's journey, it should also remind them that when it's necessary to go with life's flow, the trip can be taken in elegance and style.

Balloon Adventures of New Bedford, Inc.
564 Rock O'Dundee Road, South Dartmouth, Mass. 02748
508-636-4846

Cupid's Chapel of Love's Over the Rainbow Helicopter Wedding

GATLINBURG, TENNESSEE

Nancy wore light blue denim shorts, a sleeveless white cotton shirt, and white sandals. Jim wore dark blue denim shorts, a white polo shirt, and tennis shoes. When Debbie Schultz, their wedding coordinator at Cupid's Chapel of Love in Gatlinburg, Tennessee, saw them, she paused and said, "That's casual. That's very casual."

There was no doubt that on their wedding day Jim and Nancy Williams of Owatonna, Minnesota, wanted to blend in with the crowd. The only thing that gave them away was the corsage of red roses Nancy wore on her wrist and the preacher holding a Bible. Otherwise, they looked just like any other tourists about to board a helicopter for a sightseeing flight over the Great Smoky Mountains. This gleaming white helicopter, however, was going to be Jim and Nancy's wedding chapel, where they planned to exchange vows in a Cupid's Chapel of Love Over the Rainbow Helicopter Wedding.

Considering that they met and courted each other over long-distance phone lines, it seemed somehow appropriate that they exchange their vows over stereo headsets in the sky. Nancy was a sales representative for a glass fabrication company in Owatonna. Jim worked for a skylight manufacturing firm in Martinsville, Indiana. Their frequent business contact over the phone gradually became personal. Soon, they were calling each other on their own time to sky-high monthly phone bills.

"We were able to talk about everything," says Nancy, "so we felt we had to meet." One weekend, unbeknownst to her family or friends, Nancy drove six hundred miles to southern Indiana to meet Jim. It was her first long car trip alone. "If I had told my friends, they would've said, 'You're going where?!!'"

Her curiosity, however, could not be quelled. Even though

Jim and Nancy Williams next to the minister and helicopter pilot

she and Jim agreed to meet as friends, they were both nervous when she rolled into town. "I thought, Oh no, she's really going to come down here," says Jim. "What if I don't like this girl?"

"I was so nervous, I almost rear-ended cars talking on the car phone trying to follow directions to his office," says Nancy.

"When I saw her, I was impressed," says Jim, still sounding pleasantly surprised. "I thought, Why would anyone this beautiful drive all this way to see a stranger?"

Nancy smiles shyly. "Seeing him in person relieved all my nervousness." She looks at Jim's boyish face and wide smile. "A face like that couldn't hurt a fly."

That evening, they had dinner at the Eagle's Nest restaurant in Indianapolis while it rotated high in the sky over America's heartland. Shortly thereafter they were exchanging heartfelt vows under the rotating blades of the helicopter, with an eagle's-eye view of the misty blue mountains, waterfalls, and lakes in the heart of the Smokies.

Gatlinburg, a quirky combination of Bible Belt morality and bluegrass and country revelry, has long been a popular honeymoon town, but it's now a major marriage mecca as well. Gatlinburg and neighboring Pigeon Forge boast twenty wedding chapels, which perform close to seventeen thousand weddings per year. A chapel seems to adorn practically every geographic feature in the area. There's the Chapel by the River, the Chapel in the Glen, the Chapel in the Valley, the Chapel in the Village, and the Chapel on the Creek, to name only a few.

"Most couples who come to Cupid's Chapel of Love wed in our white log chapel in the woods," says Rose, owner of the chapel. "Ninety-eight percent of the brides wear full traditional attire. We have brides with trains long enough to wrap around the chapel. And we have couples like Jim and Nancy who choose something a little different."

"We just kind of knew about Gatlinburg," says Jim. "We thought about getting married in a gazebo, but then we thought, Nah! Let's get a little more bizarre." They read through all the brochures from Gatlinburg and decided on the helicopter wedding because it was definitely different. The helicopter also only seats four people, so there was absolutely no way relatives could come along.

Some couples rake ancient address books to come up with an impressive number of guests to invite to the grand event. Jim and Nancy did just the opposite. Wanting to avoid any fuss, they invited no one. They told family only that they were going to get married somewhere in the Smokies. "We wanted it to be private, away from Minnesota and Indiana," says Nancy. "We also didn't want to spend a lot of money. We just wanted it to be like we were on vacation and were going to stop off somewhere and get married."

"I've always wanted something simple," says Jim. "It's bad enough to have to say 'I love you' in front of strangers, much less in front of your family. One of the few people we did tell was Nancy's ninety-five-year-old grandmother from Denmark. She's a great lady. She asked, 'Is that that little brown church?' Nancy said, 'No, Grandma, it's a helicopter,' and she laughed and said, 'Oh, you silly girl!' My mother only said, 'I got wedding pictures of all my kids. Make sure you get a good photographer.'"

As Nancy and Jim's wedding day approached, their desire to be different caused regular wedding jitters to intensify. Neither of them had ever been in a helicopter. "I worried I would get sick," says Nancy. "People at work said, 'You'll never know you're off the ground,' or 'It's just like fair rides.' But I get sick at fair rides! I took a bag on the helicopter just in case."

"We were driving around town the night before the wedding and I saw a lot of old broken-down helicopters," says Jim. "I thought if our helicopter looks in any way broken down, I'm not going up. The preacher can say the vows on the ground. But I remembered what my friends at work told me: 'Remember, that pilot doesn't want to hurt himself or die any more than you do.'"

It was a calm clear day in May when Jim and Nancy made their way to the airport for the big event. "When we got there I kept telling myself, 'Please don't get sick,'" says Nancy. "Then I asked myself, 'How can I convince this pilot not to hurt us?'"

Jim's first thoughts, on the other hand, were ones of great relief. "When I saw that shining white helicopter I thought, That's a good-looking helicopter! I wanted to make sure it wasn't a broken-down one."

They recognized the preacher because of his suit and Bible. "He started to do a crash course of the wedding right there on the ground," says Jim. "I thought he was getting ready to marry us right there. He just started going into it."

Rehearsing on the ground made sense. Once the helicopter was in the air, the sound of the rotating blades and the tight quarters made communication difficult. Jim and Nancy sat in the backseat while the preacher sat next to the pilot. "When we took off I just sat back," Nancy remembers. "I'm scared of heights, so I didn't look out for a while."

"Once we got up I joked that Nancy couldn't back out or she

was going overboard," says Jim. Once the wedding party was at cruising altitude, they donned their stereo headsets with the attached microphones and got ready for the ceremony. "Before the preacher started, the pilot gave us his views on marriage," says Nancy. "He said that fighting was going to happen and that we shouldn't go to bed mad. I thought that was nice."

"When the preacher started with the ceremony, he twisted around as best he could to see us," adds Jim, "but legwise, he couldn't get around too much. It was a good thing we had the headphones. The guy at mission control in this iddy biddy shed also had headphones and heard everything we said. After we were announced husband and wife he said, 'We got a divorce flight going out in half an hour for half price.'"

Obviously, Jim and Nancy didn't take him up on the offer. After half an hour they returned to earth a happily married husband and wife. "I felt fulfilled," says Nancy. "I felt good about everything. I didn't feel scared anymore." She laughs. "We were pretty close to God. We felt we needed a boost."

"I didn't feel just married," says Jim. "I was still in awe of the helicopter ride. It was so smooth."

"But it was also loud," says Nancy. "It was half an hour afterward and I still couldn't hear anything."

A Cupid's Chapel of Love Over the Rainbow Helicopter Wedding costs $350. Rose also offers other unusual options for couples looking to be unique. "We have horseback weddings where the couple rides out for about two to three hours and exchanges vows on horseback. We can't have them out much longer than that because their little buns get sore. Then we have Elope on the Slope where the couple gets married at the top of the ski slope. That one's not as popular because the minister has to be able to ski too. We say, bring us your dreams and we'll make them come true. We're very open-minded here."

Jim and Nancy now live in Minnesota on the edge of a vast, flat cornfield where the only thing flying overhead might be a flock of geese heading south. When they think of their long-distance romance, of their secret southern odyssey to

Gatlinburg, they smile and laugh. Dreams do come true, both over the rainbow and over the phone lines.

Cupid's Chapel of Love
706 East Parkway, Gatlinburg, Tenn. 37738
800-64CUPID / www.tennweb.com/cupid

The Schooner Yacht Wendameen
ROCKLAND, MAINE

The skies of Rockland, Maine, can be dreary and gray, the water of Penobscot Bay choppy and chill. Stiff breezes blowing in from the Atlantic could tear through the warmest clothing, but Captain Neal Parker would still rather be sailing than strolling the seaside streets of Rockland or exploring the surrounding pine-covered, rocky hills.

"The crummiest day on the water far exceeds any day on the shore," declares Parker, who navigates his historic sixty-seven-foot schooner *Wendameen* among the islands and inlets of Penobscot Bay. "On a breezy day, the schooner could be going only seven or eight miles per hour, but you feel like you're doing 120 in a Chevy convertible. The sails fill and you hear the water rushing under the bow and the gentle creaking of the boat—every movement is a thrill."

Parker's love of sailing stands him in good stead with his neighbors. Camden, just north of Rockland, is home to the nation's largest fleet of schooners, the elegant masted vessels whose powerful yet graceful sails take to the wind like eagles of the sea. Colonial Americans first used schooners as merchant and fishing vessels, but by the twentieth century the steamship took over and schooners became strictly pleasure craft. It was then that commercial sailors began derisively referring to the relatively slow schooners as windjammers.

Today, however, windjammers—far from being the scorn of the seas—are elegant and graceful adornments to any waterfront, and every summer people from all over the country travel to the Rockland/Camden area to sail along Maine's

Postcard of the schooner *Wendameen*

dramatic coastline. Here, points of rocky land reach out like gnarled fingers, grasp the blue waters of Penobscot Bay, and send them hurling onto the stony shores. Because of this rugged beauty, Maine has also drawn couples to its seaside villages to tie the knot—Camden has even been called a "marriage magnet"— but couples eager to chart a truly unique wedding course seek out Parker and tie the sailor's knot aboard the *Wendameen*.

Every summer, Parker takes passengers on one-night cruises aboard the schooner into the protected waters of Penobscot Bay with its many pine-covered emerald islands. Whether guests help sail or just lie back, all aboard delight in the symphony of wind and water; watch the gulls swoop and soar; enjoy a hearty dinner cooked on board; marvel at the sunset; stargaze; and dance on deck to the music of George Gershwin and Paul Whiteman played on the *Wendameen*'s original Victor Gramophone.

"People think of sailing and being out on the water as a romantic experience," says Parker. "There's a beautiful harmony as the vessel responds perfectly to the elements. Couples envision their lives having such harmony. I've never been on a schooner where a fight breaks out after the wedding!"

There's also no fighting over where exactly the nautical nuptials will take place, as Parker himself doesn't know on any given day what his itinerary will be. "When people ask, 'Where are we going?' and I say, 'I have no idea,' they look at me like they can't believe it. Most people are so used to having an itinerary. But taking a cruise on a schooner is not like a flight schedule when you always know where and when you'll land. Our destination always depends in part on the wind and tide conditions. That's the pleasure of it—finding a new harbor where different boats come and go, being someplace new at night. But once people get into the groove, they find it exciting."

Couples wedding aboard the *Wendameen*—an Indian word meaning "fisherman"—can either sail with other passengers on a regular overnight cruise—$155 per person including dinner and breakfast—or charter the whole boat, which accommodates fourteen guests, for $1,250.

Anyone marrying aboard the gracious schooner quickly realizes that Parker's affection for his boat is as deeply felt as a couple's love for each other. In fact, when Parker first discovered the schooner abandoned on a mud bank in Connecticut, it was love at first sight. He laughs. "She looked up at me with those take-me-home-from-the-pound eyes, and I knew I wanted to restore her. At the time, the only thing I knew about the boat was that she was old, but once I learned her history, she took on a whole different life for me, and I wanted to restore her as closely as possible to how she was when she was launched in 1912. But you never feel like the owner of the boat. You always feel more like the custodian. It's exciting to think that people will be taking her out fifty or one hundred years from now."

If, as Parker insists, a boat exudes whatever life has been on board her over the years, the *Wendameen* has quite a personality. Chester W. Bliss, a wealthy socialite from Springfield, Massachusetts, launched the *Wendameen* in 1912 and used her to entertain from his summer mansion in New England. Notable guests included writer Katherine Porter and playwright Eugene O'Neill. Bliss also frequently sailed the *Wendameen* to Maine to pursue sport fishing and hunting.

In 1916, the Uihlein family of Milwaukee—owners of Schlitz Breweries—bought the *Wendameen* and sailed her on Lakes Michigan and Superior. Chicago attorney Paul L'Amoreaux acquired the *Wendameen* during the Roaring Twenties. During Prohibition, he frequently entered the schooner in the 320-mile Mackinac Race. It ended in Canada, where he loaded the *Wendameen* up with whiskey and champagne.

By the mid-1930s, the *Wendameen* was back on the East Coast in the possession of wealthy yacht broker G. W. Ford of New York, who planned to restore the now aging craft. But then came World War II, and Ford laid the *Wendameen* up so the Navy wouldn't requisition her as an antisubmarine vessel. After the war, Ford was too busy to restore the *Wendameen* and sold her. The subsequent owner left the fallen schooner to decay on the Connecticut mud bank for nearly fifty years until Parker was smitten with her in 1986.

It took him two years to raise enough money to get the *Wendameen* back to Maine, where restoration began in 1988. Two years later, on July 1, 1990, the schooner sailed for the first time in fifty-seven years; and in 1992, she was placed on the National Register of Historic Places. Soon, couples began seeking out the historic craft for a memorable wedding at sea.

Jan and Charles Anthony of Hampstead, New Hampshire, knew that a wedding aboard the *Wendameen* would be a perfect way to have a low-key yet adventurous celebration where the guest list would, by necessity, be limited to the number of people who could fit on the boat.

"My father used to fly, so I've always wanted to sail or fly," explains Jan, a stay-at-home mother who met Charles, who works in printing sales, on a blind date. "It's a real sense of freedom. When Charles and I were visiting Camden, the light just went off that a schooner would be a perfect place to get married. Actually, our first idea was to elope to Bermuda, but

Jan and Charles Anthony have a champagne toast aboard the
Wendameen

when we told my parents, my mother threw a fit! They wanted
to be involved. But then we also wanted our four children from
our previous marriages to be involved too."

"I'd sailed before, and it's always been a wonderful
experience," says Charles. "When you're out on the water and
things are going well all you think about is sailing. Jan and I are
both romantic, but we're also pragmatic. Getting married on a
schooner was beautiful, but it was also a very controlled
environment. There wasn't a lot that could go wrong. In fact,
nothing could really go wrong because we planned so very little."

While Parker assures potentially nervous couples that there's
virtually no chance of getting seasick on the relatively calm
waters of the bay, some family members still were not convinced
that a wedding at sea would be smooth sailing. "We took Jan's
parents out to dinner and gave them a glass of wine before we
asked them how they felt about a wedding on a schooner," says
Charles.

"They weren't too thrilled at first," adds Jan, laughing. "They thought they'd have to spend the night in the middle of the ocean! All they wanted to know was whether they'd be able to see land. Once we told them we'd be within swimming distance of land and that there were no sharks, they were okay with the idea. They were happy that I was happy."

"We couldn't have picked a better day than the August day we sailed," recalls Charles. "The sun was out, the wind was blowing, and we were just cruising along. Captain Parker said it was one of the best sailing days he had ever seen. He has such a passion for his boat, and it was a joy to watch him engage in the pure art of sailing. The boat really did come alive. We had eight guests along with our children, and everyone got involved in raising and lowering the sails and raising the anchor. It was so much more fun and interesting as opposed to everyone just sitting around in a tuxedo."

Since it's pretty hard to hoist an anchor in a cummerbund or wedding gown, casual is key when it comes to *Wendameen* wedding attire. Jan wore a blue tropical-print dress and sandals—Parker urges brides not to wear heels so the finish of the beautifully restored wood deck isn't damaged—Charles wore shorts and a shirt, and their children, ages seven to fifteen, wore shorts and polo shirts.

"We had no real plans for when the wedding would take place," says Jan. "We were just going to go with the flow until we felt the time was right. For most of the day we were all so caught up in the views and the experience. We had maps out and were spotting all the islands. The boat was leaning way over in the water, almost sideways, and water was splashing in our faces! You could see the hills and the islands and the Owls Head Lighthouse and lobster fishermen. There wasn't a bad view. It was all so beautiful."

But as the afternoon waned and the intensifying yellow light of evening reflected off the blue water and green islands, Jan and Charles knew the time was right. Captain Parker anchored the *Wendameen* in a secluded harbor and led Charles and Jan through the short and simple vows. "Everything stood still," says Charles. "The water and the air. It was like the whole world stood still to listen to us for that fifteen minutes."

"We didn't write our own vows," adds Jan, "so they weren't even personalized, but I was still crying! It was very special."

After champagne and a dinner of vegetable lasagna, the newlyweds put a record on the gramophone and danced their first dance, not under a multicolored disco ball but under a thousand points of light. "Every star in the galaxy was out," says Jan, still amazed at the heavenly display. "There were four thousand million more stars than you see anywhere else. You could see every star ever made."

As the chill night air settled over the water, Jan and Charles joined their guests in the schooner's tight but cozy cabins. "There was just enough room to close the door and climb into bed," says Charles.

After a night anchored on calm waters, everyone rolled out of his berth for a breakfast of fresh muffins and coffee before heading back to Rockland for a 10:00 A.M. landing. "The next day was definitely a hat day!" laughs Charles. "Everyone was ready for a shower!"

There was no silk and satin at Jan and Charles' *Wendameen* wedding, no second-guessing the guest list, no distant relatives sitting despondently over cake and coffee—and that's exactly as they wanted it. "In a traditional wedding, people get so caught up in what everyone is wearing and who's with who," says Charles. "In our wedding aboard the *Wendameen,* people focused on the day at hand and all the different experiences. It was like the whole day was the ceremony. If you were bored, then there was something you were missing."

"It was a very simple but extraordinary day," concludes Jan.

When the *Wendameen* was launched over eighty years ago, bejeweled socialites were the first to dance on her deck under the New England stars. It's no longer necessary to be a member of the upper crust to set foot aboard the gracious schooner, but couples who do decide to exchange their bands of gold in the shadow of the *Wendameen*'s crisp white sails definitely come away feeling like a million dollars.

Schooner Yacht *Wendameen*
P.O. 252, Rockland, Maine 04841
207-594-1751 / www.midcoast.com/wendameen

2

The Depths of Love

Our ancestors the cave dwellers are not remembered for their refined manners. "Neanderthal" is synonymous with loutish, unmannerly, unsophisticated, crass, boorish, backward, and dirty. No wonder the first response to a cave wedding is open-mouthed incredulity. Cave weddings, however, are not a prehistoric practice.

Every year hundreds of couples across the United States go underground to wed among stalactite and stalagmite formations that rival any elaborate floral arrangement. Perhaps it's human nature to want to make hospitable the dark, mysterious underground, but cave marriages are alive and well in the twentieth century, and each chilly chamber of romance boasts its own unique wedding area.

Niagara Cave in Harmony, Minnesota, has a wooden pulpit and pews in its ten-seat Crystal Wedding Chapel. At Cumberland Caverns in McMinnville, Tennessee, couples wed in a vast underground dining room beneath a three-quarter-ton crystal chandelier. Florida Caverns in Marianna, Florida, has a Wedding Room, as does Indian Echo Caverns in Hershey, Pennsylvania.

Heavenly weddings take place deep underground in the Palace of the Angels—also known as the Wedding Room—in the

Caverns of Sonora in Sonora, Texas. Couples wed surrounded by shimmering, translucent white calcite formations in what is considered one of America's most beautifully decorated caves.

Couples at Moaning Cave in Vallecito, California, might be doing just that when they rappel 180 feet to the cave's huge main chamber to take their vows. Several brides have donned a white jumpsuit and helmet to take this ultimate plunge. Less adventurous guests use the hundred-foot spiral staircase to make the descent.

After a sandwich and soft drink in Carlsbad Caverns' Underground Lunch Room, couples can step into a small neighboring alcove to tie the knot in this vast New Mexico cave. Part of the National Park system, it is one of the largest and most highly decorated caves in the world.

While most couples are content to surface immediately after the ceremony, one couple spent their honeymoon in a cave. Once during Art Linkletter's television show "People Are Funny," which aired in the 1950s and 1960s, a newlywed couple was chosen from the audience and awarded an all-expenses-paid honeymoon trip "deep into the heart of the romantic Ozarks."

That heart happened to be a cold one, and it lay in Meramec Caverns in Stanton, Missouri. During the trip, the couple got a little closer to the cave than they expected. In order to claim their "real" prize, they had to dress in leopard skins and stay underground until they found the "key to civilization" hidden somewhere in the cave.

Tour guides say the couple slept in a little stone nook—now known as the Honeymoon Room—and, when not looking for the key, passed the time chasing each other around with Styrofoam clubs, to the delight of tour groups. On the tenth day, it's said, they found the key and returned to Hollywood to claim their prize—$10,000 and a trip to the sunny Bahamas.

Far from being reduced to barbaric behavior, however, most couples who wed underground are awed and humbled by the glorious beauty found deep in the heart of Mother Nature.

Luray Caverns
LURAY, VIRGINIA

The wedding zone. It's the area many couples pass through on the rocky road to the altar. Like dazed and confused drivers weaving on a rainy night through miles of pylons in some endless highway construction zone, couples navigating the wedding zone steer through a maze made up of guest lists, invitations, chapel rental, flowers, photographer, gowns, tuxedos, entertainment, and food.

Dani and Nyk Englander make their way into
Luray Caverns' Cathedral chamber

When Dani and Nyk Englander of Warrenton, Virginia, decided to wed in Luray Caverns in the Blue Ridge Mountains of

Virginia, they knew that preparing for this unconventional event would require them to make numerous trips through the wedding zone. There was another zone they had to pass through, however, one they never anticipated, and it came at them on their wedding day. The drip zone.

Because they were married in January, Nyk and Dani had feared that a snowstorm might make navigating mountain roads treacherous. Instead, they had to contend with a mountain meltdown. "It was seventy degrees that day," says Dani, a performer and early intervention nurse. "Everything was melting, and there were a lot of drips in the cave. When we were setting up the chairs, we had to keep moving them out of what we called the drip zone, but it seemed everywhere we moved them, there were drips. We just had to keep wiping them off and hope that people wouldn't mind getting wet."

"Before the ceremony started, I was waiting with my grooms-men in a little side room in the cave," says Nyk, a trainer for a computer company who met Dani through a friend. "I kept getting dripped on. I have a shaved head and the water kept rolling off it onto my tuxedo, so my groomsmen kept moving me around, saying, 'You're in the drip zone!'"

But since it was water that started creating Luray Caverns' grand formations 450 million years ago, Dani and Nyk were willing to accept its plentiful presence at their wedding. It was a small price to pay for the glorious surroundings. "The beauty of God is so magnificent in Luray Caverns," says Nyk. "It's not a matter that God directed someone to build something for his glory. By his own hand he created this majestic sanctuary."

Whatever ethereal architect created the cave's formations, Nyk and Dani's admiration for the cave is universal. Luray Caverns, a U.S. Registered Natural Landmark, attracts half a million visitors annually from all over the world. So exquisite are the formations that a sign at the cave's entrance warns visitors that they can be arrested for touching them. It takes 120 years for a formation to grow one inch. Oils on the human skin can permanently stop that growth as well as soil and destroy the colors.

Luray Caverns is one of the world's most finely illuminated caves, but the naturally bright colors of the formations themselves are the stars: pure whites, glittering golds, glistening creams and tans. With Luray's many breathtaking formations, it's like walking through the gilded palace of an underworld king.

Pluto's Ghost is a towering column of pure white calcite. The fifty-six golden folds of Saracen's Tent make up one of the most perfectly formed drapery structures in the world. In Giant's Hall, monumental columns stand forty-seven feet tall and more than thirty-five feet in diameter, while glittering stalactites hang from the ceiling like the trails left following the explosion of golden firecrackers.

But the focal point of the Luray Caverns tour is the Cathedral, a large round chamber where stalactites hang like shimmering candelabra. Shortly after the cave's discovery in 1878, six hundred people attended a dance in this room illuminated by hundreds of candles in chandeliers hung from stalactites.

Music lovers still have reason to visit the cave, thanks to Leland Sprinkle, an electronics engineer and organist who invented Luray Caverns' world-famous stalacpipe organ in 1954. This amazing instrument produces music of symphonic quality when electronically controlled rubber-tipped plungers strike stalactite formations.

Sprinkle tapped on over three thousand different stalactites over a three-and-a-half acre expanse to get the right range of sounds for his organ which can be played either manually or electronically. Each cave tour is treated to the classic "Oh, Shenandoah,' one of twenty songs the organ is programmed to play. A plaque near the organ reads, "Man's genius and the hand of God are in perfect harmony."

In a period when man's "genius" is turning the surface of the planet into a disharmonious compendium of pollution, noise, and bad design, it's no wonder that couples come underground to seek a wedding site far below it all. A local couple were the first to wed in the cave in 1890. Since then there have been hundreds of weddings in the cave's Cathedral. Some couples have even named their first child Luray Virginia.

"Most people are overwhelmed by the experience of the cave," says Jim Logan, who has organized special events in the cave. "We had a Japanese couple who were married in Japan but who flew over here just so they could have a second wedding in the cave. We have about four to eight weddings a year. It also seems to be getting popular for all kinds of events. We recently had our first bar mitzvah in the cave."

It costs $400 for the couple and up to twenty guests to use the cave immediately after closing hours—there's an extra charge for additional guests.

"Nyk and I were driving around one day and ended up in Luray," says Dani. "When the tour guide said there had been weddings in the cave, we just looked at each other and knew that's where we'd get married."

Despite the elegance of the cave's formations, there's also a certain informality to a cave wedding that appealed to Dani and Nyk. "We never wanted a traditional wedding," explains Dani. "We're both very casual. There's nothing formal about us, and there's something so formal about a typical church wedding. We wanted something where people could relax and have a good time."

"Luray Caverns is a very honest place," says Nyk. "I can't say that most churches are honest places. I had seen a lot of things in churches that were so unlike the nature of God. But I wanted something more than a bland chapel or a justice of the peace."

At first, their families were astounded at their choice of locations. Dani laughs. "My mom said, 'A cave? Why a cave?' When she'd go shopping for a dress she would come home and say, 'I didn't tell them it was for a cave wedding.' All our guests asked, 'What do you wear to a cave wedding?'"

Nyk also laughs. "My mother just said, 'Why? Why would you get married in a cave?' People think of a cave as being damp, dark, and cold, devoid of color, devoid of light, devoid of most things that a wedding is about—light, color, beauty, warmth. But I told my family, 'If you go there, you will know what I mean.'"

The only person who was initially thrilled with the location was the minister they had chosen, the Reverend Doctor Angus McDonald. "He went out there to see the cave before the wedding," says Nyk, "and he went crazy over it. He loved it. Every time we'd see him he'd have another cave fact for us. He was so excited. He was our greatest ally."

Despite the couple's professed casualness, their wedding with a hundred guests was a pretty formal affair by cave standards and offered some logistical nightmares. "If guests are hiking forty-five minutes into the cave, they want to sit down for the ceremony, so we felt we needed chairs," says Dani. "It was kind of a nightmare to carry them all down there, but our guests were really helpful and took them back up afterward." She laughs. "We thought, Here our guests came to a wedding and we make them work!

The fifty-four-degree temperature of the cave did not stop Dani from wearing an off-the-shoulder gown, but because of the damp cave floors, she did take some precautions with the long white dress. "I had it hemmed kind of short," she reports. "I had a train, but I had it permanently bustled. The seamstress said, 'I don't think you want this permanently bustled,' and I said, 'Yes, I do!' But in Luray you go up a hill and down a hill and the dress drags. By the time the ceremony started it was so dirty."

Nyk and Dani rode to the cave from their hotel in separate limousines. "Visitors to the cave were hanging around to see us come in," says Dani. "Everyone was taking pictures." A short flight of steps in the visitor's center leads people into the cave. Nyk and his groomsmen entered first, followed by their guests, who were escorted to the Cathedral by two violinists, the haunting music resonating throughout the cave's vast spaces.

After everyone was settled in their damp chairs, Nyk emerged from his drip zone, Dani made her entrance, and the ceremony began. "The minister incorporated references to the cave throughout the ceremony," says Dani. "He spoke of how you have to have wear and tear and trauma for something beautiful to develop. He was just incredible."

Music was important to Dani and Nyk, and they had wanted several songs played on the stalacpipe organ, but because the passage leading to the control box was full of water from the rain, they could not change the preprogrammed songs.

"The only song we could play was 'Oh, Shenandoah,'" says Dani, "but that was okay because it's such a beautiful song. Before it started, there was an incredible silence. You could hear drip, drip, drip, then 'Shenandoah' started. It sounded gorgeous."

The whole ceremony was incredible to all involved. "Our wedding was beyond anything I could possibly imagine," says Nyk. "To be looking into Dani's eyes and to see the backdrop of the cave and the candles and the anticipation that she was going to be my wife. It was more magnificent than anything I had ever experienced. It was overwhelming."

Their guests thought so too. "My sister is a lot more conservative than I am," says Nyk, "and at first she wasn't too excited about a cave wedding, but on the label to the video she wrote, 'Wedding of the Century.' Everyone thought it was magnificent."

Benton Stebbins, one of the cave's discoverers, planned to call the cave the Wonder and Beauty of the World. Although the name never stuck, Luray Caverns and the surrounding Blue Ridge Mountains are without doubt both wondrous and beautiful. A poem inscribed above the stone fireplace in the gift shop says it all:

> Here nature, with her magic wand,
> Dispensed her gifts with lavish hand;
> Her largess filled the earth and air.
> When further space could not be found,
> She carved these caverns underground,
> And stored a world of grandeur there!

Luray Caverns
Box 748, Luray, Va. 22835
540-743-6551 / www.luraycaverns.com

Howe Caverns

HOWES CAVE, NEW YORK

Many people say the bride glows with happiness on her wedding day, but at Howe Caverns in Howes Cave, New York, more than just the bride glows. "We've had a neon wedding where the clothing of the wedding party—socks, ties, shirts, everything— was all neon pink, green, and yellow," says John Sagendorf, general manager of the cave, which is situated in the foothills of the Catskill Mountains in upstate New York. "We've also had a chromium wedding where the bride wore a bright silver gown. One guest said, 'There's more chrome on the bride than on my Cadillac.'"

Generally, however, the only item in Howe Caverns guaranteed to glow is the six-inch-thick heart-shaped calcite stone imbedded in the brick floor of the cave's Bridal Altar. Lit from below, the heart glows a warm yellowish red and provides a toasty spot for couples to stand in the fifty-two-degree cave.

"Its definitely a cool place," says Debbie Vickery of South Glens Falls, New York, who wed Kevin Vickery at the cave's Bridal Altar. "You don't have to worry about passing out, like in a church."

In fact, the cool air that permeates Howe Caverns was what led Lester Howe, a local farmer, to discover the cave in 1842. When Howe noticed that his cows repeatedly stood out in the hot sun near the same clump of dense bushes, his curiosity was piqued, and he decided to investigate.

One day he followed his cows to the spot and felt a cool stream of air coming from the bushes. Pushing them aside, he discovered a dark hole in the ledge. Determined to know where the hole led, he returned the next day with rope and an oil lamp and squeezed himself into an amazing new world. Subsequent exploration led to the intricate web of passageways, vaulted chambers, and subterranean waterways. He quickly received worldwide attention for his discovery and opened the cave to an eager public. Next to Niagara Falls, it was the leading tourist attraction in New York.

Photo of the first wedding in Howe Caverns—the 1854 wedding of Harriet Elgiva Howe to Hiram S. Dewey in a room then called the Bridal Chamber

Perhaps eager for even more publicity, Howe arranged for his own daughter to marry in the cave's Bridal Chamber, the first of nearly four hundred weddings to take place in the cave over the years. On September 27, 1854, Harriet Elgiva Howe and Hiram S. Dewey proved the extent of their love by venturing into the cave for the big day. A photograph shows the couple, she in white gown, he in black tuxedo, standing before a white-robed minister atop a tall rock formation. Torches and lanterns surround the couple, while two men in hard hats and soiled clothes, clutching oil lamps, climb a ladder to reach the site.

No record exists of the obstacles Harriet and Hiram had to overcome on their way to the altar, but like the cave's first intrepid tourists, they no doubt had to do a fair share of tricky and sometimes strenuous maneuvering to reach the wedding site.

Lester Howe realized that not every bride would be as willing as his daughter to crawl through the cave's natural entrance, wade through water, or climb over massive, slippery jumbles of fallen rock just to get married, so he worked to clear and widen the more difficult passageways. In 1855 he wrote, "Now, ladies can pass through the entire length of the cave with as much facility as gentlemen, and in nearly every instance they seem to take greater delight in performing the journey than their companions of the opposite sex."

Twentieth-century technology helped ease the way even further for future couples. A lodge was built over the cave entrance, and in 1929 an elevator was installed that took guests 156 feet into the depths of the cave in only thirty seconds. After the addition of electric lights and brick walkways, one early guidebook writer declared, "No rubbers are needed, and white shoes may be worn." That year also saw the creation of the present-day Bridal Altar, where about thirty couples marry every year.

"Some of my friends and family thought I was crazy for getting married in a cave," says Debbie, who met Kevin, a chef, through a friend. "They said, 'Why would you pick something like that so far away?' But I didn't think it was weird. It can't be too strange if other people do it. Plus, I've always liked caves. It's neat to be down underground, and they fix them up so nice with the lights that you don't need to worry about decorations."

There is much below to hold the attention of couples and their guests. Lester Howe himself wrote that the cave offered "greater inducements than any other place or section of the country that can be found within the wide spreading limits of the American continent." Ancient formations along the one and a half miles of passageway include the Chinese Pagoda, an eleven-foot-tall ivory-tinted calcite stalagmite resembling an intricately carved Oriental temple. Couples can experience the

Debbie and Kevin Vickery stand above
the cave's calcite heart

romance of Italy when they view the Leaning Tower of Pisa, a
cylinder of calcite that resembles its Italian namesake, or take a
gondola-like boat ride on the underground Lake of Venus. The
Winding Way, a narrow 560-foot passage that makes an intricate
series of **S**-turns, is one of the world's best examples of water
erosion.

Several brick stairs lead to the Bridal Altar, which occupies a
long, narrow, low-ceilinged chamber just off the cave's main
passageway. The calcite heart glows in the floor before a small
nook where the officiant stands. Yellow lighting illuminates

nearby rock formations, while the trickling of the underground River Styx provides natural musical accompaniment.

Legend has it that whoever stands on the calcite heart will be married within a year, and it worked for Debbie and Kevin. "We visited the cave before we were married," says Kevin. "It was the first time I had ever been in a cave. I thought it was pretty neat. When we saw the Bridal Altar, Debbie and I stood on the heart and she mentioned getting married there. I thought it'd be a good idea. We got married almost a year after we visited the cave."

Like many people who wed at Howe Caverns, Debbie had been married before and was looking for something simple yet unique. "My first wedding was in a church and my second was with a justice of the peace, so I thought I'd try something different and start at the bottom this time. The only way to go is up. Plus, I wasn't about to spend a lot of money on a big wedding."

There is no charge for getting married in the cave. The bridal party and any of the couple's children are admitted free; others pay the regular admission price—$11.50 for adults, $6.00 for children. Group rates are also available.

The Vickerys had a small wedding with about thirteen family and friends. Debbie wore a floor-length teal gown with white lace trim, and Kevin wore a tuxedo. They arrived at the cave in a limousine and naturally took center stage as they made their way to the Bridal Altar on a busy Saturday afternoon in April. Since the cave is never closed to accommodate a wedding, couples must expect and be receptive to "uninvited guests."

"A tour guide was just about to take a group down when we arrived," says Debbie. "He asked them if they could wait a couple minutes for us to go down. A lot of the people were excited and asked if they could watch. We wouldn't have minded, but the guide thought it might be too many people."

There's room to accommodate approximately one hundred people around the Bridal Altar, but since there's no seating, guests must stand throughout the ceremony. Debbie jokes, "At least they can't fall asleep if they're standing up."

There's little chance of that, considering the atmosphere. "We had just gotten married when a tour group came through," she says. "They were all clapping. We didn't have a lot of our friends there, so it was nice that we had a welcoming crew."

Over thirteen million people have visited Howe Caverns over the years, proof of the pull that the dark, mysterious subterranean world still holds for us. A reporter with the *Cobleskill Index* of 1929 captured this feeling when he wrote, "As you wend your way through these underground chambers you are held in a strange thralldom. There's a stillness so profound that it entrances you....And yet the work is going on hourly, minutely, as it has for centuries because the tiny drops of lime-laden water, dripping like liquid diamonds, never stop."

As long as Howe Caverns' formations continue to form and draw crowds, couples will follow their beating hearts to the cave's glowing calcite one to declare their burning love on this warm and precious stone.

Howe Caverns
Howes Cave, N.Y. 12092
518-296-8900 / www.howecaverns.com

Cosmic Cavern

BERRYVILLE, ARKANSAS

"There's trout in that lake as big as a small child," says Randy Langhover, owner of Cosmic Cavern in Berryville, Arkansas, as he describes the scaly inhabitants that swim through the cave's Mystery Lake. Even though the fish that swim through the chilly blue green waters of the lake help attract twenty thousand visitors a year to Cosmic Cavern—a trout is even featured on the cave's logo—they detracted from the sacred atmosphere of the wedding ceremonies that used to take place inside the cave.

"They can cause a lot of commotion," says Langhover. "If people feed them, they can jump up to five feet high, and when they dive back down they make a lot of noise. It got to be real distracting for couples, so they stopped getting married near the lake."

The splashing of subterranean fish did not, however, stop couples from wedding in Cosmic Cavern altogether; they just moved the ceremony to the Silent Splendor, a recently discovered area of this Ozark cave, the beauty of which is truly heavenly. It's also known as the Oh My God Room, and when the tour guide illuminates the chamber, visitors know why. So numerous, pristine, and delicate are the formations that people literally gasp "Oh, my God!" at first sight.

Pure white soda-straw formations hang from the ceiling. One of them is nine feet tall, the tallest in the Ozarks. Glittering golden-hued stalagmites and stalactites reach from wall to wall and back into the recesses of the deep and narrow chamber. A twenty-five-foot wall of onyx looms beyond the room. The 1993 discovery of this area made national news and gave couples good reason to climb down the steep flight of stairs that leads into the cave from the gift shop for a wedding of truly cosmic dimensions.

But it's not just newly married couples who have had otherworldly experiences in the cave. In 1972, former cave owner Martin Buehler changed the cave's name from Mystery Cave to Cosmic Cavern to reflect the special powers he felt the cave possessed. Although the cave's mystery—the source of its lake water—still remained, Buehler renamed it to reflect his belief that it was a place where heaven and earth met, a place of infinite potentiality.

"He was a real hippie-type fellow," says Langhover. "He could've been John Lennon's twin brother. He was really into the Zen Buddhist, yin and yang type stuff. He felt you just couldn't get any earthier than being in the cave. He even designed the cave's logo to be a yin and yang symbol."

A sense of natural balance was not, however, present in the first wedding at Cosmic Cavern in 1977. "That girl got married in the cave because she wanted to make an old boyfriend mad," says Langhover, who was managing the cave at the time. "I guess she thought the publicity she'd get would be a way of getting back at him. It turns out she only stayed married for six months.

"After that Martin decided he wanted to marry couples too, so he sent for one of those one-dollar preacher licenses through the mail. He did very informal weddings. They'd all go back there in their Levi's and he'd ask them things like, 'Do you promise to do his dishes and take care of his dog? Do you promise to be on your best behavior for her and make sure your dishes are done?' After the weddings they'd have big wine tailgating parties in the parking lot."

This kind of thinking isn't very common in the Ozark Mountains, however. Even though Cosmic Cavern is only twenty miles from Eureka Springs, Arkansas, described by Langhover as a "haven for counterculture types," it's also only a short drive from the seven-story-tall Christ of the Ozarks statue, the second largest statue of Christ in the world. So when Langhover took over the cave in 1980, the fish took the spotlight on the cave's logo. He kept the name Cosmic Cavern only to avoid confusing tourists. He charges $25 for a cave wedding, which must take place after operating hours.

All weddings at the cave have not been as laid back as the first affairs. "We've had several formal weddings," says Langhover. "One time, the bride was worried she'd get clay all over her long white dress going through some of the tight passageways, so she took some blankets down into the cave and got dressed behind the blankets before the wedding and got undressed in the cave afterwards."

Although Donna Diehm of Norman, Oklahoma, was also a little concerned that she'd get her off-white tea-length lace dress soiled with the infamous red clay mud of the region, she didn't let it stop her from marrying Randy Diehm in what has become their favorite cave.

"We started going to caves several years ago," says Donna, an executive secretary, who met Randy, a salesman for floor coverings, while bowling. "We were looking at a map and saw a bunch of caves in the area and we thought it'd be a neat vacation to visit all of them. Now we go to caves all the time. They each have their own character. It's just amazing that it took years and years and years to create the formations."

Cosmic Cavern was only the second cave Randy and Donna had visited. They were impressed not only by the flight of stairs leading into the cave but by its breathtaking formations. Randy was so impressed that he later joined Langhover on a "wild tour" of the cave, where they ventured back into less explored areas. Randy and Donna became friends with Langhover, and Cosmic Cavern was one of the first places they thought of when they decided to marry.

"We had thought about Vegas," says Randy, "but I personally didn't want to get married and go gambling. That didn't seem very personal. When I thought of the most natural place to get married I thought of the cave. We're very down to earth. We're not earthy people, but we like nature, and the cave was special to both of us. Going to caves is something we'd never done with anyone else. It's something we created just for ourselves. We both enjoyed Cosmic Cavern so much I thought no other place would be better."

"When Randy suggested it I thought, Yeah!" says Donna. "Where else could you go that was a creation of God's that nobody's spoiled? The difference between the cave and Vegas was astronomical. Getting married in the cave was also a reflection of our relationship with each other. We're very open and natural with each other. It's so different from the relationships we've had in the past."

Getting married in a nontraditional setting also allowed Randy and Donna the freedom to create their own ceremony. They both had been married before and were anxious to avoid the traditional wedding hassles. "With a traditional wedding, you have to please everyone in the family and not just yourself," says Donna. "You think, So-and-so can't come because they don't get along with so-and-so. And then there's all the little hassles like mailing out invitations. I was so worn out following my traditional wedding. I only remember the tedious things about it, but I was so excited following my cave wedding. The biggest challenge was just conveying to our families that we were inviting only a small group of friends."

Randy and Donna had about ten friends at their wedding. They got married on a snowy day in January when the sixty-three-degree cave was the warmest natural setting around. "The weather was perfect," says Donna. "Snow covered all the rolling farmland surrounding the cave. I felt like Cinderella."

Their friends, none of whom had been to the cave, were eager to witness the ceremony. "Only one person was a little concerned," says Donna. "One gentleman we invited was very claustrophobic. He has a large-caliber body, and he was kind of scared about walking through some of the narrow cave passages. He didn't know what he was getting into." It turned out he had no problem getting into the cave, physically or mentally. "All our guests were in awe of the cave and the Silent Splendor area where we got married," says Donna.

The setting also allowed for more freedom during the ceremony. "During a traditional wedding, the bride and groom face away from the crowd," says Randy. "We were facing our friends so they were able to see our expressions while we said our vows. They were participating right along with us. We also got to see how our friends reacted too."

"Even the men were touched," says Donna. "They got close to each other there. At a traditional wedding people are just there to see something happen. They never really get involved."

Randy and Donna were married by a local minister in a simple ceremony. For music, they had taped versions of favorite songs by the Eagles, Barbra Streisand, and Whitney Houston. "It was a very casual environment," says Donna. "Our music was a little too loud when it first started playing, so I asked a friend to turn it down. You could never have done something like that in a traditional wedding where you're just terrified if you're walking down the aisle at the right time. After we were married our friends cheered and clapped and said, 'Way to go!' You don't hear that in a traditional wedding."

For Donna and Randy getting married in Cosmic Cavern was also a spiritual experience. "You couldn't go in a cathedral church that would be prettier," says Randy. "It was very sacred. The stalactites were our altar. Going to a cave is like going to heaven. I feel like I'm with God."

"It's like you're walking in God's house," says Donna. "He made all those formations. No one could make something look that beautiful. It's like you're home in the Lord."

Whether couples feel more at home with Eastern or Western spirituality, there's a universal belief that all of Cosmic Cavern's varied splendors are worth praising.

Cosmic Cavern
Route 4, Box 392, Berryville, Ark. 72616
870-749-2298

Bridal Cave

CAMDENTON, MISSOURI

"We actually had a couple who wed in sheepskins, just like cavemen," says Steve Thompson, general manager of Bridal Cave in Camdenton, Missouri. "The groom carried a papier-mâché club, and when the wedding was over he grabbed his wife by the hair and pulled her out of the cave." Thompson shakes his head in disbelief when recalling the ceremony. "They were already three sheets to the wind when they got here."

Given their state of induced euphoria, it's surprising the wedding took place. Another couple was almost not as lucky. "We had a lady who showed up to get married in a white bikini," says Thompson. "The man was wearing a suit, but the preacher refused to marry them until she put on a cover-up. So she puts on this white lace see-through thing which looked worse than the bikini. The preacher reluctantly married them."

And then there are the brides who can't get enough dress. "One bride wore this big Southern-belle-type hoop skirt, but when she went to go in the cave her dress wouldn't fit through the entrance. The guests were already inside the cave, so she made them come out. Then she put on her street clothes, carried the dress inside the cave where she put it on, then had the guests come back in."

Not all the weddings at Bridal Cave are so offbeat, but as the granddaddy of all wedding caves—more than seventeen hundred weddings have taken place in the Bridal Chapel since the first wedding in 1949—Bridal Cave has seen its share of odd ceremonies in addition to the many traditional affairs. "When the cave opened in 1948, no one anticipated that there'd be weddings here," says Thompson, "but people were attracted to the legend, and they began to ask about getting married in the cave."

According to local legend dating from the 1800s, Conwee, son of Osage Chief Neongo of the Big Hills, wanted to marry Wasena, daughter of Elkhorn, Chief of the Little Hills. When Wasena spurned Conwee's advances, he kidnapped her and her companion, Irona, and held them captive in the cave. Rather than marry someone she did not love, Wasena escaped from the cave and jumped to her death off a nearby cliff, still known today as Lover's Leap.

Irona, however, had long loved Conwee's brother, Prince Buffalo. Following a period of mourning for Wasena, Irona and Prince Buffalo chose to be married in the lovely stalactite-adorned room where she and Wasena had been held captive. Today, that room is known as the Bridal Chapel, and couples continue to be captivated by its beauty. Couples have come from all over the United States and several foreign countries to wed in Bridal Cave, and nearly all these couples have their wedding picture displayed in the cave's gift shop.

"We have about thirteen hundred pictures here," says Thompson as he looks through the stacks of photo albums arranged by decade. "People will look through these books for hours. They get really mad if they can't find their picture or the picture of whoever they're looking for. They want to be represented here."

From grooms in military uniforms to leisure suits to tuxedos to cutoffs, and from brides in stiff A-line dresses to groovy flowered robes to traditional white wedding gowns to the white bikini lady, here is a history of bridal attire over the decades. There's also some Ozark wedding humor on display—one photograph shows a father-in-law in a coonskin cap pointing a rifle at the newlyweds.

But couples aren't the only ones attracted to the cave's beauties. Fifty thousand people visit Bridal Cave every year. Situated in Thunder Mountain Park, the cave overlooks the Lake of the Ozarks, a popular recreation spot in southern Missouri. Entering the cave is relatively easy; several flights of stairs descend from the gift shop down a hillside to the cave entrance, which looks out over the lake.

For visitors who might think weddings are the main Bridal Cave attraction, a sign at the entrance of the cave announces the date of the next wedding and the name of the couple. Interesting formations along the tour include an entire cave wall covered with tumbling white flowstone known as the Frozen Niagara, columns of glimmering white calcite known as Stairway to the Stars, and ceilings dripping with lovely pink and rosy red soda-straw formations.

Although the entire tour takes visitors through some tight passages requiring squeezing and stooping, the Bridal Chapel is just a short distance into the cave. A winding paved pathway illuminated with small trail lights leads to the chapel, which accommodates about seventy-five guests. Weddings take place in front of an impressive twenty-five-foot tall drapery formation looking like a shimmering golden curtain or a wall of elegant icicles. A large cone-shaped stalagmite serves as a natural altar, and creamy white flowstone, like wedding cake icing, covers the walls.

Since the cave is a relatively warm sixty degrees, guests won't need to bundle up, but they might want to wear a sweater to protect themselves from the drips that fall pretty regularly from the lofty cave ceiling.

These chilly drips were not a deterrent to Tracy and Darrell Mathany of Kansas City, Missouri. "The cave was very romantic," says Tracy, an accountant, who met Darrell, a sales representative for a lumber company, through a friend. "We had looked at some churches in Kansas City, but the cave was as nice as any church setting, and it would be something to talk about and remember. We'd both been married in a traditional wedding before and were looking for something more low-key with less hassle. We'd been to the cave before and just thought it'd be cool to get married there. Our family and friends all loved the idea. They wanted to know how we came up with it."

Darrell was also eager to do something different. "Since we each already had a traditional wedding, we thought, Why do it the same way? Bridal Cave was also a place where we could do pretty much what we wanted. Our guests could come in tank tops and shorts or they could come in tuxedos."

If bigger is better, Tracy and Darrell had one of the most memorable weddings in Bridal Cave history. Nearly 115 people crammed into the Bridal Chapel, one of the largest groups in the cave's history. They came in everything from dresses and heels to jeans and cowboy boots.

"We invited about 175 people," says Tracy. "We told them we couldn't guarantee where they'd be standing during the wedding or if they could see anything, but they came anyway. I think they were curious."

As avid boaters, Tracy and Darrell rented a forty-two-foot houseboat and arrived for their wedding by boat, docking below the cave entrance. Darrell, dressed in a tuxedo, waited in the gift shop while Tracy got ready in the restroom of the Rock Shop, another gift shop close to the cave entrance. She wore a long white halter-style gown with a white lace headpiece. "It was raining, so I didn't use the bridal lounge in the cave office," says Tracy. "The lounge was a little bit farther away from the cave entrance. I thought I'd get dripped on enough in the cave."

Once Darrell and the guests took their places in the Bridal Chapel, Tracy made her entrance to the recorded pipe organ strains of the bridal march playing from a CD player hidden behind a stalactite. "We brought in one chair for Darrell's dad, but otherwise everyone else was standing," says Tracy. "Because we had so many guests, it was pretty cramped. We had people stretched back into the cave who couldn't see the ceremony. Still, everyone couldn't believe how nice it was and what a great idea it was. A lot of them had never been to the cave. If any of them thought a cave was dark and depressing they changed their mind."

During the short ceremony, a local minister pronounced Tracy and Darrell husband and wife, and they took their place in Bridal Cave history, couple number 1,599. Following their wedding, a tour guide presented them with a lifetime pass to the cave. This pass is included with all wedding packages, which run from $325 to $425.

Whether or not Irona and Prince Buffalo were the first couple to celebrate a subterranean wedding ceremony in Bridal Cave, their story started a trend that has resulted in many many happy endings.

Bridal Cave/Thunder Mountain Park
Route 2, Box 255, Camdenton, Mo. 65020
573-346-2676 / www.bridalcave.com

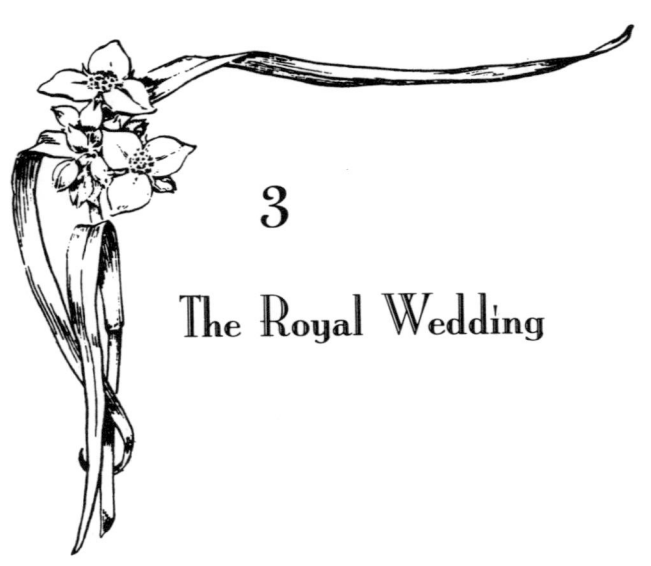

3

The Royal Wedding

Although the United States declared itself a democracy more than 220 years ago, Americans still yearn for that blue-blood treatment. Since the observance of wedding ritual has always been a sign of status, some couples take full advantage of the situation and choose a location that amplifies their sovereignty.

Prince Charming weds his bride in a Walt Disney World Magic Kingdom wedding. The fairy tale begins when the bride arrives in Cinderella's glass coach complete with costumed footmen and six white ponies. A majordomo carries the wedding rings to the altar in Cinderella's glass slipper, while a trumpeter heralds the bride's entrance. The ceremony takes place in the rose garden of Cinderella's Castle.

What was once the second-class smoking room aboard the *Queen Mary,* the largest passenger ship ever built, is now a first-rate wedding chapel. The *Queen Mary's* Royal Wedding Chapel hosts approximately six hundred weddings a year from the ship's "throne" in Long Beach, California, where it's rested since 1964 following thirty years of ocean crossings. Couples and their guests spend the night aboard ship in the restored first-class staterooms of this twelve-deck, eighty-one-thousand-ton reminder of the glory days of ocean travel.

In 1849, sugar planter John Hampden Randolph had one of

the largest and finest homes in the South built as a way of attracting eligible suitors for his daughters. The Nottoway Plantation in White Castle, Louisiana, is an invitation to elegance for couples enamored of southern aristocracy. The White Ballroom, complete with original crystal chandeliers, intricate, lacy frieze work, and hand-carved Corinthian columns, provides a stunning wedding setting.

Cats have always been perceived as regal beings, and at Gillette Castle in East Haddam, Connecticut, couples are surrounded by photographs of castle builder William Gillette's passion—cats. Built in 1914, this twenty-four-room fortress was patterned after a medieval Rhenish castle and was home to Gillette—an actor and playwright—and about twenty of his favorite felines. One can even see the bell used by Gillette's cook to call the cats to dinner. Summer weddings at the castle afford a splendid view of the Connecticut River.

Couples looking for the real thing, an authentic royal wedding in America, head to Berkeley Springs, West Virginia, to wed in Berkeley Castle. Colonel Samuel Taylor Suit built the castle in 1885 to entice an Alabama debutante to marry him, but since the castle's present owner proclaims himself a direct descendent of James I of England and James VI of Scotland, this darkly romantic stone edifice on a hillside proudly declares itself "America's only royal castle." The George Washington Dining Room is a popular reception site.

On a couple's wedding day, they are indisputably the "royal we," but as the following locations show, a royal wedding in democratic America takes on a myriad of interesting forms.

Medieval Times Dinner and Tournament
LYNDHURST, NEW JERSEY

Cultural critics in New York City say that once you're outside the Big Apple, you might as well be in the Dark Ages. Anyone traveling west from Manhattan through the Lincoln Tunnel into neighboring Lyndhurst, New Jersey, knows exactly what they mean; that is, if they turn down Polito Avenue and head toward the concrete castle that is Medieval Times.

Although a torture chamber with pleasantries such as thumbscrews and neck grippers does occupy the dungeon museum of the castle, it's the positive side of the era that takes center stage for the thousand people who each evening unabashedly don a paper crown and experience Medieval Times Dinner and Tournament.

Michael and Michelle Cubria and the wedding party on the grounds of Medieval Times

One of seven wildly popular establishments nationwide and in Canada, the Lyndhurst Medieval Times transforms everyday American citizens of the twentieth century into privileged royalty of eleventh-century Spain for an evening of pageantry, jousting, feasting, chivalry, and romance.

When visitors leave their "steeds" in the parking lot and walk through the castle door, they're in for a knight to remember. "Welcome, lords and ladies," bellows Count Don Raimundo II in his bright velvety costume as he and his countess hand out paper crowns to one and all. As the newly appointed nobility mingle with their fellow royalty in the Hall of Arms, surrounded by colorful tapestries and suits of armor, they find themselves gradually adopting the formal speaking style of their illustrious host, moving their arms with a tad more flourish, walking a bit taller, laughing a bit more heartily.

The festive mood continues when trumpeters of the realm sound the call to table and the aristocrats proceed to the Grand Arena for the royal jousting tournament and unfettered feasting. Long, narrow tables rise in tiers around a sand-filled arena. Each section of the audience, or "kingdom," is represented by a splendidly garbed knight for whom they'll root in the tournament.

While period music plays, serfs and wenches serve up the four-course banquet. Guests take their soup from a pewter bowl with handles and tackle the whole roasted chicken with their bare hands—there were no utensils in the Middle Ages—but so thrilling is the show, it's easy to forget about greasy fingers.

Amid swirling klieg lights and mist, the six splendid Knights of the Realm appear on grand Andalusian stallions. Thus begins an impressive display of horsemanship as the knights compete in the intricately choreographed Tournament of Games and the Battle of Champions. Whether tossing javelins, engaging in hand-to-hand combat, or charging at each other full gallop with steel swords, the brave knights valiantly fight on for the honor of their wildly cheering kingdom. The evening culminates when the champion knight chooses his Queen of Love and Beauty from his kingdom of fair maidens.

Given the grandiloquent display of courage, strength, and grace, given the royal treatment that every guest is heir to, it's no wonder that weddings at Medieval Times are popular events. "It's a different twist on pomp and circumstance," says Laurie Rovtar-Piro, public relations and promotions manager. "When the castle opened in 1990, we never thought about doing weddings, but then people kept calling wanting to know if they could get married here. We now do about ten weddings a year."

The ceremony takes place in the castle's Hall of Arms, where a trumpeter heralds in the wedding party. After the ceremony, guests enjoy the banquet and tournament, then dance the night away in the castle's Knight Club while partaking of the sculptured castle cake. Wedding packages begin with the $500 rental of the castle. Dinner and show is $38.49 per person. Extras can include a knighting ceremony, cheering banners, medieval favors, and dungeon passes.

"We wanted something people would remember," says Michael Cubria of the Bronx, who wed Michelle Cubria at Medieval Times. "The only thing different about the traditional weddings I've been to has been the two people. I would've been okay with getting married in a church, but I doubt I would've had much fun. Tradition is nice in its place, but Michelle and I will be sharing our lives for a while. We wanted something as special as possible. A traditional wedding is so commercialized and aimed at the brides. It's hard for a man to get involved with the planning.

"We both have an affinity for the medieval and Renaissance period. Anytime I've gone to Renaissance festivals, I've always gone in costume. I'm attracted to the gallantry, the honor, the adventure, the whole castle thing. I want to be a little bit regal. The Medieval Times castle isn't like a castle in Great Britain, but its still impressive." He laughs. "After being there, I felt at home. I thought, I could live here!"

"I like the romance of the period," says Michelle, who met Michael through their work in the tobacco industry. "The way they spoke and acted, the chivalry. You don't have that anymore. Since weddings are supposed to be about romance, we thought Medieval Times would be a good place to get married. We're creative people, and planning the wedding was something we could do together. A lot of brides don't remember much about their traditional wedding. But getting married at Medieval Times was like starring in your first school play. You never forget it."

Michelle and Michael wanted to remain faithful to the time period and researched medieval costumes and celebrations on the Internet. "Obviously, we weren't living in medieval times," says Michael, "so we didn't know exactly how they did things, but most people coming to the wedding didn't know what to expect at all, so the bottom line was that we just wanted to have fun."

Their fun began with creating their own scrolled invitations to the wedding at Castle Lyndhurst. "We wanted the event to sound regal, so we referred to the wedding as the joining of the House of Cudemo with the House of Cubria," reports Michael.

Gathering costumes was also an enjoyable challenge. "We didn't want any chintzy-looking costumes," says Michael. "I wanted the whole blue-blood thing. I ended up renting a wonderful costume that was a replica of the outfit King Henry VIII wore when he wed Anne Boleyn—full of royal reds and golds. A performer at Medieval Times even asked me if I was new because my costume looked so authentic. I'm really thinking about buying it!

"During rehearsal for the ceremony in my street clothes, I kept laughing every time I walked down the hall, but once I put on the costume, it empowered me. I became more serious, and I wanted to make sure I was walking regal enough."

Michelle wore her mother's wedding dress, an off-white damask gown with an empire waistline. The only adjustment she made was to have royal blue inserts put into the draped sleeves to give it a medieval feel. She did her hair in ringlets and wore a pearl tiara. "It was fun," she says. "I got to dress up and act a little theatrical. It felt more like a play than a wedding."

Some of their sixty-five guests, none of whom had been to Medieval Times, also came in costume. Michelle's brother even wore a suit of chain mail that he had made especially for the event.

At the sound of the trumpet, Michelle and Michael walked into the Hall of Arms accompanied by period music from the movie *Robin Hood Prince of Thieves*. After Michelle and Michael recited some love poems they had chosen for the event, they were pronounced the new lord and lady. "It all felt very regal, very royal," says Michael. "I even got knighted!"

Although the event resonated with meaning, it was actually quite meaningless—at least from the legal point of view. "We didn't want to hassle with getting a wedding license in New Jersey," says Michelle, "so we got legally married by a justice of the peace earlier in the day in Yonkers. We did it on the same day as our Medieval Times wedding even though it was kind of hectic. Otherwise we thought we'd have two different wedding anniversaries."

"The legal wedding was more like getting your driver's license," adds Michael. "The language is pretty stiff and it's not very emotional. It took us time to create our vows for the Medieval Times ceremony, so it was more from the heart."

After the ceremony, the guests delighted in the show and feast. Michelle and Michael did make one small concession to modern times. "We used silverware," says Michelle. "We couldn't expect our guests to eat greasy chicken with their fingers. We didn't want it to be half regal and half peasantry."

During the tournament, Count Don Raimundo announced the Cubria's marriage to the entire kingdom. As the crowds cheered, Michael stood up and waved royally, while their knight, who ended up winning, threw Michelle a bouquet of flowers. "We had a great time," says Michael. "It was way too short. The next morning we woke up and it was back to reality. The fairy tale was over. I thought, I'm not a lord and Michelle's not a lady—at least not a medieval one. We wanted to do it all over again. When you get married, you are literally king and queen. You feel like you're in a different world."

The actual medieval times may have been full of grueling hardship and dark despair for the thousands of people who weren't royalty, but for modern-day medievalists and the lords and ladies who wed in Castle Lyndhurst, the times shine.

Medieval Times Dinner and Tournament
149 Polito Avenue, Lyndhurst, N.J. 07071
800-828-2945 / www.medievaltimes.com

Medieval Times, Buena Park, Calif. / 800-899-6600
Medieval Times, Kissimmee, Fla. / 800-229-8300
Medieval Times, Schaumberg (Chicago), Ill. / 800-544-2001
Medieval Times, Dallas, Tex. / 800-229-9900
Medieval Times, Myrtle Beach, S.C. / 800-436-4386
Medieval Times, Toronto, Ont. / 800-563-1190

Bishop Castle
RYE, COLORADO

It's not every couple who'd want a stainless steel fire-breathing dragon competing for attention on their wedding day, but Lisa and Jerimy Noon of Colorado Springs were only too eager to wed in the shadow of the dragon's toothy grin. It's the first thing they saw peering over the trees when they discovered Bishop Castle on a camping trip in the Rocky Mountains outside of Rye, Colorado.

"We felt so magical the moment we found the castle," says Lisa, a freelance photographer. "At first we thought it was a church, but the dragon peeking over the trees confirmed that we weren't entering a church with rules."

"So much love went into the castle," says Jerimy, a sheet metal worker, artist, and model who met Lisa on the sidewalk outside their apartments. "It was quite a struggle for Jim Bishop to build it with all the opposition he faced, but it's very motivating to see what one person can do."

Jim Bishop, the owner and single-handed builder of the castle, has never been one to avoid a challenge, especially when a principle is involved. His passion for justice and action on a

Bishop Castle and its fire-breathing dragon head

grand scale started in high school. "During my junior year, some cheerleaders came in and said they needed some help in the parking lot," says Bishop, "so I went out and they had this trunk load of live chickens in their car all dyed different colors. They were going to use them in a stunt at the football game, but those chickens had been out in that trunk all day suffering in the heat! Those chickens had feelings too! I came unglued! I just went in and put my books in my locker and never went back!"

At fifty-three, Jim Bishop still acts on principle, only instead of standing up for chickens he's become a cheerleader for the common man through the ongoing construction of his remarkable Bishop Castle. Twenty-eight years ago, when Bishop began building a stone cabin on a plot of mountain land, he never anticipated the fantastic direction it would take and the battles he'd come to wage over it.

"As I worked on the building, people started telling me it looked like a castle," says Bishop of the elaborate three-story medieval structure that he has worked on nearly every day for the past twenty-eight years. It is, according to Bishop, this country's biggest one-man project, always open free to the public. "The idea for the castle came from the people. It's the people's castle, and it's the only true fighting castle in the world. We're up in siege against the government! We have enemies!"

As the castle grew, Bishop battled with the forest service over his right to gather rock from surrounding national forest lands; he battled the Colorado Highway Department over his right to put up road signs to attract tourists to the castle; he and his wife, Phoebe, fought an eight-year paperwork battle with the Internal Revenue Service to get tax-exempt status for the castle—25 percent of castle donations go to the Bishop Castle Foundation for Newborn Heart Surgery. He battled with Colorado tourism officials to get the castle listed on the map as a tourist attraction.

Throughout these battles his only weapons have been perseverance and his invocation of the "power of the public" to overcome government control and bureaucracy. "I think if you got to get permission all the time to be free, needing permits for this and permits for that and mandatory insurance, you're really paying for your freedom. When that American flag flies over the castle, it means what it means—freedom, liberty, and justice."

Those concerned with government regulations may have other points of view, but Jim Bishop is never shy about pointing out his. In his booklet "Castle Building: From My Point of View" he writes: "The Bishop Castle is a monument to hard working poor people at no expense to the tax payer or anyone else. It is a landmark. It promotes public pride and spirit, is inspirational, and shows what a poor man, or anyone, can do in a free country. It is a fight for freedom to keep the government under control."

Bishop's passion for his project is uncontrollable. "I feel great," he says. "I can get as much work done in three hours as most people do in a week. I get more and more ideas all the time. If I lived to be a hundred, I couldn't do it all."

But Bishop does work to do it all. When he's not running his ornamental iron business in Pueblo, he's hauling materials up to his castle. What he's accomplished is almost unreal. Decorated with ornamental iron, the stone castle stands amid towering pine trees bordering the San Isabel National Forest. Flag-festooned minarets tower alongside turrets and flying buttresses. Exterior stone stairs rise to meet tall, arched windows. It's truly a magical, mystical, distinctly intriguing structure.

"I got ideas from a hodgepodge of places," says Bishop, "from *National Geographic* to cathedrals and castles in Europe." Future plans include a mausoleum tower—the ashes of several people have already been scattered over the castle—solar-powered, wrought-iron-and-glass scenic elevators, waterfalls, a draw-bridge, and a remote control for the fire-breathing dragon.

Bishop Castle's very own stainless steel smoke-bellowing fire-breathing dragon head was born from discarded stainless steel hospital trays rescued from a Pueblo dump. The dragon's snarling visage looms from the top of the castle; its lower jaw measures seven feet. "It used to be that smoke came only from its nostrils, but now I got a propane torch in there and the flames come shooting out. One day I'll get it to where it's remote-controlled and I can just walk around and push the remote and run it."

While the dragon first drew Lisa and Jerimy to the castle, they returned many times and developed a friendship with Bishop. When they decided to marry, there was no doubt they wanted to wed at Bishop Castle. "It's such a magic place," says Lisa. "It's very powerful and enchanting. It's also out in nature. I'm more myself when I'm not flooded with materialism all around me. So much of marriage is commercialized. People feed off other people's dreams."

"The castle is enchanting," says Jerimy. "When Lisa and I are

Lisa and Jerimy Noon kissing on the ground
of the castle

together, it's very mystical. We couldn't imagine getting married
anywhere else. We also thought it'd be a very powerful and
inspirational place to share with others."

But just as Bishop faced confrontations with people who did
not share his rocky vision, Lisa and Jerimy found that the road to
the altar of their choice was to be occasionally rocky as well. The
main objection they faced was from Lisa's mother, whose idea of
a royal wedding tended more toward Versailles than medieval
gothic.

"My mother had been to the castle a while ago," says Lisa.
"She thought it was a very dangerous place and perfect for a
lawsuit with all the rocks and metal and low ceilings."

There were other challenges as well. "My sister has cerebral palsy and uses a wheelchair, so my mother worried that the castle wasn't accessible, that there was no running water, no bathrooms. But there is a toilet about fifty feet down the mountain. It's not within smelling distance. The castle smells very clean." says Lisa. "Also, because Jim's always working on the castle, there's heavy equipment nearby. A cement mixer is not what some people want near the altar."

This generational clash isn't uncommon at weddings, and in this case could only be resolved by both mother and daughter getting their way. "In the end we had to have two weddings— my wedding in the castle and the next day my mother's wedding at the Trianon in Colorado Springs. It's a boarding school now, but it was built in 1907 as an estate and was modeled after the Grand Trianon at Versailles. Once we separated the weddings, she was happy."

"My parents from Massachusetts were rooting for us," says Jerimy. "Lisa and I planned to be married with a Renaissance theme. My parents enjoyed Renaissance fairs and were excited about a castle wedding. All our friends thought the idea of the castle was cool. They were glad they didn't have to go somewhere boring."

"We did so much of the preparation ourselves," says Lisa. "Jerimy made the swords and I hand-embossed three hundred invitations. It gave us time to think about the commitment of marriage."

Despite Lisa's mother's fears, the castle wedding with its 125 guests was a success. Lisa, Jerimy, and their attendants camped out in the castle the night before and got ready at a nearby friend's house. "It was a little bumpy for my sister to get to the castle from the parking lot," says Lisa, "but she enjoyed it." The entire wedding party, including Lisa's mother, dressed in Renaissance attire. Lisa wore a mid-length cream-colored dress with laced bodice, and Jerimy wore dark pants, a shirt with puffed sleeves, and a vest. The men carried the swords that Jerimy made for them.

Jim Bishop was there, but his participation was somewhat limited. He came encased in an elaborate suit of armor. "The armor's plenty heavy," he says. "It's hard to climb stairs, and it'll pinch you. It also makes a lot of noise."

The ceremony, officiated by a judge who was a family friend, was held outside the castle underneath an eave. Some guests watched the wedding from various levels of the castle; others gathered on the grounds. Lisa and Jerimy walked down an aisle of raised swords, while a friend played period guitar music. "Because our wedding was in a difficult place to get to, the people who went really had their blessings with us. It was very romantic. Even my mother broke down and cried during the ceremony."

In keeping with the public spirit of the castle, tourists were in plentiful supply at the wedding. Although they were fascinated by the event, they also took the power of the public a little too far, at least for Lisa and Jerimy. "They felt pretty comfortable taking pictures of us," says Jerimy. "Some of them were getting kind of demanding and saying, 'Stand over here,' or 'Stand over there' so they could get pictures. Finally, I had to ask them, 'Are you a tourist or are you a guest?'"

"It was kind of hard," says Lisa. "People kept asking me, 'Where's the bathroom?' I'd point to my wedding dress and say, 'Don't you see who I am today!' But when you do something unusual you have to bend and go with the environment."

The environment at their Trianon wedding the next day couldn't have been more different. At this sophisticated affair, Lisa wore a formal gown with a long train—although Jerimy still wore his castle costume. "I enjoyed both weddings," says Lisa, "but it was rather tiresome to have two of them."

"We were able to have a better reception with the second wedding," says Jerimy. "At the Trianon, we could hook up a DJ and have a place to party. And a place to go to the bathroom."

Jim Bishop never charges for weddings at his castle—over thirty weddings have taken place in recent years. "The couple can make a donation if they want, but I don't care to know what it is. I don't look when they put it into the donation box. If they're embarrassed or nervous or poor, I ask no questions. Their money mingles with money from the tourists' donations all day. Everyone's welcome. There's no hard feelings."

Jim Bishop may have enemies, but he also has thousands of admirers—sixty thousand people from around the world visit the castle each year. "When I dropped out of school, they told me I wouldn't amount to nothing," says Bishop, who relishes the attention his castle receives. In "Castle Building" he writes, "All I really want is my name on it, and the publicity and recognition for doing it. In the honor and glory of GOD, but also in the honor and glory of myself. If I said anything else, I would be a liar and a hypocrite!"

In a voice as heated as the fire that spews from his dragon's mouth, he concludes, "It's Jim Bishop's castle! It's my art form! It's a world-class monument to freedom and justice! It's the American dream!"

Jim Bishop, castle builder, is indisputably king of his hill.

Bishop Castle
HCR 75 Box 179, Rye, Colo. 81069
719-564-4366

Isis Oasis

GEYSERVILLE, CALIFORNIA

"At first, my parents from Germany were very confused by Isis Oasis," says Thomas Schenkel, a physicist living in San Francisco. "They couldn't identify with it and didn't know what to do. They would've liked a traditional church wedding. Instead, my mother looked around and saw all these pagan Egyptian things, and that would mean something bad for her. But the ceremony put that in the background for her. After the ceremony, my parents both had very positive feelings about the place."

Isis Oasis, a ten-acre retreat in Geyserville, California, has

Postcard of Isis Oasis owner Loreon Vigne standing in front of the Temple of Isis

been the site of many revelatory weddings since its founder, sixty-five-year-old Loreon Vigne, created it on the site of a former Baha'i school in 1980. "I've always felt an affinity for the era of the ancient Egyptians," she says. "It's full of mystery, and magic, and wonder."

So too is modern-day Isis Oasis. There's nothing barren or forbidding about the lush vineyards surrounding Isis Oasis in northern California's wine country. Rather, Isis Oasis is a fertile gathering ground for those seeking to nourish body, mind, and spirit.

Isis was one of the most important goddesses of ancient Egypt, and for good reason. When her husband Osiris was murdered and dismembered, she tracked down his body parts and pieced him together so he'd be able to rule as god of the underworld. She was thus honored for her restorative powers. As nurturing mother to the sky god Horus, she was also honored for her powers of protection. Often depicted wearing a throne on her head, she was widely revered. Temples were built in her honor in Egypt, and her cult later spread to Greece and Rome.

Thousands of years later, the appeal of Isis made its way to Ireland and Lady Olivia Robertson. It was there in 1976 that Robertson founded the Fellowship of Isis, an organization whose purpose was to promote love, beauty, and truth while revering and conserving nature. The fellowship ordained priests and priestesses, although all members were free to maintain other religious allegiances.

Lady Olivia's "mission" took hold. Eager to experience the feminine side of a deity, thousands of people around the world joined the fellowship and created Iseums to honor their muse. Isis Oasis is surely one of the most distinctive places where devotees of the goddess gather. Here one can do everything from study Egyptian yoga to honor the lion goddess Sekhmet and the cat goddess Bast, just as the ancient Egyptians did, during the annual All-Hallows Celebration.

Visitors check into Isis Oasis at the front obelisk. From there, they're free to wander the grounds, view the collection of exotic animals and birds—including ocelots, llamas, and peacocks— receive a massage, soak in the pool or sauna, eat a vegetarian meal, or spend the night in a pyramid.

The center point of Isis Oasis is the Temple of Isis, a nondenominational church dedicated to earth-based spirituality. Modeled after an ancient Egyptian temple, complete with gold pillars and hieroglyph-adorned walls, the Temple of Isis offers a quiet place for people to meditate while reflecting on the four elements—earth, air, water, and fire—symbols of which occupy each corner of the temple.

It's this balanced accord with the elements that draws couples to marry at Isis Oasis. "Couples from all different religious and spiritual backgrounds marry here," says Loreon, who performs many of the ceremonies. "I even did a Zen wedding where the only thing I said was 'You are now married.'"

Most ceremonies take place under the massive outstretched arms of Isis Oasis' five-hundred-year-old Douglas fir tree.

Loreon has even created a special tree ceremony, which emphasizes a couple's need to sway in different directions while still meeting on harmonious ground. Other popular wedding spots include the Temple of Isis and the Redwood Theater, built in the 1930s.

Couples reveling in the royal treatment they receive in the goddess' abode stay the night at some of California's most unique honeymoon accommodations. Although some guests stay in the rustic twelve-room lodge decorated with an ancient Egyptian motif, couples seeking cozier quarters can retreat to the tipi, yurt, or geodesic dome. Couples really feeling the call of Isis cuddle up inside the twelve by twelve pyramid with a skylight and a mattress on the floor. "It's built according to ancient specifications, so you get a lot of charged energy in there," says Loreon. Those more in spirit with the surrounding vineyards enjoy the uniquely restful Wine Barrel Room, an actual twelve-foot wine barrel complete with skylight and wicker bed. "It's cozy and unique," says Loreon, "and it still smells like wine. You have good dreams in there."

It was on such congenial grounds that Thomas Schenkel and Leslie Kirk Campbell wanted to celebrate their wedding. Thomas, a native of Germany, met Leslie when he enrolled in her school for creative writing to improve his English. As thinkers and writers they sought a spiritual place where they could create rituals personal to themselves.

"We're not religious," says Leslie, "but we didn't want just a civil service. We wanted a special place and a special service to create intensity, a service that would express ourselves and our lives."

"We wanted ritual," adds Thomas, "but if we had had a traditional church ceremony all my friends would've asked, 'How could you, an intellectual person of the nineties, do that?' We were lucky in that California has the infrastructure for a postconventional ceremony."

"I knew I didn't want a traditional ceremony," says Leslie. "I recently went to a traditional wedding where I felt I was just out there with all the other guests. The couple didn't even know I was present. It was important to us that we thought about all the people at our ceremony, that everyone have a chance to speak. They weren't there just playing roles. They were our friends. It was more like, 'I'm your friend and I'm going to play the cello,' or 'I'm your friend, I'm going to perform the ceremony.'"

As Loreon's niece, Leslie was familiar with her aunt's adventurous spirit and knew that Isis Oasis would be the perfect wedding spot. "From early on she inspired me toward the arts. She'd do things like paint big butterfly wings on her eyes and not care what people thought. She raised ocelots in the city when she lived in San Francisco, and in her house she had unconventional things like old wheelchairs for people to sit on. She was very courageous in her striking out. Also, since Thomas and I were coming into our marriage with equal balance and power, I was attracted to the strength of the female energy in the land."

Leslie and Thomas took Isis Oasis' spirit of calm into the planning for the event as well. "I looked at the preparation for the wedding as a meditation," says Thomas. "So many details can drive you nuts. But the planning provides a great chance to deal with your partner under stress. It was a good exercise. It felt purifying."

They were married on the spring equinox in Isis Oasis' elegant redwood theater. Stained-glass windows hand-crafted by Loreon and depicting majestic peacocks filter the light into the redwood interior. "The theater has such an innate sacredness," says Leslie. "It was also spring and a full moon and I was six months pregnant, so there was a lot of female energy."

They had sixty guests, including Thomas's parents from Germany, neither of whom had been to the United States. Since they did not speak English the ceremony was bilingual and was performed by Klaus Schüller, a friend of Thomas' and a former Benedictine monk from Germany. Because Thomas and Leslie weren't sure if he'd be able to marry them in the United States, they were legally married several days before by a justice of the

Leslie Campbell and her husband
Thomas Schenkel on the grounds of
Isis Oasis

peace. "Some of our family
thought the ceremony at Isis
Oasis was a bit redundant," says
Leslie, "but the power of the
word comes from you, not the
law. The ritual ceremony had the
power, not the legal one."

Wanting the ceremony to be
spiritual and not totally pagan,
they incorporated into it readings
from different religious traditions, poetry, and music ranging
from Vivaldi's "Four Seasons" to
"Amazing Grace." Leslie wore a
white lace dress, and Thomas
wore a suit. Afterward, Loreon
released two white doves while
speaking of how love requires
freedom, not cages.

"It was all very magical for us," says Leslie. "What everyone
said when they spoke was so meaningful and honest, so unlike a
traditional ceremony where everything goes by in a blur and the
couple is just glad it's over. Then to go outside in the sun and see
flowers all around, and the animals, and the unbelievable
sounds of peacocks and birds. It was beautiful."

"A lot of people cried and said, 'You made us all believers
again,'" says Thomas. "I think they believed once again in
authentic rituals that work and that open us up to a transcendent
reality."

After the ceremony, nearly everyone stayed the night and
enjoyed Isis Oasis' grounds, pool, and sauna. "It was important
to us that our guests stay and enjoy themselves and not be in a

big rush to leave," says Leslie who spent the night with Thomas in the Enchanted Cottage, a small cozy abode on a knoll off by itself, with its own fireplace and hot tub. Judging from the enthusiastic response of their guests, no one was in any hurry to do so.

Weddings at Isis Oasis cost anywhere from five dollars per person for small day ceremonies to $1,800 to rent the entire Isis Oasis for the ceremony and overnight stay.

In ancient Egypt, the preservation of the cosmic order depended on the strict adherence to rite and ritual when honoring the deities. Thankfully, the only thing affected by the diverse wedding rituals that take place at Isis Oasis is the contentment of the couple and the happiness of their guests. But judging from the joy Thomas, Leslie, and their guests felt and the final happiness of Thomas' doubtful parents, the world's varied deities and Isis herself were no doubt swinging on the stars.

Isis Oasis
20889 Geyserville Avenue, Geyserville, Calif. 95441
800-679-RETREAT

Chapel in the Palms

KAUAI, HAWAII

No sooner do planes hit the tarmac in Hawaii than their mainland passengers are treated like royalty. Leis—traditionally used as offerings to the gods—are thrown over tourists' necks as their every whim is catered to. But long before Hawaii became the common man's kingdom, the islands were home to actual chiefs, kings, and queens who ruled over their lush valleys and mountains for centuries. If tourists venture beyond their beachfront high-rise, they'll find the peaceful places apart from surfers and swimmers that the island royalty called home.

Kauai, the most isolated and least developed of the Hawaiian islands, has always been a place apart. When King Kamehameha the Great gained control of all the other Hawaiian islands in 1795, Kauai alone remained unconquered, a separate kingdom. Puna, Moikeha, Kaumualii, Queen Kapule—the names of the island's chiefs and royalty roll off the tongue like water over the rocks of Kauai's towering waterfalls. Throughout the island one can spot the ancient stone temples where priests performed ancient chants and solemn ceremonies.

But as important as these native royalty are to the history of Kauai, it seems a more recent king with an equally resonant name has also left an indelible impression on the island—Elvis Presley, King of Rock and Roll. No sooner had Hawaii become the fiftieth state in 1961 than Elvis' movie *Blue Hawaii* introduced mainlanders to the islands' charms.

As son of a wealthy pineapple king, Elvis preferred crooning melodious melodies with island natives over attending to big business. His movie marriage to Joan Blackman in Kauai's Chapel in the Palms on the grounds of the Coco Palms Resort, however, has resulted in big business for Kauai native Larry Rivera, composer and entertainer. Since shortly after Elvis' death, Rivera has been coordinating Chapel in the Palms Weddings, faithful re-creations of Elvis' *Blue Hawaii* wedding complete with all the royal touches: canoe paddlers, conch shell blowers, and floral arch bearers.

"Elvis Presley loved Kauai," says Rivera. "He came here often and had his own suite at the Coco Palms. He was fabulous and kind and sincere and honest. He made you feel like the star. People from all over the world come to Kauai for a Blue Hawaii wedding Elvis Presley–style. A planeload of couples from England recently came here just for a Blue Hawaii wedding."

The Chapel in the Palms sits in the midst of a forty-five-acre coconut grove on the grounds of the Coco Palms Resort, a classic of Hawaiian kitsch with its palm-frond chandeliers, clamshell washbasins, and evening torch-lighting ceremony. Elvis wasn't the only king to be attracted to the surrounding natural beauty. The lagoon on the property and the land surrounding the Coco Palms has a truly regal history. Along a nearby ancient footpath, high chiefs were borne in their canoes to their homes by the lagoon—the path was once forbidden to commoners on the penalty of death. Queen Deborah Kapule, the favorite wife of Kauai's last high chief, King Kaumualii, made her home near the lagoon until her death in 1855.

The Chapel in the Palms now makes its home next to the lagoon. With its shaggy palm-thatched roof and steeple, the twenty-seat chapel has been the site of thousands of weddings since it was built in 1954 for the movie marriage of Rita Hayworth in *Sadie Thompson*. It was Elvis' *Blue Hawaii* wedding, however, that captured the imagination of couples looking for a royal wedding Hawaiian-style, and Larry Rivera was there to make their dreams of royalty a reality.

Rivera is himself an island dignitary of sorts. He began composing and singing traditional Hawaiian melodies at the Coco Palms almost immediately after it opened in 1953. He's performed all over the United States, appeared on the television show "Fantasy Island," and recently released his twelfth recording.

Like all royal events, a Blue Hawaii wedding follows certain rituals. The celebration begins when the groom, dressed all in white with a red sash around his waist—the sign of royalty—climbs aboard a double-rigged canoe covered with fresh tropical flowers. Two Hawaiian men clad in red *malos*—loincloths—paddle the canoe across the lagoon to meet the bride, while Larry Rivera, also on board the canoe, strums his guitar and serenades with melodies from *Blue Hawaii*.

Once the couple is united on board the canoe, they travel to the Chapel in the Palms. Upon landing, island women bearing flower-covered arches greet the couple and escort them to the chapel. Before them walk two men blowing the conch shell, signifying the arrival of royalty and the beginning of an important ceremony. Larry all the while follows along singing about love—aloha—and beautiful tropical Hawaii. After the ceremony, the chapel bell joins the sound of the conch in celebrating the happy union.

Chris and Deedre Pettersen ride to the Chapel in the Palms with Larry Rivera

Because of insurance reasons the Coco Palms has yet to reopen following Hurricane Iniki in 1992, but Larry Rivera continues to arrange about a hundred Blue Hawaii weddings a year in the Chapel in the Palms. A ceremony costs $1,570.

Chris and Deedre Pettersen of Los Angeles did not choose a Blue Hawaii wedding specifically because of Elvis, but they nevertheless felt his love for the islands. Chris, vice president of a commercial bank, and Deedre, a fitness consultant, met by chance in the lobby of a university and instantly felt attracted to each other. They likewise felt an instant connection with the islands upon their first visits.

"I first saw Hawaii on a business trip," says Deedre. "The

moment the plane landed in Waikiki, my heart opened up and I started to cry. Hawaii has a very special loving feeling. The compassionate people, the tropical feel, the weather. It was paradise. It felt like home, and I'd never been there. My heart yearns for it still."

"I was born in Honolulu," says Chris, "but moved when I was small. My parents always spoke of the islands as paradise. When I returned as an adult, I knew they were right. If Hawaii is paradise, then Kauai is the garden of Eden. It's so lush and uncrowded compared to the other islands. You can't help but be awed by its beauty and think that someone greater than ourselves created it."

When Chris and Deedre became engaged while vacationing in Kauai, they knew they wanted to marry there as well. "A concierge at our hotel told us that we had to speak to Larry Rivera, that he was a dignitary of sorts, an ambassador to Hawaii," says Chris. "We called him and he was so in tune with people. He loves the island and wants you to enjoy and appreciate it. A Blue Hawaii wedding sounded perfect."

"We're spiritual people," explains Deedre, "but we hadn't found a church in Los Angeles to feel comfortable in. A Blue Hawaii wedding was a happy medium since we wanted the spirit and essence of Kauai. Some of our friends wondered why we had to go so far away, but we felt so connected with the island."

Neither Deedre nor Chris wanted a traditional wedding. "I'd recently gone to a wedding with about four hundred guests," says Chris. "But when you asked anyone about the wedding, the first thing they said was, 'There was a lot of people there.' Everything just came down to numbers."

"I had the gown and the church wedding in the early eighties," adds Deedre. "At first, I had to do a lot of work inside to let go of the idea of a traditional wedding. But I'm forty. I'm not a princess anymore."

The Pettersons, however, were treated like royalty for their Blue Hawaii wedding. Chris dressed all in white with the red Hawaiian sash around his waist, while Deedre wore a white halter gown with a lei of purple orchids and a wreath of flowers for her hair. Their eight guests also got into the spirit, wearing Hawaiian shirts and leis.

A local minister performed the ceremony, concluding with a prayer in Hawaiian and a butterfly release into the blue Hawaiian skies. "The wedding was beautiful," says Chris, "beyond what I'd hoped for. The idea of traveling across a lagoon to pick up my bride accompanied by gentle, strong people so in spirit with the music. It was hard not to cry. It was like being in a dream. Deedre looked so beautiful. All of a sudden you realize what's important in life."

"The ceremony is so symbolic," agrees Deedre. "The man leaving his world, coming to the woman in her world, and then both going together to a new world."

Chris and Deedre believe they were married in the true spirit of aloha, the spirit of love and welcome, and speak rapturously about the royal treatment they received from everyone on Kauai. "I'm not the same person I was before our wedding," says Chris. "It made me appreciate that there are beautiful people out there who don't live in a metropolis, and when they give you their word they mean it. Larry has such a magical energy about him. Whenever we're down and depressed we listen to his CD's."

Elvis even found a way to make his presence known. "Larry's microphone wasn't working when he sang 'Blue Hawaii' on the canoe," says Deedre, "so in the video he dubbed in Elvis singing the song. So I guess you could say that Elvis sang at our wedding!"

The royal courts of Kauai are part of history, but for couples who follow the Hollywood example of Kauai's other king and have their dreams come true in a Blue Hawaii wedding, history is still being made.

Chapel in the Palms Weddings
1092 Kamalu Road, Kapaa, Kauai, Hawaii 96746
808-822-3868

4

Shop Till You Drop: In Search of the Perfect "Chapel"

Americans are arguably the world's most avid shoppers, and nothing can set a couple to arguing more than shopping around for a place to hold the most important event in their life. Wedding sites, therefore, come in all shapes, sizes, and locations to please even the most eclectic shopper.

The thirty-five-thousand-ton battleship U.S.S. *Alabama* docked in Mobile, Alabama, provides couples enamored of the glory days of World War II a militaristic setting for their wedding. In the shadow of 139 giant war guns and sundry missiles, submarines, and other war equipment, couples pledge a life of peaceful coexistence.

Couples seeking saner ground travel to Dunseith, North Dakota, for a wedding in the International Peace Garden's Peace Chapel, which straddles the Canadian border. Couples have also wed in the shade of the International Forest of Friendship in Atchison, Kansas.

In 1814, a group of German religious dissenters called the Harmonists shopped for a utopia in southern Indiana. Their historic community, now called New Harmony, today attracts shoppers seeking values in antiques and crafts, but one building in the community still attracts those who want no object to come between them and God—not even a roof. The Roofless Church appeals to couples who desire God's love to rain down on them.

A really wild wedding can be had at the Philadelphia Zoo. Couples marry at the Rare Animal House with its beautiful view of the Impala lawn and the city of Philadelphia; at the Reptile House where Egyptian cobras make excellent icebreakers; or at the Treehouse, home to magical oversized habitats where guests can rest their feet by sitting on larger-than-life caterpillars. Zoo staff guarantee that the charm and personalities of the untamed guests will fascinate one and all.

Up until the late 1930s, Elkton, Maryland was known as the wedding capital of the world. Because of the surrounding county's liberal marriage laws, nearly ten thousand couples a year traveled to Elkton to wed. The town was even mentioned in movies such as *Guys and Dolls* and *The Philadelphia Story*. Today, the fourteen-seat Little Wedding Chapel is the only remaining chapel, and about eight hundred couples wed here each year. Historically, they are in good company since luminaries such as Babe Ruth and Joan Fontaine wed here as well.

High-tech couples have a number of online wedding chapels toward which they can point their browsers. The Knot at www.theknot.com calls itself the largest and most comprehensive wedding resource on the Internet. In 1997, this site celebrated the first-ever Wedding Day holiday by getting thousands of couples worldwide to participate in an online exchange of vows. The Knot aims to carry on the tradition each year on the third Saturday of every June. Although several legal weddings have taken place ontline, most are symbolic ceremonies taking place on sites like the Knot, the Cheap Chapel, and GlamOrama's Weddimatic Commitment System, all catering to couples still doing some window shopping.

In the wedding industry, one size never fits all, but hard to please "chapel" shoppers should never despair—the perfect fit is out there.

Lady Cyana Divers' Underwater Wedding

ISLAMORADA, FLORIDA

One of the last things a bride and groom seem able to do on their wedding day is kick back and relax, but for couples deeply in love with each other, to kick back and relax is literally the most important thing they can do when they don their scuba gear and take the plunge for an underwater wedding.

"I call myself Justice of the Pisces," says Gloria Teague of Lady Cyana Divers in Islamorada, Florida. For the past eight years this scuba instructor and notary public has been marrying couples under the waters of the Florida Keys.

The Keys have long been populated by people with an almost mythic resistance to anything resembling routine. In fact, Lady Cyana Divers takes its name from the mythical father/daughter diving team of Scyllias and Cyana, who dove beneath the Aegean Sea to cut the anchor lines of the invading Persian fleet.

Early explorers of the Keys battled voracious mosquitoes and stifling heat, engaged in conflicts with the Seminole Indians, and endured isolation from the mainland to seek their fortunes from sunken ships.

With the completion of the Overseas Highway in 1928, the installation of electricity in 1942, and the beginning of mosquito control in 1952, the Florida Keys quickly became a divers' paradise. There are more dive shops per square mile in the Keys than anywhere else in the world, and couples from all over the world have come to Islamorada to marry underneath the brilliant multihued waters.

When couples marrying on solid ground turn queasy at the prospect of walking down the aisle, what compels these couples, many with no previous diving experience, to sink below the surface and kick their way down a watery aisle? One obvious reason is location. The warm indigo waters of the Keys are home to the longest living reef system in the continental United States. More than six hundred varieties of magnificently colored tropical fish swim among the reefs and the shipwrecks of eighteenth-century Spanish galleons.

Islamorada, or "the Purple Isles," was named by Spanish explorers centuries ago. The surrounding water's varied colors—blues, indigos, purples—and the golden light that reaches through to illuminate the roseate coral formations rival the colors of the most magnificent stained-glass windows of the grandest cathedral.

"It takes an adventurous person to marry underwater," says Teague. "They're serious about marriage, they're just not serious about the ceremony. With an underwater wedding, couples don't put their relatives through a laborious church wedding that's over in half an hour."

Simply preparing to take the watery plunge is fascinating. Couples with no diving experience spend several days learning the ropes before they tie the knot. They spend day one in a swimming pool learning correct breathing and kicking techniques. On day two they practice actual diving before going through with the ceremony on the third day.

"Sometimes people will panic," says Teague. "I had a bride who decided she just couldn't do it. She was afraid of the water and afraid of the pool and was crying. I had to take her aside and ask her, 'Do you want to get married underwater or not?' But I worked with her, and she went through with it."

Couples choose the preferred location for their ceremony from a wide variety of reefs and shipwrecks in the Islamorada area. They can either go out on the regularly scheduled daily depture of Lady Cyana Divers' boat ($40 per person) or charter the whole boat for a private ceremony ($650). The ceremony itself costs $195.

Once the couple is underwater, the watery ritual begins. Because speaking through the diving equipment causes a person's voice to sound garbled and hollow, rather like an underwater Darth Vadar, most communication, even the vow exchange, takes place by writing on special underwater slates that Teague and her staff design and hand-paint for each couple.

"We gather in the presence of friends, family, and fish," she begins as she points to the words on her slate. Fish do show up for the ceremony, and they often stick around. "Sometimes you see fish that make you wonder why you're in the water," says Teague. "But they're really harmless. During one couple's wedding, a five-foot barracuda sat over the groom's shoulder and stared at the bouquet of flowers for the whole ceremony, like it was the best man. Another time a small nurse shark decided to join the ceremony and lay the whole time underneath a ledge. The bride loved it."

The ring exchange and kiss are the trickiest part of the ceremony. "We keep the rings on large clips, like a dog collar, so they don't float away," says Teague. "For the kiss, couples grab their partner's harness with one hand while removing the regulator from their mouths with the other. They tip their heads, kiss, put the regulator back in, and breathe."

While air bubbles travel upward, guests on board uncork the other bubbles for the revelry that takes place when the couple surfaces. Some couples even have their guests dive down with them. Guests can also snorkel and observe the ceremony from a higher elevation. "Oftentimes the best part of the ceremony is the reaction of other people on the boat," says Teague. "One couple on board thought it was such a good idea they came back and renewed their fortieth anniversary vows underwater."

Besides the standard diving equipment, what a couple wears is limited only by their imagination. "I've had brides in full-length wedding dresses and veils. We practice a special kick in the dress so that it doesn't get wrapped around her legs in the water. Grooms have worn everything from traditional tuxedos to tuxedo T-shirts to skimpy black swimwear and bow ties, like Chippendale dancers. I've had couples in Roaring twenties swimsuits, cowboy hats, brass diving helmets from 1932, and mermaid costumes. One couple who married in mermaid attire

Scott and Laura Leupold float behind the
Christ of the Deep statue

even produced a video showing the groom catching his mermaid
bride and returning her to the sea where they become mermaid
and merman. Even if the couple wears just a swimsuit, I can
usually convince the bride to wear a veil and garter."

Scott and Laura Leupold of Hinckley, Illinois, were already
certified divers when they decided to marry underwater. "I've
been swimming all my life," says Scott, a nurse anesthetist. "I
grew up at the pool and was on the swim team and dive team, so
I had thought about a dive wedding. I like a little challenge,
something a little iffy, but I wondered how we'd get a minister to
go underwater. I read about Gloria in a dive magazine and told
Laura about it."

"I thought a dive wedding would be great," adds Laura, a radiology technician who met Scott at work. "I love being in the water. It's so quiet and peaceful, like being in outer space. Anybody can get married in a church, and a traditional wedding is stuffy and expensive. There's so much pomp and circumstance, and people buying you gifts you don't need. Our wedding was more bold and daring. Our parents were miffed that we weren't inviting anyone, but they don't like to swim anyway. Also, with an underwater wedding you don't have to do your hair or wear makeup, and it doesn't matter if the weather's bad because you get wet anyway."

In keeping with their simple philosophy, Scott and Laura wore standard dive suits for their wedding, his blue, hers pink. Laura wore a garter, around her leg, and Scott attached a carnation boutonniere to his suit. Laura also carried a bouquet of red carnations and baby's breath.

They wed in a private ceremony at the base of the Christ of the Deep statue in the waters of John Pennekamp Coral Reef State Park. "It seemed appropriate to have the wedding at the base of the statue," says Laura. "You got to have Christ in mind when you do anything. During our ceremony the sun was hitting the statue and beams of light were coming from Christ's arms. We felt such awe."

After the ceremony, Laura did the traditional bouquet toss, only with a twist. "I fed my bouquet to the fish," she reports. "They loved the baby's breath. They were like little piranha around my face." She and Scott then swam off to explore on their own for a while, newlyweds in a kaleidoscope of color.

"I keep a log book of all my dives," says Scott. "For that day I wrote: Underwater one hour and five minutes. Depth 28 feet. Air temperature 82 degrees. Visibility 50–60 feet. Wedding. Best dive of my life.'"

Gloria Teague assures couples that any wedding jitters they have will get washed away on the outgoing tide once they see the ease there is in gliding down the aisle. Couples like Scott and

Laura would certainly agree that an underwater wedding in the tropical Keys ensures a flood of warm memories.

Lady Cyana Divers
P.O. Box 1157, Islamorada, Fla. 33036
800-221-8717 / www.ladycyana.com

The Round Barn of Arcadia

ARCADIA, OKLAHOMA

"I was sitting with my grandfather on his porch when the Round Barn's roof caved in," says Jeannice Calkins of Oklahoma City. "It sounded just like a tornado. It was a devastating feeling. We just stood there with our mouths open, and my grandfather said, 'Well, there it goes.' All the time when I was growing up I just thought about it as an old barn with holes in it. It wasn't until the roof caved in that I realized the history and beauty that could be lost. Since it's been restored, I tell everyone about the barn. I could sit in the upper floor all day and watch people's reactions when they see the dome for the first time. It makes you feel good."

The Round Barn of Arcadia, Oklahoma, made Jeannice feel so good that she and her husband, John, decided to be the first couple to wed in its warm embrace following its restoration in 1992. "People were so happy after the barn's restoration," she says. "When John and I decided to get married there, everyone said, 'I'll be there with bells on,' and they were. Almost everyone came with bells on their shoes."

It was a glorious celebration in commemoration of a glorious resurrection. In 1988, the Round Barn sat along Route 66 like a proud beauty struggling to remain dignified despite years of hardship. Its once-graceful circular planks were rotting and pulling away from the outside. Windows in its shabby sides appeared like the dark hollow eyes of a gravely ill person. Its magnificent domed roof, its crown of glory, had collapsed with a

The Round Barn restored

sickening sigh, and it was shifting off its foundation as if preparing to lay down for life's final rest.

When farmer William Odor built the barn in 1898, its innovative shape captured the imagination of Oklahomans. Grain and animals were sheltered on the ground floor, and dances were held on the upper level under the graceful dome of the wooden sky. So fine were the acoustics, it was possible to hear a pin drop on the other side of the barn—or so it was said. It quickly became a topic of conversation and a landmark for travelers.

But as the round barn changed hands over the decades and as the Oklahoma weather took its toll, it gradually tired out and began to lose its shape. Even though it was placed on the National Register of Historic Places in 1977, the Round Barn looked as if it was going to become history. Its beauty was definitely in the eye of the beholder. It needed more than a facelift to restore its spirit; it needed major and difficult reconstructive surgery.

Then in 1988, Luke Robison, a retired carpenter and history buff from nearby Oklahoma City, long an admirer of the barn's charms, took it upon himself to restore the soulful aging beauty. Armed with spirited tenacity, he and a group of not-quite-so-young Arcadians formed the Arcadia Historical and Preservation Society. Their nickname—the Over-the-Hill Gang. Their motto—"Think Round." Their goal—to provide the tough love and cold cash that would help the barn regain its status as the most shapely beauty for miles around.

But thinking round was easier than doing round, especially for a group of preservation novices. The architectural challenges the project posed were immense. When the domed roof collapsed just three weeks after the society was formed, many people thought that was the end of the barn, but just as many were moved by the Over-the-Hill Gang's commitment to the decaying old structure and donated cash, equipment, and thousands of hours of labor.

Supplied with equal amounts of imagination, determination, and love, Robison and the Over-the-Hill Gang gradually returned the Round Barn to the glorious beauty of its prime. So astonishing and nearly miraculous was their labor of love that the National Trust for Historic Preservation in Washington, D.C., gave them its prestigious National Honor Award in 1993.

Today, thousands of travelers from around the world cruising Route 66 stop at the Round Barn of Arcadia to admire its shape and story. "People love the barn," says Eula "Toodie" Teuscher, the seventy-two-year-old retired teacher who is now the current president of the Arcadia Historical Society. "I recently received a letter from a friend of mine who had her ninetieth birthday party in the barn. She wrote, 'When we have the desire to save the history of our ancestors, that's just a little piece of heaven in our hearts.' The barn is a symbol of Oklahoma's frontier heritage. It helps people appreciate what men in the 1890s could do without power tools. It's an engineering feat, even today."

Sitting on a small green hillside around a bend in the otherwise straight stretch of Route 66 that crosses Oklahoma, the Round

Barn with its shingled domed roof stands out against the blue Oklahoma sky. The ground floor contains a history of the barn and the restoration efforts. Ernest Lee "Butch" Breuger, who once worked the now-closed filling station next to the barn, greets visitors from behind tables of Round Barn and Route 66 souvenirs. Having appeared in several documentaries about Route 66, Breuger's as much a fixture of the highway as the barn itself. He proudly displays his own sketches of the Round Barn along with photos of other round and nearly round barns sent to him from around the country. Also on display are photographs of the "old" round barn, faded and forsaken, a constant reminder of what can be accomplished with heartfelt determination.

But it's the top floor of the barn that's truly wondrous. When visitors step into the loft and look up into the forty-three-foot dome, their first reaction is a whispered, "Wow!" Gently curving burr-oak rafters radiate from the peak of the dome like beams of light stemming from a star. More than thirty-three thousand golden brown shingles create the impressive domed roof. It's like looking up into a giant basket woven by a master craftsman. Footsteps resonate on the polished oak floor and voices echo under the lofty dome, while gentle winds blow in from the windows that ring the walls.

The accomplishments of the Over-the-Hill Gang have made the Round Barn a wonderful place for couples who are about to embark on a journey that will require equal commitment, courage, and spirit. Since the Calkin's wedding in 1992, there have been about two to three weddings a month in the spacious loft, which holds up to two hundred people and rents for $175. Weddings in the barn range from the Calkin's country-themed celebration with gingham and hay bales to the formal affair of Stefanie and Steve LeGrande of Guthrie, Oklahoma.

Although Stefanie and Steve grew up together in Guthrie, they both eventually moved away. Drawn by the pull of family ties, they later returned to Guthrie, became reacquainted, and eventually were engaged. It was family ties, too, that led them to the barn.

"My grandfather had seventy acres in Arcadia and took his hay to the barn to store," explains Steve, an electrician, "and some of Stefanie's relatives were involved in the restoration of the barn. It's always seemed to be a part of the family somehow."

"It was in the process of decaying when we were growing up," says Stefanie, a veterinary technician, "but it was always a landmark to give directions. Anytime you talk around here of someplace historic or significant, you think of the Round Barn. I had been to a birthday party at the barn when I got the idea of marrying there. It was so beautiful with all the open windows."

"When she came home and told me about marrying in the barn, I thought it was incredible," adds Steve. "I didn't want a regular church wedding where everyone just shows up at the church and it's the same old thing. I've been in about fifteen weddings. I wanted ours to be different. I've done some carpentry work, so I appreciate the work people did on it, especially on the dome. I thought it'd be the perfect place."

"We also didn't want to be right in town," says Stefanie. "We wanted something in the country, something peaceful. In the barn you could have the windows open and hear the birds." She laughs. "One of the reasons we didn't get married in our church is that we couldn't have the windows open!"

Despite the rustic setting, the LeGrandes wore formal attire. Stefanie wore a floor-length off-white gown with embroidered roses, and Steve wore a tuxedo. Their 125 guests sat in folding chairs set up in a semi-circle around the platform that stands in the center of the barn. "At first we wondered how we were going to set up chairs for the families," says Stefanie, "but then we realized that we loved the concept of family and friends all in a circle. There was no bride's side and groom's side, no division between friends and family. No matter where you sat, you were always part of the circle."

Getting Steve's ninety-eight-year-old grandfather into that circle was somewhat of a challenge. "We had to sit him in a chair and carry him up the flight of steps to the loft," says Steve. "It was a little awkward, but it worked."

Everyone agreed that the service was lovely, although the barn was a bit hot—there is no air-conditioning. "Our cake was leaning over because it was so warm," says Stefanie.

The guests who had not been to the barn since its restoration were quite impressed with the beautiful results, especially as the sun set and highlighted the warm browns ands golds of the wood. Following the ceremony, the LeGrandes and their guests spent the evening dancing by torchlight under the graceful dome, just as in Odor's day one hundred years ago.

Every eye that now beholds the Round Barn of Arcadia sees beauty. As circular wedding bands symbolize unending love, so the barn stands strong and round and true, an indisputably dignified and commanding presence in this town of three hundred people. Truly, this once faded beauty has been barn again.

> The Round Barn of Arcadia
> Arcadia Historical and Preservation Society
> P.O. Box 134, Arcadia, Okla. 73007
> 405-396-2398

Chapel of Love, Mall of America

BLOOMINGTON, MINNESOTA

On the wide open plains of the Midwest, church steeples and grain elevators share the horizon as they rise to the heavens. Soybeans, corn, cattle, and God demand equal attention and respect in the breadbasket of the nation.

But once ribbon-straight country roads begin twisting into the complicated knots of suburban interstates, housing developers uproot farmers and plant pseudo-estates. Super America convenience stores overthrow king corn, and the tiered parking lots of shopping malls dwarf houses of worship.

In Minnesota, land of ten thousand lakes, baptism into the cult of patriotic capitalism became easy when the Mall of America opened in 1992 in Bloomington, a suburb of Minneapolis. The nation's largest retail emporium and the most visited destination in America, the Mall of America covers 4.2 million square feet and houses more than five hundred stores, fifty restaurants, eight nightclubs, fourteen movie screens, one LEGO Imagination Center, one eighteen-hole Golf Mountain, one Underwater World aquarium, and one seven-acre Camp Snoopy indoor amusement park.

According to the mall's public relations department, Mall of America compares more than favorably in terms of sheer size with other countries' cultural landmarks. More than twenty St. Peter's Basilicas in Rome would fit inside the mall. Masterpieces by Michelangelo compete with a three-story-tall inflated Snoopy sitting Buddah-like in the center of the park that bears his name. Children frolic and play in the belly of the beast.

Compared to Mall of America's 4.2 million square feet, Russia's Red Square is a teeny 800,000, while the forty acres of gardens surrounding Buckingham Palace would easily fit into the mall. But perhaps the most sacrilegious statistic—at least to those who believe baseball rather than shopping is America's most spiritually imbued pastime—is that seven Yankee Stadiums would fit inside Mall of America. "Where have you gone, Joe DiMaggio?" takes on new meaning here.

Forty-two million people a year pass through the mall's red-white-and-blue, stars-and-stripes emblazoned doors, including over two million foreign tourists. On holiday weekends when out-of-towners make pilgrimages to the mall, the wait for a spot in one of the twenty thousand parking spaces can seem like an eternity. If patience is a virtue, these parkers are blessed in abundance as they await their turn to slide into a slot that will allow them easy entrance to the promised land.

In fact, the seven-story parking garage is one of the first things visitors see when they approach the Mall of America from the sprawling, soaring maze of highways, hotels, and motels that sprout and thrive on the fertile grounds surrounding the mall. As high stone walls surrounded and protected cities of old, the tiered gray-cement garage stands guard around the cherished goods of our consumer culture.

Four giant department stores anchor the Mall of America and prevent it from floating away on its own tide of enthusiastic promotions. "There's a place for fun in your life" is the mall's motto. Now one only has to find it amid the lights and noise and seemingly endless procession of stores that line the aisles to the altar of the almighty dollar. Souvenir shops even sell T-shirts professing, "Shopping is Life. Nothing Else Matters."

But in the Mall of America, not all aisles lead to fashion, food, and trinkets. One aisle actually does lead to something no amount of money and glitz can buy—true love.

Nestled at 240 North Garden between the Reminisce gift shop and the Minne Sew Ta monogramming shop, across the aisle from the glowing red lights of the General Nutrition Center, the Chapel of Love specializes in fanning and feeding the flames of passion. It's here that couples shopping for a wedding bargain tie the knot, where the "something borrowed" of wedding traditions isn't always money.

White pillars frame the doorway of the glass-fronted Chapel of Love, which also houses a gift boutique. A simple gold heart over the entranceway reminds shoppers and couples that true love needs no frills. But once inside the Gifts of Love boutique, the marriage-minded are surrounded by the frills that make love profitable for the Chapel of Love. Everything from pearl-and-lace-encrusted baseball caps to bride-and-groom bubble gum can be had for a price.

The seventy-five-seat chapel with its white wooden pews lies concealed behind frosted glass doors. Tastefully decorated in shades of ivory and moss green with twining floral arrangements adorning the simple podium and the rafterlike ceiling, the Chapel of Love's understated interior seems far removed from the screams of riders on the Ripsaw roller coaster two hundred feet away, the fabricated thunderstorms that roll on schedule through the Rain Forest Café, or the alcohol-inspired musings of star-crossed lovers at Planet Hollywood nightclub.

A small bridal dressing room allows brides to prepare out of sight of the tide of package-toting shoppers that inevitably floods the entrance to the chapel whenever a wedding takes place.

Comments from onlookers run from the appreciative and positive—couples fondly recall their own weddings and want to walk down the chapel's aisle—to the cynical and scornful. "A wedding in a mall?" a traveler from Holland scoffs. "Never! What's next? A funeral parlor?" Meanwhile, another onlooker wonders whether "these types of marriages" last longer than "church-type marriages." Even the archbishop of the Minneapolis/St. Paul diocese condemned the Chapel of Love when it opened for stripping marriage and family of their sacred and dignified character.

But Sue Bostrom Mills, senior wedding consultant, is used to incredulity. "There are two questions visitors always ask," she says. " 'Can you really get married there?' followed by 'Who would want to get married there?' "

But the Chapel of Love definitely appeals to a wide variety of shoppers. Since its opening in April 1994, more than fifteen hundred couples from thirty-five states and four foreign countries have wed here. A Dream Wedding at the chapel can cost as little as $195 and be over in twenty minutes. If money's no object, a Mega Wedding runs $3,295 and includes limousine service and luxury hotel accommodations.

In fact, Tairie Starr, a wedding consultant at the Chapel of Love, was so enamored of the setting that she and her husband, Bill, who works in shipping and receiving had their own wedding in the chapel. "Its pretty! It's cute! I mean, churches don't look like that," she declares. "It's got those white pews, and it's already decorated so you don't have to do anything to it."

Unlike most people, Tairie says she was never fazed by the idea of a mall wedding. "I didn't really know people reacted so negatively until I started working there. All day long I hear, 'Can you really get married there?' and 'How much does a divorce cost?' One lady even said to me, 'This is really asinine. Who would get married in a circus like this?' But once I get these people inside and calm them down and talk seriously about the chapel, they understand. I mean, we have ministers here who pastor local churches. They're not people who got a license to marry someone from the back of a magazine. These are real people."

Bill, whom Tairie met through the personal ads of a Christian dating service, was a bit more tentative at first about a mall wedding. "The idea took some getting used to," he admits. "I was concerned about what people would think. I always used to laugh at these people who get married when they're doing things like jumping out of an airplane. I thought it was disrespectful to get married that way. I always thought you were supposed to get married in a church, that it was more sacred and traditional, but Tairie convinced me. She made the chapel sound interesting. When I went to see it, there was something there that I felt good about, that I felt at peace with.

"Also, when I'm in the mall or in a large public space, I feel lost in the crowd, and I like that. Basically, I'm not comfortable with an audience. Getting married in a church, you're part of a much bigger display, so even though I was definitely on stage at the Chapel of Love, in a way it seemed relatively small compared to a church."

Although the pastor from their church officiated at their wedding, Bill and Tairie did not get married at their church primarily because it was so big and unadorned compared to the chapel. "It was going to take a lot of time and effort and money to make it look like a wedding was happening there," says Tairie. "It just has folding chairs and it just isn't pretty. Plus we didn't need the space. With only seventy-five guests, it would've looked like no one showed up."

Although the walk down the aisle in the Chapel of Love is pretty straightforward, the maze of the mall can present problems to anyone not familiar with its layout. It's one thing to wander in search of a bargain, it's another to get lost en route to your own wedding. "Because I hadn't been to the mall that much, Tairie and I went through the motions of navigating the mall and getting to the chapel about three or four times before the wedding," recalls Bill.

For their wedding, Tairie wore a long white satin gown and Bill wore a tuxedo. They navigated their way effortlessly through the crowds and met their guests in the chapel. Although the frosted glass doors are shut during the ceremony to maintain privacy, the service is broadcast into the gift shop, so curious shoppers can eavesdrop.

After Tairie and Bill's short traditional ceremony, they made their way through the crowd that invariably gathers around the store when a wedding takes place and back out into the mall. While many newlyweds stop at Camp Snoopy for a spin on the carousel or a ride on the coaster, Tairie and Bill headed straight for their reception at Mrs. Knott's Restaurant in the mall.

"We got a lot of attention from shoppers," says Tairie. "People were smiling all around. Security guards congratulated us, and one woman came up and gave us a hug. Seeing a bride and groom just makes people happy."

Although some of their friends were a little surprised at their choice of locations, they all agreed that the wedding was lovely. "A lot of our guests said, 'It's not what I thought it was going to be,'" reports Bill. "They thought a wedding at the Mall of America was going to be a funny thing, a big joke, but our wedding couldn't have been nicer in a church."

Despite the Chapel of Love's detractors, Mills remains upbeat. "We're working in a very positive, uplifting environment. We're assisting people in orchestrating probably one of the most important days in their life.

"I personally believe in marriage, and I'm thrilled whenever I see two people become a couple. I also feel this to be somewhat of a stewardship in my personal life. To make a reverent, spiritual setting available to people and to provide them with clergy so they can start their married life off with the unity of God.

"The sacred, after all, is where you want it to be. We just happen to be in the Mall of America."

Chapel of Love, Mall of America
240 North Garden, Bloomington,Minn. 55425
800-299-LOVE / www.chapeloflove.com

Empire State Building
NEW YORK, NEW YORK

When King Kong beat his furry fists in a lovelorn frenzy atop the Empire State Building in New York City, he set an example for other passionate suitors eager to scale the skies to profess their love. Since his famed 1933 ascent of America's grandest cathedral of commerce, countless lovers have followed in his footsteps to exchange words of endearment high above the bustling streets of midtown Manhattan.

Although the building is no longer the world's tallest, the mystique surrounding the 102-story Empire State Building remains timeless and immeasurable. Since opening in 1931, the graceful Art Deco tower has stood for what's grandest and noblest in the human impulse to rise above and dominate our surroundings.

Every year 3.5 million people from nearly every country on the planet visit the observation decks for a view of one of the world's most vibrant and powerful cities. On a clear day the view extends as far as eighty miles into five states.

When the elevator doors open onto the eighty-sixth-floor Observatory visitors are drawn to the outdoor terrace as if towards the shore of the sea. Language barriers are forgotten as strangers gesture to strangers to have their picture taken looking out over the shimmering waves of concrete. Taxicabs glide like golden fish among the massive ships of commerce and industry. Central Park appears a verdant oasis amid miles of cement and steel. And in the distance, Lady Liberty lifts her lamp beside the golden door.

At night, the Empire State Building rises like a glimmering needle into the star-spangled fabric of the evening sky. Its tower lights have set the mood for the city and the nation, commemorating everything from presidential to World Series victories. The Freedom Lights—revolving beacons of light 1,095 feet above the street—symbolize a welcome to this country and the unlimited opportunities of America. All things seem possible in this airy empire.

It's this feeling of confident idealism that attracts lovers eager to believe in the infinite possibilities of their own life together. About a dozen wed throughout the year in the glass-enclosed observatory on the 102d floor, but it's the Valentine's Day wedding contest sponsored by the Thirty-fourth Street Partnership that draws the most interest and attention. Started in 1994, the contest requires that couples write an essay titled "Why I Want to Get Married at the Empire State Building." Thirty-four winners receive a free wedding for up to fifteen guests, including wedding rings and champagne toast.

"We've received hundreds of entries from all over the world," says Eileen Aluska, assistant director of the observatories, who helps choose the winners. "We look for interesting stories, like the couple where the bride's father was a stonemason who laid the foundation for the building. We also look for couples who might not be able to afford a big wedding, although the couples have to get to New York themselves."

The weddings take place in a private room on the eightieth-floor sky lobby with views north into Central Park and east toward the impressive silver spire of the Chrysler Building. Couples walk a red carpet to a special greenery-bedecked pagoda accompanied by live piano music. The first wedding gets underway at 7:30 A.M., and the last one finishes up at 8:00 P.M. Four different judges announce couples husband and wife throughout the day.

But any wedding fatigue on the judges' part couldn't compare with the joyous fatigue felt by Trevor and Karen Sinden. It was a long way from their four-acre Inkstand Meadow Farm in Kent, England, to New York City, but the Sindens were determined to wed in the Big Apple.

"New York just seems like the place to get married," says Trevor, an electrical engineer who had visited New York the year before with Karen. "A lot of places in England close up early. In New York, you can be out all night. You can eat when you want to. It's a twenty-four-hour-a-day place. Karen and I are extroverts, and as we get older we like to try different things."

"When Trevor surprised me with a Valentine's Day trip to New York, we decided that it was finally time to get married," says Karen. "We'd been together nine years, but we'd concentrated on raising our children from our previous marriages. We had earlier planned a wedding at a country home in England, but then my father died and I didn't think I could handle a big wedding, so we got on the Internet to look for places where we could get married in New York and decided on the Empire State Building. There's not a single person who doesn't recognize it. It has that one and only shape. It goes up and up and up. It's America. It's New York. Even the name's got a ring to it."

"The Empire State Building comes to mind almost immediately when you think about America," says Trevor. "It has character. It's not just a block. Even though other buildings are bigger and taller, there'll never ever be another Empire State Building."

There were, however, some glitches to overcome. Trevor and Karen did not know about the Valentine's Day contest, and when they called to make wedding arrangements for Valentine's Day, they were told that it was all booked. But when a couple canceled at the last minute, Trevor and Karen were asked to send a fax saying why they wanted to get married at the Empire State Building. They immediately composed a response saying how romantic and energetic New York City was for them. When they faxed it back, they were assigned the 5:00 P.M. wedding slot. Karen quickly packed up her wedding dress, and several days later she and Trevor were off to America. The only person they told about their wedding plans was Karen's mother, who was quite pleased they were finally getting married.

"We landed in New York the day before Valentine's Day," says Karen. "After a long flight we still had to rush around and get a money order for the marriage license, so we took a taxi to the post office and a taxi to the municipal building—this great big mundane building—where everyone but everyone in New York was queuing up for a license whether they were getting married on Valentine's Day or not. There was a queue of people coming out of the office and up the corridor and down the corridor. A lot of people were getting married right there in that municipal building. I thought it very bland.

"But there were so many people there. I started to worry because you had to have the license twenty-four hours before your wedding and the office was getting ready to close for the day. I started to cry because I didn't think we'd get the license in time. I thought, No one else in this queue is planning to get married in the Empire State Building. But we made it with twenty minutes to spare. Then we could relax."

The next day, Valentine's Day, Trevor and Karen took a limousine from their hotel to the Empire State Building. Karen wore a long narrow-cut white lace dress, and Trevor wore a suit and tie. On the flight from England, they had met a couple who were celebrating their wedding anniversary in New York, and they agreed to be their witnesses. "I asked them if they'd be available and they were quite pleased to do it," says Karen.

Getting married late in the day was a relatively quiet event as the media that had taped some of the earlier weddings for live broadcasts were gone. "It was more of a ceremony than we thought with the red carpet and the piano player," recalls Trevor. "I had tears in my eyes. It was very emotional. We had come all that way, and it wasn't easy to arrange all the details. We couldn't believe we were getting married in New York."

"We thought someone was going to wake us up from a dream," says Karen. "We had rushed around and then queued up and now there we were in front of a judge, and we had done it all on our own. We were on cloud nine, but everything went by so fast. We also didn't know that they were going to give us a ring. We had already got one, but I thought, I can't not have our Empire State Building ring, so now I wear both of them!"

After the Sindens' ceremony, they were presented with a laminated card showing their membership in the Empire State Building's Valentine's Day Wedding Club. "We don't know quite what it does," says Karen, "but when you think how many people there are in the world and how many people get married at the

Empire State Building on Valentine's Day, there's not that many people, maybe around 136, so far. We consider ourselves lucky. We still can't believe sometimes that we got married at the Empire State Building."

When the couple returned to England, their friends and family were thrilled with the news of their romantic New York wedding. "I put my dress on several times for my family," says Karen, "because once you put it away, you put it away for good. I even wore it down to the village pub to have a drink."

When Faye Wray agreed to star in *King Kong,* she was told she'd have the tallest, darkest leading man in Hollywood. Although the love that awaited her at the top of the Empire State Building was certainly not what she had in mind, there's no doubt that modern lovers can be nothing but pleased with their romantic rendezvous high in the Manhattan sky.

Empire State Building
Fifth Avenue at 34th Street, New York, N.Y.
212-736-3100 / www.esb.nyc.com

Married in Madison County

WINTERSET, IOWA

Passing cars cause clouds of white dust to rise from the winding gravel roads of Madison County, Iowa. The clouds billow toward the boundless blue sky, then resettle upon the tall green cornstalks that line the rolling roads that lead to Madison County's historic covered bridges.

Cornstalks are not, however, the only things clothed in white along the back roads of southern Iowa. Ever since *The Bridges of Madison County*—Robert James Waller's best-selling novel turned film—made popular Robert Kincaid's and Francesca Johnson's star-crossed romance, couples from all over the country have donned their white wedding finery and traveled to Winterset, Iowa, to star in their own rendition of Waller's sentimental tale.

Front view of the Roseman Bridge

Photographer Robert Kincaid was a drifter and a dreamer who met a kindred spirit in Iowa farm wife Francesca Johnson. When he rolled up to her tidy farmhouse in his battered pickup and asked directions to the Roseman Bridge, they began a romance so intense, so poignant in its fleeting reality that readers forgot the definition of fiction and were convinced that Robert and Francesca's story was real.

Soon, thousands of tourists from around the world flocked to the picturesque town of forty-five hundred people to see the bridges Kincaid photographed. One Japanese fan was so enamored of the story that he flew to Des Moines forty miles north of Winterset, took a taxi all the way from Des Moines just to see the bridges, then flew right back to Japan.

But lovestruck tourists were not content merely to gaze at the six historic bridges. They also wanted to look longingly on other sites frequented by Robert and Francesca. An official blue highway sign now points the way to "Francesca's House," a stately nineteenth-century farmhouse that stood empty for years before the movie crews shooed out the raccoons and catapulted it into fame. The house has been propped exactly as it was in the movie, and couples eagerly re-create their favorite scenes. They dance in the kitchen and lie in the claw-foot bathtub, now a hot spot for photographs. One couple even got married in the kitchen and had their reception in the dining room.

They drive through the intersection where Francesca made the decision to stay with her family; eat a meal at the Northside Café where Robert ate; sit in Harry the Pickup; stay in room 13 of the Village View Motel, the orange-carpeted room where Waller stays when he's in town. The Montross Pharmacy's coffee shop even created its own *Bridges* dessert, Francesca's Regret—a hot apple dumpling covered with cool ice cream. Tourists often ask if posters of the dessert are available for sale.

But it's still the 1883 Roseman Bridge, where Francesca pins the note inviting Robert to dinner, that draws the most crowds. A gift shop in the shadow of the bridge sells everything from pieces of the bridge salvaged during its 1992 renovation—wood that "dates from the time of Robert and Francesca's visit"— to glass vials of sand gathered from the Middle River beneath the bridge, to ceramic mugs that gradually reveal Robert and Francesca dancing inside the bridge when hot liquids are poured in.

As real-world lovers twirl away in the dusky shelter of the covered bridge, oblivious to the business of the mundane world, it's the wedding business that has Pat Nelson dancing. "My family didn't eat a meal in the months after the movie came out. I had to have someone come in and help me clean my house," says this Winterset native, who arranged nearly fifty weddings on Roseman Bridge in the months following the 1995 release of the movie.

Before *Bridges* mania hit Winterset, Nelson had coordinated special events for the Chamber of Commerce. When it became swamped with wedding inquiries, Nelson took over and started Married in Madison County. Now she coordinates weddings for fans of the book from all across the United States, most of whom choose to marry at Roseman Bridge. Nelson's packages run from $550 to $1,025.

"Couples like the extent of the commitment that Robert and Francesca had to each other, that they found their soul mate," says Nelson. "Even though Robert and Francesca didn't stay together, their relationship was rock solid. During the wedding ceremonies, couples get lost in their own world. They shut everyone out. They always want the minister to say what Robert says to Francesca: 'This kind of certainty comes once in a lifetime.' They look in each other's eyes and cry. The women cry. The guys cry. In fact, for half of the weddings, it's the guy I work with in making the arrangements. They think it's so romantic."

Michael Comstock of Genoa City, Wisconsin, was one of those romantics. *The Bridges of Madison County* was the first movie he and his wife, Dorothy, a supervisor of a condominium, saw together while dating. "We both sat and cried," says this dispatcher for a trucking company. "My tears were rolling nonstop. It was so touching. After I saw the movie, I bought the audiotape and drove down there myself. I'm a romantic at heart and wanted to see what was there. The drive was wonderful. Listening to the book while driving, I felt like I was Robert Kincaid when he sets out on his trip.

"When I saw the Roseman Bridge I was in total awe. A wedding was going on, and my jaw dropped to the ground. What a beautiful place! What a feeling! How all bridges in life join two things together and how this bridge was bringing two people together. When I walked away, I knew that I wanted to get married there."

It's no wonder Michael had such an interest in the story. His relationship with Dorothy has many elements similar to the tale of Robert and Francesca. He first saw Dorothy at a craft show where she had a booth. "When I came around the corner, she was bent over brushing her long hair. She wooshed it back and that was it. I was immediately attracted to her."

He bought a coat hook from her and later on exchanged several words at the pop machine. "I left that day with nothing but regret. I went home and wrote a two-page letter and went back the next day to give it to her, but I got really nervous and couldn't do it. It was my eight-year-old son who said, 'Dad, give it to me, and I'll give it to her.' He did, but I was too nervous to stay and see her reaction."

Dorothy, meanwhile, had been wondering who this man was who kept hanging around the craft fair with his son. "I remembered when he bought the coat hook he kept looking at me strangely. I thought there was something wrong with me! When I saw him walking around the next day I thought he must be there with his wife. It's not common for men and boys to be at a craft fair alone.

"When I read the letter, I turned fifty shades of red. I mean, this guy had paid to get back into the fair just to bring me a letter. He went through every encounter we had with each other, told me how beautiful I was, that he doesn't usually do something like this. I was afraid he was watching somewhere and laughing at me, but I was impressed that he'd follow through on his feelings."

It was several weeks, however, before she responded to the letter, as she was going through a separation from her first husband. She and Michael eventually went on a date and began calling each other regularly. When they saw the movie together in the beginning stages of their relationship, Dorothy admits feeling awkward because of the similarity of their relationships. "I related to Francesca quite a bit. Her job was her family. She took care of everyone and lost herself. At the time, I also felt very little gratitude. I was the mom and wife and did everything and got lost in the shuffle."

Eventually, Michael and Dorothy's relationship led to marriage, and when it came to choosing a location, Michael thought immediately of the bridges of Madison County. "I asked

Dorothy, 'How would you like to go to the bridge?' and she thought it'd be very romantic."

"Winterset is full of down-home people," says Dorothy. "That's how I was born and raised. I love the idea of gravel roads and nothing but corn and rivers around. At first I was somewhat hesitant about planning a long-distance wedding, but when we found out that Pat arranges everything, we knew it'd be a good idea."

They were married on Roseman Bridge on a warm and windy August day in front of thirty guests. They rode to the bridge in an antique horse-drawn buggy driven by a man in a gray coat and top hat. "It was so nice to go up and down the gravel roads and see so much of the day," says Dorothy, "all the farms and hills and trees. It was lovely. On our way to the bridge a limousine passed us on a gravel road and the people in it stopped and took pictures of us."

Their guests were waiting at the far end of the 107-foot-long bridge when Michael and Dorothy arrived. Dorothy, wearing a long white sleeveless dress, and Michael, wearing a tuxedo with a western-style tie, followed their children as they strewed rose petals down the white runner leading into the bridge. "Doe Eyes," the theme from the movie, played on a CD player. Michael and Dorothy walked across the resounding wooden planks of the bridge while warm sunlight streamed through the windows. Following the simple ceremony, they released two white doves and had a champagne toast.

"Everyone was crying," says Michael. "It was wonderful!"

Meanwhile, a group of camera-ready tourists had gathered at the other side of the bridge. "Pat had tacked up a note asking tourists to please be patient while the wedding was going on," says Dorothy. She laughs. "But in our video we have all these other people at our wedding."

Following the ceremony Dorothy and Michael had a reception at the Summerset House, a Victorian mansion turned tea room and inn. The previous day, they had visited all the spots from the movie, so after the reception, they headed to their bridal suite, room 13 at the Village View Motel.

Although Dorothy and Michael's Roseman Bridge wedding was inspired by the flickering world of film and fantasy, they feel their real-world relationship will be as steady and true as the old bridge itself.

"Roseman Bridge has withstood a lot of time and will probably stand there many more years," says Dorothy. "It can be old, but it'll still stay. Just because it's old doesn't mean it has to fall apart, kind of like a marriage."

Married in Madison County
511 West Benton Street, Winterset, Iowa 50273-1026
800-841-5336 / www.bridgeweddings.com

St. Augustine Lighthouse
ST. AUGUSTINE, FLORIDA

Coordinating a wedding can be a dizzying experience. While under siege by heightened emotions, couples must navigate through a seemingly boundless sea of details in order to safely reach the shores of wedded bliss. But for couples who wed atop the St. Augustine Lighthouse in St. Augustine, Florida, simply getting to the wedding site can be the most dizzying detail of all. It's a 219-step climb up a cast-iron spiral staircase to the top of the 165-foot tower, the twelfth tallest lighthouse in the United States.

Although the mere thought of such an ascent makes many people feel lightheaded, it hasn't stopped several couples a month from braving the stairs to wed on the light's outdoor observation deck. And where the bride and groom decide to wed, there others must follow.

"The justice of the peace who married us was a little overweight, so he started climbing up the stairs about fifty minutes before everyone else so he'd have time to catch his breath for the ceremony," says Carrie Straub, who wed David Zugasti at the top of the distinctive black-and-white striped tower.

But it's the breathtaking panoramic view over sandy beaches and downtown St. Augustine—our nation's oldest city—

The St. Augustine Lighthouse, St. Augustine, Florida

with its lovely Spanish-influenced architecture that makes the climb tops on the agenda for over a hundred thousand visitors each year. "I've seen eighty-eight-year-old women with heart problems climb to the top," says Francine Baumann, gallery coordinator of the St. Augustine Lighthouse Museum located in the restored keeper's house. "People have always found lighthouses romantic, but it amazes me what many people will go through to get to the top. At least the designer of the lighthouse included eight wide landings along the way."

Since the Pharos of Alexandria—the world's first lighthouse and one of the Seven Wonders of the World—was built in the third century B.C. off the coast of Egypt, lighthouses have appealed to the romantic imagination. Standing solitary vigil during raging storms along treacherous coastlines and manned by keepers whose devotion to the lifesaving beams of light have bordered on the heroic, lighthouses have stood as beacons of hope, sources of comfort and guidance on life's high and turbulent seas.

But far from anticipating a stormy relationship, couples who wed at the St. Augustine Lighthouse are attracted to the positive appeal of the brilliant light. "The idea of the light guiding you through good times and bad is very romantic," says David, a native of Spain and a tour guide at the lighthouse who met Carrie, a college instructor, through a mutual friend.

"The lighthouse is a very calming place," says Carrie. "Although David and I are spiritual people, we're not religious, so neither of us wanted a traditional church wedding. That would have been a mockery for us. Even though we wanted to boil the ceremony down to its essence, we wanted a more pristine environment than some chapel where couples go for a quickie wedding.

"I definitely believe the lighthouse is the most romantic setting in St. Augustine," says Baumann. "When it's all lit up, it's like a big fairy tale. Owls perch in the windows at night, and it's very magical. A lot of couples also get engaged at the top of the tower. They'll come down all excited and say, 'We just got engaged up there!' We always have champagne on hand so we can give them a toast."

On a clear day, being high in the sky is a joy, but sometimes bad weather casts a shadow on the celebration. "There was a couple who married on New Year's Day," recalls Baumann. "It had been raining, and when there's a change in temperature outside, condensation forms inside the tower, and the stairs and railings get all wet. Basically, it rains inside the tower. Usually if the tower's closed to the public because of bad weather, it's closed for any weddings too, but the bride showed up in a full wedding dress and heels, so I made the couple and their guests sign disclaimers that if anyone got hurt, we'd not be responsible. I walked up the stairs before everybody and dried the railings as they came up. When they got to the top, it was like they were married in the middle of a cloud."

As dramatic as some of the wedding weather can be, the long history of a guiding light in St. Augustine is just as dramatic. In the sixteenth century, Spanish settlers were the first to erect a wooden watchtower at the inlet, from which they scanned the seas for signs of enemy vessels. The British replaced this structure in 1737 with a taller tower so they could get a better view over the treacherous, ever-shifting sands—called "crazy banks"—near St. Augustine. When the United States acquired

Florida in 1821, Congress provided funds to reconstruct the crumbling tower, and in 1824, the lamp was lighted on Florida's first official lighthouse.

At the outbreak of the Civil War the light was ordered extinguished to reduce naval superiority of the Union, and it remained dark until 1867. It was the eroding shoreline, however, that finally forced the old tower to be permanently abandoned. In 1872 construction began on the present black-and-white striped tower, which was lit on October 15, 1874. By 1876, the keeper's stately red-brick home, trimmed with white Victorian gingerbread, was ready for its first inhabitants.

But less than a hundred years later, technology made obsolete the role of the steadfast and dedicated keeper. In 1936, the light was electrified, and by 1955 control of the lighthouse was completely automated. While the St. Augustine Light House remained an active aid to navigation, the keeper's house stood vacant and decaying. When an arsonist's fire gutted the house in 1970, its future appeared dark and grim.

But the allure of the noble light would not be extinguished. Recognizing the history and potential of the property, the Junior Service League of St. Augustine began a fifteen-year campaign to raise the money necessary to restore the house and tower. Its heroic efforts led to the creation of the St. Augustine Lighthouse Museum, which opened in the keeper's house in 1988. By 1991, the refurbished tower was ready to welcome eager climbers. As lighthouse lovers from around the world made their way to St. Augustine, the future of the property looked bright.

In 1994 the first wedding took place at the top of the tower, and it has remained a popular wedding site since. "As a tour guide at the lighthouse, I had seen a lot of couples get married there," says David. "The place is beautiful, it's in nature, and it's historical. It's the perfect setting."

Despite the tower's height, David and Carrie's wedding was very down to earth. "We had about twelve guests at the wedding," recalls Carrie, "so we could live in the moment of it and never worry, What do I have to do next? Formality didn't bog down the ceremony. It was very beautiful and emotional."

The closest David and Carrie came to formality was their wedding attire—and even that posed some problems, at least on Carrie's part. "When I went shopping for shoes to wear with my calf-length dress I saw a pair I liked, but at the time my only thought was, Oh! I like these shoes!" She laughs. "It didn't click till I got to the tower on our wedding day that their three-inch heels might make climbing the stairs kind of difficult. There's a lot of open grillwork on the stairs, so I ended up climbing with the balls of my feet. I made it just fine, but it was actually harder to climb down the steps with the heels."

Although David claims that he holds the speed record for climbing the tower—"I can make it to the top in fifty-seven seconds"—come their wedding day, things moved at a more relaxed pace. "None of our guests objected to the climb," says Carrie. "Most of them had never been to the lighthouse, so they were excited about going up. We took our time and were laughing and joking all the way up, saying things like, 'We're almost there!' David followed behind everyone and videotaped the climb. We had a very simple ceremony at sunset, although the weather was kind of cloudy. People were laughing and crying. It was the perfect wedding. At the reception we gave each of our guests a button from the gift shop that says, "I climbed the St. Augustine Light."

Up to thirty-five people can fit at the top of the red-capped tower, although guests at larger weddings might be left in the dark during the ceremony—the circular observation deck makes it hard for everyone in a large group to see around the massive Fresnel lens. Simple weddings can take place any time during or immediately after operating hours for $25. Couples can also rent the lighthouse's oak-shaded grounds or the gallery on the upper level of the keeper's house, beginning at $1,000. So popular is the site for weddings that plans are in the works to offer complete wedding coordination services.

While the St. Augustine Lighthouse attracts couples on the Florida coast, other lighthouses nationwide provide couples with equally illuminating wedding experiences. The glass-enclosed sixty-foot tower of the Big Bay Point Lighthouse in Big Bay, Michigan, rises 120 feet above the rocky, forested coast of Lake Superior. Its remote location on a narrow point of land in Michigan's Upper Peninsula with views of the Huron Mountains makes it quite a find for couples seeking to keep a low profile.

Couples spend their honeymoon in the old keeper's house, now a bed-and-breakfast, with excellent views of one of the world's wildest and woolliest lakes. Lucky couples are treated to a dazzling display of the aurora borealis at this true northern light.

On the West Coast, the Heceta Head Light Station in Yachats, Oregon—also a bed-and-breakfast—offers couples an electrifying view of the Pacific shore. Considered one of the most beautiful lighthouses in the world and one of the most photographed, the whitewashed tower, built in 1894, sits perched on a cliff 205 feet above the vast Pacific Ocean. From this lofty perch visitors observe the dramatic interplay of wind and water.

Couples marry on the sandy beach below the lighthouse or on the grassy lawn outside the keeper's house. With a beam of light visible twenty-one miles out to sea, the Heceta Head Light has a powerful pull. One couple even traveled with their whole family from Japan just to wed at Heceta Head.

Finally, couples eager to remain in the dark hop on the mailboat to get to the Keeper's House, a bed-and-breakfast alongside the Isle au Haut Lighthouse in Isle au Haut, Maine. Located on a small, sparsely populated island, the Keeper's House is short on electricity—there is none, nor are there telephones or auto traffic—but long on character. Bordering the rugged wild woods of Acadia National Park with views out into the Atlantic, the Keeper's House and its rustic grounds provide earthy couples a heavenly wedding setting.

Gaslights, candles, and kerosene lanterns provide romantic

evening illumination, while the rose-colored blink from the 1907 lighthouse keeps time with beams from three other Maine lighthouses visible across the horizon.

Over the years, lighthouses have saved countless lives as they've sent their beams penetrating the fiercest gale, but now they also save an ever-growing number of couples from navigating headlong into the sound and fury that often engulfs a traditional wedding. Whether a couple marries on the grounds of a lighthouse or takes to the tower, a lighthouse wedding is always a bright idea.

The St Augustine Lighthouse and Museum
81 Lighthouse Avenue, St. Augustine, Fla. 32084
904-829-0745 / www.stauglight.com

Big Bay Point Lighthouse
#3 Lighthouse Road, Big Bay, Mich. 49808
906-345-9957

Heceta Head Light Station
92072 Highway 101 South, Yachats, Oreg. 97498
541-547-3696

The Keeper's House
P.O. Box 26, Isle au Haut, Maine 04645
207-367-2261

5

Something Old, Something New, Something Borrowed: Themed Weddings

The word "theme" used to be a dirty word, conjuring up images of lined yellow notepads, thick pencils, and in-class essay exams. But "themes" are now big business as Americans seek to turn everything from buying a shirt to eating out to getting married into a drama-filled and entertaining experience.

Star-struck couples "film" their wedding in the Chinese Theater courtyard at the Disney-MGM Studio at Disney World in Orlando, Florida. Screaming fans and autograph hounds greet the couple as they arrive in a star motorcade down Hollywood Boulevard for an official handprint ceremony at the Chinese Theater. The evening ends with a personalized fireworks display.

In the battle to be the biggest, brightest, and boldest in Las Vegas, resorts have grown increasingly grandiose. With more than four thousand rooms, the medieval-themed Excalibur resort is a powerful presence on the mighty Strip. This white-turreted castle complete with moat and drawbridge is also home to the Canterbury Wedding Chapel, site of merry medieval weddings. A full range of costume rentals means brides and grooms can pack light.

On a much subtler scale is the Native American ceremony arranged through Sedona Weddings that takes place among the red rocks of Sedona, Arizona. From a medicine man performing the ceremony to a traditional circle dance, this wedding, performed atop Bell Rock, sets the spirit soaring.

At the Fantasy Inn and Wedding Chapel in South Lake Tahoe, California, the intimate thirty-seat wedding chapel is decorated in a tasteful Olde English decor. It's the themed accommodations, however, that get fantastic. Couples can choose anything from the Romeo and Juliet suite, modeled after a fairy tale castle, to the Rain Forest suite with its jungle motif and spa to the Antony and Cleopatra suite with its Roman pillars and ivory-draped royal-palace bedchamber.

Even more outrageous are the forty-five themed rooms at the Adventure Inn and Wedding Chapel in Reno, Nevada. The adventure begins in a chapel complete with two waterfalls and satin doves. Then it's off to outrageous accommodations such as the Adam and Eve suite, where couples are tempted by the sweets of their own fruit tree orchard, or the Super Ocean suite with its eleven-foot clamshell bed, waterfall, and lagoon. Couples feeling wild at heart check into the Cave Suite, a replica of a prehistoric cave hewn out of molten rock with ferns and mushrooms growing from its walls. Those feeling a tad roguish head for the Pirate Suite, where they walk the plank into the Jacuzzi.

But themed wedding accommodations predate the theme-happy 1990s. The Madonna Inn in San Luis Obispo, California, was the first to offer bizarre bedding. Opened in 1958, the inn remains a classic in overnight kitsch with its 109 different themed rooms. Although the Caveman Room with its rough-hewn rock walls and leopard-print bedspreads may be a bit primitive for some newlyweds, other rooms are specifically geared toward the softer side of new lovebirds. The Cloud 9 room has golden cherubs floating from the ceiling, and spiral stairs in the all-pink Love Nest lead to heavenly bliss. A little more down-to-earth is the Bridal Falls room with its natural stone walls and cave waterfall shower.

Whether a couple chooses a themed wedding or a themed wedding night, all involved in the production have no problem rating the event a unanimous A+.

Ohio Renaissance Festival
HARVEYSBURG, OHIO

Theatergoers enduring a bad production of Shakespeare might depart into the midnight hour thinking that people in sixteenth-century England did nothing but walk around in tights, intone incomprehensible sentiments to glazed listeners, and stab people with bloody daggers. They would as soon suffer one of Shakespeare's infamous insults than spend a whole day around people speaking and acting as if they just stepped from the pages of *Hamlet*.

But thanks to the popularity of Renaissance festivals, Shakespeare and the entire Elizabethan era have a chance of redemption from the good intentions of amateur thespians. At the numerous festivals nationwide, the ebullient spirit of the Elizabethans thrives, and time travelers revel in the wit, gaiety, and grace of the era.

Since 1989, the Ohio Renaissance Festival in Harveysburg has carried people back to the fictional town of Willy Nilly on the Wash in 1572. In this thirty-acre re-creation of a sixteenth-century English village, nearly two hundred costumed peasants, merchants, jesters, and royalty roam the streets entertaining and educating thousands of visitors each season. With the recent addition of St. Peter's Chapel, it's a perfect spot to stage an enchanting wedding and a boisterous reception.

It's this incomparable atmosphere that compelled Rise and Kurt Huffman of Fairborn, Ohio, to wed at the Ohio Renaissance Festival. "At one traditional wedding I went to, the only thing the guests seemed to be enjoying was comparing everything to other weddings they'd been to" says Rise. "Meanwhile, the poor bride was stressed out by everything. I knew that when I got married, I did not want people sitting around comparing my wedding to others. Kurt and I had been to the Renaissance festival when a wedding was taking place, and it looked like a lot of fun. There's so much activity at the festival. Meanwhile, our serious side could be addressed during the religious ceremony."

"We wanted to do something offbeat but something with pomp and circumstance," agrees Kurt, an office manager who met Rise, a telecommunications salesperson, through a singles group. "At a typical wedding and reception, it's difficult to keep guests entertained. At the Renaissance festival, if our guests couldn't find something to do, it was their loss.

Guests never have to worry about getting stuck for hours at a table making small talk with distant relatives. At the Renaissance festival, everyone is free to stroll the streets with Shakespeare and exchange witticisms or discuss politics with Queen Elizabeth. The only mudslinging likely to take place is between the Beggars of Mearth, a trio of actors who perform witty versions of literary classics while cavorting about a giant mud pit.

Potential spats between sparring relatives can be averted by directing the feuding parties toward the armored jousting tournaments, the Human Combat Chess Match—a life-size chess board where costumed performers fight for each square— or the Gamer's Pub, where they can throw real battle-axes, shoot a full quiver of arrows, or try for a prize with an authentically reproduced Divinci slingshot. If they still feel the need to make contact, they can throw tomatoes at the Village Idiot as part of Veggie Vengeance.

For guests who do enjoy each other's company, colorful maypole and country dances replace the electric slide. There are also plenty of places to buy a unique last-minute wedding gift. More than a hundred artisans create crafts from the Renaissance period in daily demonstrations of glassblowing, jewelry-making, weaving, leather crafting, and more.

Finally, there's always the simple pleasure of walking around munching a turkey leg and sipping a pint of ale while enjoying nonstop live and lively Renaissance music

"Weddings at the festival are so magical. It's such a romantic setting," says wedding coordinator Kathleen Keefer. "Usually people who get married have a wedding and then everyone just sits and listens to the DJ. Here, the performers and crafters participate in showing the couples a really good time. Weddings are becoming more popular every year. We even have one booked for the year 2000."

The spirit of romance is not reserved only for married couples. During Romance Weekend, a wooing contest results in many engagements. Men have even dressed in shining armor and proposed to their girlfriends at the joust or in front of Queen Elizabeth.

Wedding-day romance begins with a bridal procession, featuring costumed characters and a bagpiper, from the front gate to St. Peter's Chapel. The 120-seat open-air chapel has wood-beam ceilings, decorative benches, a cobblestone floor, and a steeple and bell tower.

Couples wanting plenty of sixteenth-century "thee's" and "thou's" in the ceremony will not be disappointed. Bishop Nicholas Bullingham of Worcester, a.k.a. Robert Keefer, pastor of Pleasant Ridge Presbyterian Church in Cincinnati and Kathleen's Keefer's husband, uses a wedding ceremony straight from the 1559 Book of Common Prayer.

Happily married, the couple rides in a horse-drawn carriage to the private outdoor reception area. Later in the day, they may accompany Queen Elizabeth on the royal pavilion during the armored joust or take part in the village maypole dance as honored guests.

"My parents had never been to a Renaissance festival," says Kurt. "My mother was very enthusiastic about it and the costumes. My father liked the idea too, but he made it clear he wasn't going to wear tights! He ended up wearing a suit of plastic King Arthur–style armor. He wore it all day and had a

Rise and Kurt Huffman and their wedding party

great time. Even though his armor was plastic, a lot of visitors at the festival thought he was the king."

Most of their 120 guests dressed in period costumes, going for the spirit of gallantry rather than historic reality. "Some of the guests couldn't get costumes from the sixteenth century and had to move to the seventeenth," says Kurt. "My groomsmen looked like the three musketeers, but they looked great."

Rise wore an ivory dress with lace sleeves and a red lace train—red being the color of royalty. A garland of fresh flowers held her veil in place. Kurt dressed like a "pompous buccaneer" in black pants and boots, black gold-trimmed jacket with gold vest and white ruffled shirt, and a black hat with a red plume. "If it had been 1572, we were so overdressed as far as showing wealth, we would've been executed." Kurt laughs. "Under law at that time, no one dressed above the queen."

"I was treated like a princess," says Rise. "That's what every bride wants on her wedding day. As I walked with my attendants up to the wedding area, people at the festival were bowing to me all around. When I approached the stage, the guys in the wedding party took off their hats, swooped down, and formed a military arch with their swords. I started to cry. It was that warm feeling you get when you walk into a surprise party. It was the combination of everyone there supporting us and the honor of walking through the arch."

Following the ceremony, there was English country dancing and a reception with cheese, breads, fruit, and mulled cider. Kurt and Rise even had an authentic wedding cake for the period—individual petits fours. "We were told that visitors might not be able to distinguish us from the performers and that they might join us at the reception and start eating," says Kurt. "That didn't happen, but we did invite the real performers to the reception. They did a wonderful job singing and dancing for us. We even got to be in the Queen's parade and walk before Queen Elizabeth."

"I was kissed by several festival-goers," reports Rise. "I told them I wasn't a performer, but they didn't care. In fact, we were having so much fun, we felt like performers and even started to talk with accents!"

Everyone loved it," says Kurt. "One of my groomsmen was not really into the idea of a Renaissance wedding, but after the event he said anytime we wanted to renew our vows to let him know."

The Huffmans enjoyed the day so immensely that the following year they auditioned and were hired as performers at the festival. Their role, however, is a bit humbler; Kurt acts as a church sextant, and Rise is his wife. "We're basically peasants, and as poor as church mice," says Rise. "But we love it. We have more freedom to do what we want than if we were rich."

Wedding packages at the Ohio Renaissance Festival run from $1,000 to $3,000, largely depending on the number of guests. The King and Queen package ($3,000) includes hand-blown perfume bottles for the bridesmaids and leather pouch neckwear for the groomsmen, and two hand-blown glass wedding goblets for the couple. A Vow Renewal package is also available for $250.

Quite unwilling to let her beloved Romeo go, Juliet whispered, "Good night, good night! Parting is such sweet sorrow." Likewise, modern lovers who wed at the Ohio Renaissance Festival reluctantly leave the stage at day's end. And their guests, far from feeling trapped by the stifling restrictions that make a traditional wedding seem like an endless production, follow them to the gates, wishing there could be an encore.

Ohio Renaissance Festival
P.O. Box 68, Harveysburg,Ohio 45032-0068
513-897-7000 / www.renfestival.com

Captain Memo's Pirate Cruise

CLEARWATER BEACH, FLORIDA

The life of a pirate was doubtless one of unspeakable hardship and brutality. Stories abound of violent mutinies, shipwrecks on uninhabitable islands, and frightful cruelties inflicted upon captives. The stories of the ferocious Blackbeard and similar rebels of the sea send chills up the spine.

Given this horrifying history, it might seem somewhat strange to have a pirate-theme wedding aboard a pirate ship. Will guests unhappy with the seating arrangements be forced to walk the plank? Will a gold-hungry couple force their guests to commandeer passing pleasure boats in search of bigger and better wedding gifts? Will resentful relatives declare a mutiny and abandon the couple on a desert aisle?

None of the above happens when couples head to Clearwater Beach, Florida, and set sail with Captain Memo on his ship, the *Pirate's Ransom*. At Captain Memo's, couples who refuse to be held captive by the constraints of a traditional wedding experience the positive side of pirate life—freedom, joviality, and adventure.

With a crew of swashbucklers, including the likes of Typhoon Tom, Mutiny Michael, Tricky Tracey, and Stowaway Steve, weddings that take place aboard the *Pirate's Ransom,* a seventy-foot reproduction of a pirate ship, as she plies the waters of the Gulf of Mexico are worlds away from your traditional affair.

Couples looking for role models for adventure need look no further than the ship's owners—Captain Memo and his wife, Panama Pam. A suit and tie used to be Captain Memo's daily garb when he sold life insurance in southern California under the name Bill Wolzencraft. One morning, however, he realized that he could no longer dress up every day only to face repeated rejection, so in 1976 he and Pam—who used to be a teacher—pulled some money out of the bank and set out for the Caribbean on a thirty-foot sailboat.

"We planned to be gone three months," says Pam, "but we had so much fun we cashed in our retirement savings and settled in Panama." The Spanish-speaking Panamanians called Bill his Spanish name, "Memo." Since he had a boat, he became Captain Memo.

Several years later, a Canadian travel company invited Captain Memo to Florida, where it planned to have him run a pirate ship. Up for a new challenge, Captain Memo and Panama Pam set sail for Florida with fifty dollars in their pockets. Three thousand miles later, they learned that the Canadian company was all talk and no action.

Undaunted, the determined duo painted their boat, added some sails, and sewed up some pantaloons, bandannas, and sashes. The rest, as they say, is history. Today, passengers outfitted in black-paper pirate hats and armed with plastic pistols enjoy the antics of Captain Memo the Pirate and his crew of colorful corsairs as they raise the Jolly Roger and head out into the Gulf of Mexico aboard the blood-red *Pirate's Ransom.*

Although a sign aboard the ship cautions that children left unattended will be sold as slaves, it's the child in every adult pirate that must be set free in order to enjoy the antics of these boisterous buccaneers. From treasure hunts to musical chairs to the painting of black eyepatches and sinister mustaches, all aboard get carried away on a sea of frivolity.

It's this combination of fantasy, fun, and romance that entices about a hundred couples a year to greet their guests with a hearty "Ahoy, Mateys!" and marry aboard the *Pirate's Ransom* in a ceremony officiated by Captain Memo or one of his crew. "Couples have married in everything from tuxedos to bare feet," says Pam. "But even though the atmosphere's lighthearted and there's a lot of game playing on board, the ceremony is respectful. The captain's not acting crazy and running around the deck."

Wedding packages run from a simple pre-cruise wedding at $50 plus the regular cruise fare of $28 per person up to a private evening cruise with beer, wine, and champagne starting at $1,000.

The novelty of a wedding on the high seas is what compelled Doug and Lisa Burton of Brooksville, Florida, to wed on Valentine's Day in full pirate regalia. "We like odd things," explains Lisa, a receptionist, who met Doug, a former Navy pilot who now owns an office-cleaning company, through work. "Our house is full of things like medieval paintings and dragonflies and gargoyles. We saw Captain Memo's in the phone book and were attracted to the aura of fantasy about a pirate wedding. When we saw the bright red pirate ship, there was no doubt that that's what we wanted to do."

Their friends responded positively. Lisa's mother, however, was not as enthusiastic. "She was initially against a pirate wedding," says Lisa. "She thought it was making a mockery of the vows, but we feel very serious about our vows. Still, I wasn't sure if we had the nerve to go through with it."

They did, and they did so with flourish and style, dressing in dashing pirate costumes for their dramatic evening-cruise wedding. Doug and Lisa were overtaken with pirate fever long before their wedding day, though. They hand-printed their invitations on burnt-edged scrolls, then stuffed them in long-necked glass bottles and hand-delivered them to their guests.

They read, "Once upon a time in the near future, a galley called the *Pirate's Ransom* will hoist anchor and lower sails to embark on a journey that will sail the high seas of eternity. Upon

Lisa and Doug Burton and their attendants

this pirate ship, Lisa Ann Chastain and Douglas George Burton will claim their new found treasure as they exchange vows of matrimony. Please join us amidship as we make this fairy tale a reality." At the bottom of the invitations, a pair of crossed swords embraced a heart.

Their costumes were just as elaborate as their invitations. Doug dressed as a gallant captain in a black and red jacket, black satin pants, and black boots. A string of red beads stood out against the white ruffle of his shirt, and he carried a silver knife at his side. His best man, similarly attired, had a stuffed parrot perched on his gold epauletes.

Pirate women were few and far between, so Lisa chose a Renaissance-style cream-colored satin gown with a gold-trimmed bodice. Her eight-year old daughter, Ashley, wore a matching dress, while her attendant wore a bright blue silk gown with gold chiffon sleeves. Nearly all their fifty guests came in costume, including Lisa's mother.

Captain Typhoon Tom—their bearded, suntanned officiant—looked every inch the seafarer in his black pants, billowing white shirt, black bandanna, ponytail, and gold earring. In case of unexpected marauders, he wore a dagger strapped to his side.

As the sun set over the Gulf of Mexico, Scottish bagpipes played the wedding march while Lisa made her way up from the ship's hold and the ceremony began: "I bid you remember that the marriage you are about to enter before me is as solemn and binding as though it were performed in a place of worship by a member of the clergy," intoned Typhoon Tom. "It has been said that when people marry, they embark upon the sea of matrimony. I hope that your trip will be a long one. All long trips contemplate some dark and even stormy weather. Your marriage is the ship on which you sail. With the understanding of each other and the ability to give as well as take, your ship will carry you safely home."

Before the *Pirate's Ransom* returned home, however, there was pirate merrymaking to endure, including daring entertainment by flame-throwing and rig-walking pirates. As darkness settled over the waters, the *Pirate's Ransom* pulled back into Clearwater Beach. But Doug and Lisa, the most elated swashbucklers on the seas, wanted their guests to treasure the memory of their pirate wedding just as much as they did, so upon landing, they passed out gold pirate coins to the departing buccaneers.

"The wedding turned out absolutely great," says Doug. "It was very romantic. If you want to impress your future wife, marry her on a pirate ship."

"A lot of times a wedding is so boring," says Lisa. "Ours

certainly wasn't. Even though as the evening went on I looked worse and worse because of the wind and the humidity, it was still wonderful. We were so happy!"

Although the most famous pirate to roam the west coast of Florida—José Gaspar—lived only in legend, this does not stop couples from joining up with Captain Memo for a truly legendary wedding as they set sail upon the gulf's warm waters in the company of their own heart's treasure.

Captain Memo's Pirate Cruise
Clearwater Marina, Clearwater Beach, Fla. 34630
813-446-2587 / www.pirateflorida.com

Vows' Halloween Wedding
DAVIE, FLORIDA

"At weddings, couples always say they'll be together 'till death do us part,'" says Tama Glover of Sunrise, Florida. "Will and I took that a step further. At our wedding, we were eternal. We're still going to be together beyond the grave."

To convey this touching sentiment, Tama and Will didn't play ethereal harp music or clip angel pins to their lapels; rather, they took the grave part seriously and dressed as if they had just emerged from it. "We were zombies from the crypt," says Tama, an aviation electrician in the Coast Guard who met Will, a machinery technician in the Coast Guard, at the air base. "We were the walking dead with our skin all peeling off."

Possessed by the desire to do something different with the ancient wedding ritual, Tama and Will got into the spirit of Halloween and staged a truly unearthly Halloween zombie wedding at Vows: A Wedding Establishment, a wedding chapel in Davie, Florida.

"Halloween is my favorite holiday," says Tama. "As kids we were out the door from the moment school got out till 10:00 P.M. It was great freedom to be out without your parents, to be all

Tama Glover and her husband

dressed up and having so much fun. I thought it'd be the perfect holiday to get married on. I told Will that when we got married, I wanted it to be a party. We're kids! Who wants to grow up!"

"I was intrigued by Tama's idea of a Halloween wedding," says Will. "A lot of times, a couple has a traditional wedding just to please their family, and by the time they get to the event, they just want it over with. If you have to have a big traditional wedding to please your family, you might as well just marry your family. Also, I figured by everyone having to dress up, it took the stress off us being the only ones in fancy clothes."

Tama and Will's original idea was to get married in a church with a *Phantom of the Opera* theme. "But I thought that would be boring for me," explains Tama. "I would've gone as the singer, and no one really recognizes her. People would've kept asking me, 'Who the heck are you?' Then we thought we'd go as ghosts. It'd be simple and everyone would know what we were, but then Will started taking the idea further. He's always been interested in special effects and costumes, and we both love horror movies, so we decided on the zombie theme. Whether ghosts or zombies, we were still basically dead people."

Finding a chapel to stage a zombie wedding required some phone calls. "I grew up Catholic, but I pretty much figured a Catholic church wouldn't let us do it that way," says Tama. "We called different chapels to see who would. Vows was the most cooperative, so we had it there."

Brides often spend months trying on countless gowns, then spend thousands of dollars on a dress that does a disappearing act after the wedding. Grooms, meanwhile, stand patiently while their tuxes are tailored. Tama and Will were more practical. "We went to Goodwill and found a tuxedo and a wedding dress," remembers Will. "We tore them up, then trashed them in the mud and hung them outside so it'd look like we were just pulled from the grave after being down there for a year or two."

While Tama never worried about having a bad hair day for her wedding, it was her veil that was frightful. "I sprayed those canned cobwebs in my hair to make the veil, then I stuck some plastic spiders in it. I also carried a bouquet of black roses, and Will had a black rose as a boutonniere."

Tama wasn't the only one spending time in the bathroom doing her makeup on the wedding day. She and Will spent three and a half hours in front of the mirror, and the results were deadly. "I used latex rubber and other professional stage makeup for our faces so it'd look like we were cadavers with our skin rotting and peeling off," says Will. "We also made up our necks and hands, any exposed part of our body. Since I have a theater background I knew how to do the makeup, so it wasn't uncomfortable at all."

But it wasn't just Will and Tama's wedding attire that was otherworldly. When their forty costumed guests arrived for the wedding, they entered a setting more spirit-filled than spiritual. "We made tombstones out of foam and set them around the chapel," says Tama. "We cobwebbed up everything and had skeleton parts and bones thrown around on the floor. Vows uses white lilies for their regular ceremonies, so there was a lot of those around. Of course, lilies go well in a graveyard—they're the flower of the dead. The lights were dim and there was fog. It looked just like a haunted house and definitely had an eerie feeling."

In terms of music, Pachelbel's *Canon* was definitely out of the question. "As our guests were being seated we played sounds of Halloween, things like screams and doors creaking," says Tama, "but it was kind of gruesome at one point on the tape. There was a person getting hacked to death."

Their families, naturally, were a little shocked at the affair. "I grew up Southern Baptist in El Paso," says Will. "We board up the house and lock the doors before Halloween, so you can figure how my parents felt. They kind of freaked out. They weren't able to make it for the wedding, but my sister came. She dressed as Alice in Wonderland."

"My parents are in their seventies and live in New York," says Tama. "My mother's first reaction was, 'How am I going to get your father to dress up?' Then a couple weeks later she called and was all excited. She was going to dress as a devil and use her cane as a pitchfork and get my dad a cape to be Dracula. They had a good time."

When some couples look at their wedding video, they cringe at their stiff demeanor when walking down the aisle. For Tama and Will, this was the desired effect. "We walked in to music from Phantom of the Opera,'" says Tama, "but we weren't the typical laughing couple. We were more the sullen type; we walked like zombies from *Night of the Living Dead.* We timed our walk just right because as soon as we made it all the way into the chapel, the song ended and the Phantom gave out a blood-curdling scream. It was perfect."

Tama and Will wed underneath an arch outlined with Halloween lights and decorated with stuffed ravens. Mort Wolfman, manager of Vows, officiated dressed as the King of Hearts. Tama's maid of honor was a flapper, while the eleven-year-old vampire ring bearer ended up being Will's best man.

"My real best man got called out of town on business," says Will, "but since there was nothing ordinary about our wedding we just went with the ring bearer as the best man."

Surprisingly, Will's best vampire did not carry up a set of plastic spider rings. Will and Tama wed with gold bands in a traditional ceremony. After pledging to be together forever and ever and ever, Tama and Will, spellbound with happiness, made their way down the bone-strewn aisle to more music from *The Phantom of the Opera.*

The spectral spectacle continued at the reception, also held at Vows. "We made a black coffin and used that as the head table and put candelabras on all the tables," says Tama. "We decided on a normal buffet dinner. We didn't make the food all green to look like gooey brains. We didn't want to make anyone sick, although we did use black icing for the roses on our cake. We also had a ghost and grim reaper for the cake topper."

After dinner, their guests—vampires, mad doctors, witches, cows, and pizza boxes—danced the night away to the "Monster Mash" and other fun Halloween songs. But much to Tama and Will's horror, as the midnight hour approached, their guests faded away into the dark Miami night and their Halloween wedding came to an end. "It was way too short," says Tama. "We loved our wedding, and everyone had a blast."

"We had a great time," says Will, "and we planned it completely ourselves. Anymore, it seems you don't have a wedding, you buy a wedding, and you buy just what everyone else does. If you design a wedding yourself it has more meaning. It was so much fun being with Tama planning the wedding around a theme we enjoy. That's what made it romantic."

Although the romance of supernatural nuptials might remain a mystery for some, for Will and Tama, their Halloween zombie wedding was definitely a treat of a lifetime.

Vows: A Wedding Establishment
9170 State Route 84, Davie, Fla. 33324
954-472-1186 / www.aweddingforyou.com
Chapel Weddings at Vows begin at $150.

Viva Las Vegas Wedding Chapel's Intergalactic Wedding

LAS VEGAS, NEVADA

"A lot of moms and dads come to a themed wedding and they're like, 'Oh my God, what are we doing here?'" says Ron DeCar, who arranges themed weddings for his Viva Las Vegas Wedding Chapel in Las Vegas. "All their life they've envisioned their kid walking down the aisle, wearing the same dress their mom wore. But times have changed. Couples come from back east, from places where they feel stifled. All their life it's been beaten into their brain that they have to do something traditional, so they rebel and do something crazy. Las Vegas is a wild and carefree place where people can do whatever they want."

The odds are high that few wedding ceremonies are wilder and crazier than the weddings DeCar arranges and performs in. "Not everyone likes Elvis," he says, "so now they have some options." From King Arthur to the Godfather, DeCar's themed weddings appeal to couples eager to take chances. Working with several Las Vegas chapels, he brings in settings, props, theatrical lighting, and fog to set a multitude of moods. All couples need do is lay down between $490 and $650 for a wedding that's sure to be a winner.

Weddings on secluded, romantic beaches are always popular, but where's the party in that? With DeCar's Beach Party Wedding, two swimsuit-clad muscle men carry the bride down the sandy aisle on a surfboard to tunes from the Beach Boys. A Party Hearty minister wearing swim goggles marries the couple under palm trees and a beach umbrella, while showgirls wearing bikinis and carrying pink sand pails mingle with the guests.

Why save all the music and dancing for the reception? Couples choosing a 1950s, 1960s, or disco wedding boogie down the aisle and enjoy classic tunes during the ceremony. One Nerd or Fonz, Beatnik or Hippie, Travolta or Donna Summer impersonator officiates. A bit rowdier is the Rock 'N Roll "bass-in-your-face" ceremony, where an electric guitarist rocks the couple down the aisle with an ear-splitting rendition of the wedding march. Soon-to-be in-laws are provided with ear plugs.

Real-life gangsters used to be as much a part of Vegas as Elvis impersonators. Couples captivated with the disreputable side of the town's history choose DeCar's Gangster wedding. A singing waiter hovers over guests seated at restaurant tables covered with red-checkered-cloths. "Bring the whole mob to your own family affair where our Godfather Minister will rub out your single life once and for all," says the brochure. Any objections are kept to a minimum—two armed bodyguards keep watch over the minister.

If the lights and flash of Vegas aren't otherworldly enough, starry-eyed couples may wed aboard the *Starship Vegas* in an Intergalactic ceremony. Captain James T. Quirk beams in to pronounce the couple Vulcan and Vife.

And of course, there are the Elvis weddings—both *Blue Hawaii*— and *Viva Las Vegas*–style—in addition to the more "traditional" Victorian and Camelot weddings.

Paige Harrison, her husband Tim Backun, and "guests"

DeCar insists that even if some family members come into the ceremony doubtful, they leave believers. "Parents come in a little confused, but by the time they leave they've had a very good time, and they love it."

Paige Harrison and Tim Backun of Lawrence, Kansas, know all about parental discontent. Both their mothers were incredulous when they chose to be wed in Las Vegas in an Intergalactic ceremony. "My mother was really mad," says Paige, who met Tim through their jobs at Kinko's. "She was like, 'You've got to be kidding.' My brother had a common-law marriage and my sister went to the courthouse without telling her, so she wanted me to have a big traditional wedding. But once she saw that wasn't going to happen, she got into the idea."

"My mother couldn't believe it," says Tim. "At first she was appalled, but then she and my father went to a Star Trek convention to see what it was all about and got more into the idea. She ended up doing almost all the planning and making costumes for everybody."

Neither Paige nor Tim consider themselves "hard-core" Trekkies—avid fans of the "Star Trek" series who seem to incorporate the show into many aspects of their life—but since they both enjoy the aura of fantasy about the show, they thought of doing a wedding around what they had in common. "It started out as a joke," explains Tim. "We both said that if we were to get married, it would be a Star Trek wedding and we would say our vows in Klingon. It just kind of turned into that, although the ceremony was in English."

"I told Tim the only way I would get married was in Vegas with something crazy and fun," says Paige. "I didn't want a traditional wedding with a big huge crowd of people staring at me. I look bad in white and would never wear a big white fluffy dress. We looked into seeing if they had Star Trek wedding chapels in Vegas. We were really happy when we found something close to it. When we told people we were doing a Star Trek wedding, they either really liked the idea or they thought we were really weird. But I've always been the odd one, the weird one, so it didn't bother me."

Once over the initial shock, most of their forty guests got into the spirit and came in intergalactic attire. Paige wore a short red satin dress and black knee-high boots. Tim wore a red satin captain's uniform with gold trim and black pants. Paige's mother wore a silver space top with black pants, while Tim's mother came dressed as Amanda Grayson—Spock's "earthling" mother—in a flowing white robe and head scarf. Their fathers dressed in variations of an admiral's uniform.

Although most of Paige and Tim's guests were a lively bunch, some were a bit stiff. These included the cast of life-size cardboard cutouts from the "Star Trek" series who stood around the "starship" for the ceremony.

The adventure began as music from the show accompanied Paige and Tim on their walk down the aisle. When they approached the head of the starship, swirling clouds of white fog enveloped the guests while flashes of bright light filled the room. It was then that Captain James T. Quirk and Dr. Spock—played by DeCar—"beamed" into the chapel, and the ceremony began, officiated by Captain Quirk.

"Star date, July 26, 1997. Mr. Spock, have your calculations been correct?" asked Captain Quirk as he stood before Paige and Tim.

"We've beamed down to planet Earth," said Spock.

"So these are primitive humans?"

"Affirmative, sir."

"Then the first part of our mission has been a success."

But as every Trekkie knows, space mission is a risky venture. As Captain Quirk began to speak about marriage being the final frontier and a marvelous adventure, sirens sounded and lights flashed. The *Starship Vegas* had been put on red alert, a sign of perceived danger! When nothing abnormal was found and the situation stabilized, Captain Quirk continued with the ceremony.

"Do you, Paige and Tim, promise to speak the truth, no matter what language, be it Ferengi, Vulcan, or Klingon? Then face each other and place your hands on the nebula ball of love."

As Paige and Tim held their hands over the glass ball with colored beams of electricity bouncing wildly around inside, Captain Quirk "prayed" that they would live long and prosper. Before he could proceed with the vows, however, the "perceived" danger of the red alert became a very real threat.

"Paige! It's me you want, not Tim! It's me!" one of the starship's own crew yelled as he rushed up the aisle and lunged toward Paige. While yet another invading crew member tackled the star-struck intruder to the floor, Captain Quirk yelled, "Mr. Spock, please take care of them!"

Quickly, Spock came forward and gave the interlopers the "Vulcan nerve pinch"—a single touch on the shoulder that sends enemies falling to the floor. Stunned and immobilized, the fallen crew were dragged from the chapel, and the ceremony went on, culminating in distinctly otherworldly vows.

"Do you, Paige and Tim, promise to treat each other as if you were always in the neutral zone? To care for each other when your dilithium crystals are running low and your warp drive is going slow?"

When Paige and Tim agreed and were pronounced husband and wife, they were cheered by a chorus also of a distinctly otherworldly nature. Each guest held and squeezed a tribble—the little furry creatures that rapidly multiplied and wrecked havoc on the ship in one "Star Trek" episode. These squeaking tribbles serenaded Paige and Tim safely down the aisle, starry-eyed and star-struck, into the Vegas night.

"Everyone had a great time," says Tim. "I don't think my mom knew what to expect, so she told everyone not to laugh during the ceremony. She thought it was going to be serious, but people laughed through the whole thing. It was a lot of fun."

"It certainly was different," agrees Paige. "No one will ever be able to beat it. It will always be offbeat."

After the ceremony the whole crew took limousines to the

reception at their hotel. "When the limo dropped us off, everyone must've thought we were famous," says Paige.

"They crowded around and kept asking, 'When's the Star Trek Experience going to open at the Hilton?'"

If marriage is the final frontier, then Paige and Tim's journey on the Starship Vegas set them off on the right foot. Without a doubt, they boldly went where few couples have ever gone before.

Viva Las Vegas Wedding Chapel
1605 Franklin Ave., Las Vegas, NV. 89104
800-574-4450 / www.vivalasvegas weddings.com

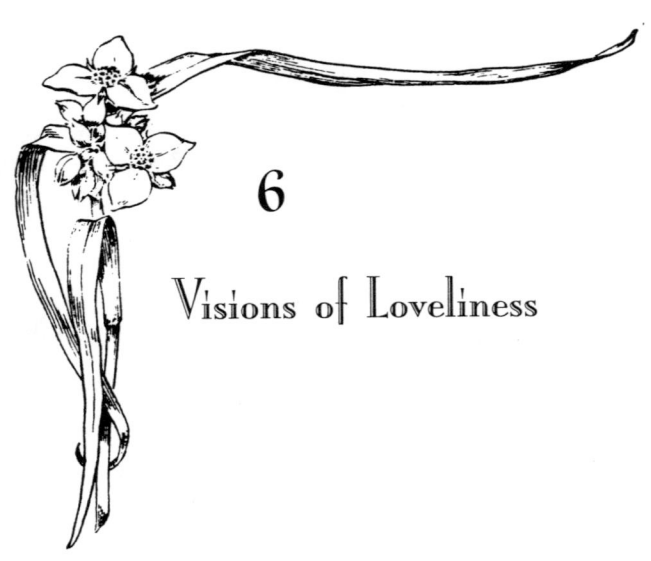

6

Visions of Loveliness

Since the first Europeans settled on these shores seeking religious freedom, America has been the home of spiritual dreamers and visionaries. Unique, often bizarre, gardens, castles, chapels, and "environments" dot our landscape, all built by people intent on asserting their moral vision of the universe.

The biblically themed Fields of the Wood in Murphy, North Carolina, is built on a scale to rival any theme park. Created by the Church of God of Prophecy, this two-hundred-acre drive-through tribute to the word of God is home to the world's largest Ten Commandments, written in letters five feet high and four feet wide. Couples have wed atop Ten Commandment Mountain with an imposing view of the mighty word.

Couples who can't foot the plane fare to the Holy Land travel instead to Covington, Kentucky. In 1958, Morris H. Coers—minister, legislator, and radio personality—re-created parts of the Holy Land on a Covington hillside and called it the Garden of Hope. Now overlooking traffic on Interstate 71, the Garden of Hope still remains a mostly peaceful site for weddings. Inside the Chapel of Dreams, couples wed atop a pink stone slab taken from the Horns of Hatton, the spot where Christ is believed to have preached the Sermon on the Mount. Couples also wed in front of a replica of Christ's tomb in Jerusalem.

A taste of Norway can be had at the Chapel in the Hills in Rapid City, South Dakota. The dream of Dr. Harry R. Gregerson, founder and speaker of the "Lutheran Vespers" radio program, the chapel is an exact copy of the nearly nine-hundred-year-old Borgund Church in Norway. Wooden dragon heads, similar to the figureheads on Viking long boats, peer from atop this most unique stave church that was dedicated to the glory of God in 1969. A grass-roofed "stabbur" imported from Norway sits next door for receptions. Nearly two hundred weddings take place here every summer.

"To God be the glory!" was Jim Reed's only response to the many architectural honors his glass chapel in the mountains outside Eureka Springs, Arkansas, won. While collecting his mail every day, Reed took note of the many people who would pull off the highway to rest and admire the mountain views. One day, the idea came to him that he should build a glass chapel on the site for these weary wayfarers. His vision became a reality when Fayetteville architect B. Fay Jones designed the chapel of Reed's dreams. Completed in 1980, Thorncrown Chapel's towering glass walls contain 6,364 square feet of glass and reach forty-eight feet into the surrounding trees. It's clear to the couples who wed here each year that Reed's vision has been splendidly realized.

Not all visions are religious in the Christian sense, though. On the eve of his wedding in Latvia in 1912, twenty-six-year-old Edward Leedskalnin was dumped by his sixteen-year old fiancee. Once in America, Leedskalnin, obsessed with her memory, began constructing a remarkable stone fortress in Homestead, Florida, in the hope that someday "Sweet Sixteen," as he referred to her, would reconsider and join him in his rocky love nest. Leedskalnin—who weighed only a hundred pounds—quarried and sculpted over a thousand tons of coral rock into massive formations, including representations of the planets, a moon fountain, rocking chairs and love seats, and an obelisk topped with the Latvian star. That Sweet Sixteen never joined him does not discourage about twenty couples a year from wedding around Leedskalnin's Feast of Love Table—a large heart-shaped stone table in an outdoor courtyard of the castle.

The bride is most often referred to as the vision of loveliness, but at the following sites, she willingly shares her title with the unique wedding settings dreamed into existence by determined idealists.

Castle Otttis

ST. AUGUSTINE, FLORIDA

Children often seek refuge in their own backyards. They build tree houses, construct ramshackle cabins, put up tents. Here they play and ponder until they make their way alone into the world and their refuges fall apart, intact only in memory.

As adults, most dreamers resort to building castles in the air, imaginary abodes where life's daily demands can be kept at bay. But rare is the adult who builds the actual castle of his actual dreams. Rusty Ickes is such a dreamer, and he built his castle in his own backyard.

The warm, sandy beaches of Spanish-influenced St. Augustine, Florida, are far removed from the cold, windswept hills of ancient Ireland, but for Ickes, a reggae musician with a wife and four children, his beachfront backyard became home to the remarkable Castle Otttis—yes, three t's—the "landscape sculpture" he built inspired by dreams and ancient Irish castles, constructed in "remembrance of and loving glorification of Jesus Christ."

Although he does not live in Castle Otttis—it has no electricity, plumbing, or running water—it is his and his community's very substantial refuge from the insistent demands of daily life.

"I was brought up Christian but my mother was a Lakota Sioux, so we were taught to honor dreams," says Ickes. "In the early 1980s I began dreaming about this castle. The dreams had no characters or plot. It was just the castle surrounded by green—it was a comforting thing."

Castle Otttis from the street

When he told the dream to Ottis Sadler, a boat builder with whom he was working on a construction project at the time, Sadler looked at him and said, "We can build that." So they did (just the two of them), in Ickes' backyard, surrounded by a sea of scrub oak, palmettos, and the Atlantic Ocean.

Ickes told Sadler, "If you put your whole heart into this, I'll name the castle after you." Ottis did, and thus the castle's name, which Ickes pronounces softly, like a long, drawn-out exclamation of wonder: Castle Ahhhhhtis.

One is awed merely by the story of the castle's creation. How Ickes and Sadler built it without any formal plans. How they used flawed concrete material rejected from other construction projects to build Ickes' perfect dream. How they worked in the Florida sun for four years to create the building, the walls of which are two feet thick.

But it's even more awe-inspiring to hear Ickes explain the religious symbolism of practically every aspect of the castle. Whether intentional or coincidental, this symbolism adds to Castle Otttis' allure. "The three t's in 'Otttis' can stand for the three crosses of Calvary or the Holy Trinity," says Ickes. "The circular O represents eternity. The 'is' a form of the verb 'to be,' as in 'I am the Alpha and the Omega, the beginning and the end.'"

His litany continues. The rejected material used to build the castle represents Jesus' saying, "the stone rejected by the builder will become the cornerstone"; a bolt accidentally imbedded in one such stone above the massive wooden front door represents the imperfection of humanity; the castle's stone turrets and crenelations represent the crown of thorns; the cross-shaped windows face east toward Jerusalem. Wind-bent oak trees around the castle represent the human ability to bend but not succumb to adversity.

Numerology also has a place at Castle Otttis. "The eighty-eight windows of the castle represent the year the castle was completed. During the summer of '88 there was also an alignment of the planets, a harmonic convergence. There are also eighty-eight keys on a piano, and I'm a musician."

Finally, a low stone wall surrounds the castle like a bow around a gift. "The castle is my gift to God and humanity," says Ickes, "but I'm not God's attorney. My thoughts are on God, but I don't try to proselytize. I welcome all people." He opens the castle the third Sunday of each month to visitors, whose donations go to local charities.

Since its completion in 1988, more than a hundred couples have wed in Castle Otttis in ceremonies ranging from Orthodox to Buddhist to New Age to Catholic. (Ickes doesn't charge for weddings in the castle, but he does require that couples make a charitable donation.) At first, couples are drawn by the castle's powerful profile as it rises three stories on an ocean-side highway lined with homes.

Ickes continuously receives letters from couples who practically beg to be allowed access to the castle for their wedding. One such couple wrote, "We hope that you will take into consideration that our admiration of your castle will manifest itself in our treating it with the utmost respect and honor."

More important, once couples step inside the gray concrete

walls of Castle Otttis, they are overtaken by the aura of serenity that imbues the rooms as they look out over the rolling waves of the sea. One bride wrote him, "It's almost as if the Castle were alive and breathing and instilling hope and sentiment into everyone that walks through the doors."

Rick and Renee Ryan at the altar inside Castle Otttis

The interior of the castle was created by master woodworker Lee Carpenter. Using cypress—the tree of life—and southern heart pine, Carpenter worked for three years to craft the altar, pulpit, pews, beams, and the spiritual symbols from many different cultures that fill the castle. In contrast to Castle Otttis' gray exterior, the reds, browns, and golds of the interior woodwork lend a feeling of warmth and peace. Red sawdust carpets the concrete floor and gives off an earthy, woodsy aroma.

Ickes, himself Catholic, sought the assistance of his parish priest in laying out the castle's main floor the way an ancient Irish Catholic church might have been laid out. The altar and pulpit stand opposed to each other because early Christians thought these elements of the mass—communion and liturgy—should be kept in balance.

Circular stairs lead to smaller rooms in the towers where Carpenter has crafted the Star of David, a mandala—an Eastern Oriental design symbolic of the universe—yin and yang symbols, and various other symbols honoring the world's many ways of praising creation.

Castle Otttis exerts a calming influence even on people who are not particularly religious, but it's usually couples with strong spiritual inclinations who decide to marry here. Such a couple was Renee and Rick Ryan of Hastings, Florida. "We wanted to get married someplace spiritual but without the limitations of the church," explains Renee, a waitress, who met Rick, a teacher, in a restaurant.

"I was raised Catholic," says Rick, "and the Cathedral downtown is beautiful, but I've always found God in more natural settings. I've always felt earth is god. When we thought about where to get married, I thought about the castle. I remember when it was being built. There were no other houses around then and it stood out all by itself. My friends and I would hang out on the beach at night when the castle was lit up with blue lights. The backdrop was awesome. As many times as I pass it, it still demands my attention, but I thought Renee might think it was dumb."

"The first time I saw the castle, I thought, What was that?" remembers Renee. "I thought it was a tourist attraction, but it always fascinated me. One day, Rick and I were talking about where to have the wedding, and at the same time we looked at each other and said, 'The castle.' It was so great I about cried!"

"At the time we didn't even know if there was an inside to the castle," adds Rick. "We worried that it might not be spiritual enough, but that feeling went away as soon as we walked in the door."

Rick and Renee left a note in Ickes' mailbox expressing interest in getting married in the castle. He contacted them, and they talked for several hours. "He asked us all kinds of questions," says Renee. "It was like he interviewed us before he'd come to a decision. He wanted to make sure we were right for each other.

"When we went inside the castle we felt total awe. Rusty had harp music and other whimsical music flowing through the castle. It was overwhelming that two men had created it. It's not what you expect from the outside, all stone and cold. Inside it felt very earthy, almost like we were outside with the wind and no glass in the windows and the sawdust on the floor."

"When I told people we were getting married there, everyone wanted to know what was inside, whether it was just cinder block, "says Rick. "When I told them what it was like they all wanted to be invited."

"My family liked the idea," says Renee. "People want something to remember. The basic church wedding you come out of there and you don't remember a thing."

The Ryans got married on a stormy day in March. A bagpipe player on the castle roof greeted their guests, while a harpist entertained from inside. Renee wore a long white gown with train, and Rick wore a gray tuxedo and ascot.

Brides prepare in the castle's Bridal Chamber, which occupies one of the turrets on the roof. If marriage is a balancing act, then here is where a woman tests her skills. To reach the chamber, she must climb a narrow circular stairway, then climb up through a wooden hatch door to get onto the roof. There are no mirrors, no amenities in the Bridal Chamber, only two wooden rocking chairs that face out toward the reflective waves of the sea.

Weather, however, forces brides to have a backup plan. "I didn't use the Bridal Chamber," says Renee. "There was a northeaster coming through, and it was too windy. In fact, there was mud everywhere outside the castle. I had to have my friends carry me inside where I got ready on the second floor."

The powerful, peaceful atmosphere of Castle Otttis was contagious to the over a hundred guests, many who observed the traditional ceremony from various levels of the castle—the main floor holds seventy-five people. "There were a lot of people there who technically should not be getting along, but we all got along and everyone loved the ceremony," says Renee.

"Even though it was a little chilly and windy inside the castle, you feel God in there. You feel a lot more strongly there about God than you do anywhere else."

"My father died about fifteen years ago," says Rick, "but I felt his presence very strongly in the castle. It wasn't one of those tangible things. It was just like a sixth sense. It was very powerful."

Inscribed in a stone at the foot of Castle Otttis' door is a quote from English philosopher John Ruskin. Ickes recites it from memory: "'When we build, let us think that we build forever. Let it not be for present delight nor for present use alone, but let it be such work as our descendants will thank us for.

"'And let us think as we lay stone on stone that a time is to come when those stones will be held sacred because our hands have touched them, and that men will say as they look upon the labor and wrought substance of them, See, this our Father did for us.'"

Ickes pats the thick walls of his castle. "One day, people will be scuba diving through this place," he says as he looks up at the massive walls, then out toward the ever-encroaching Atlantic. Until then, people can visit Castle Otttis the third Sunday of each month, stand by the altar and face the sea, and be infinitely thankful that Ickes has created this refuge, has sacrificed his backyard and a little bit of his privacy for those who remain forever children in spirit.

Castle Otttis
P.O. Box 1754, St. Augustine, Fla. 32085

The Little Brown Church in the Vale
NASHUA, IOWA

"Build it and they will come," Iowa farmer Ray Kinsella is urged in the movie *Field of Dreams*. He does, and they do. A team of baseball players haunts Ray's cornfield-turned-ballfield and helps manage a reconciliation between Ray and his dead father.

It makes a nice story. But could a place of spiritual significance really exist in the cornfields of Iowa that would inspire not merely a nine-member baseball team but more than a hundred thousand people to make a pilgrimage to it each year? Could a church rising among the corn compel more than six hundred couples to wed in its hallowed halls each year?

When the structure in question is the Little Brown Church in the Vale, the answer is an earsplitting yes. Sitting in a wooded

field outside Nashua, Iowa, the church has attracted millions of visitors from all over the world since it opened its doors in 1864. It's especially popular with couples who seek a simple site with a romantic history for their wedding.

Since World War I when records started being kept, more than 68,500 couples have traveled to Nashua to marry in the 150-seat brown clapboard church. The romance of the story surrounding its creation—a romance that wedded one man's vision of spiritual bliss with the everyday needs of a

View of the Little Brown Church in the Vale

community of pioneer worshipers—makesthe Little Brown Church stand out from the thousands of country churches that see only a handful of weddings all year.

In 1857, William Pitts, a music teacher from Wisconsin, was traveling to Iowa to visit his fianceé. When his stagecoach made a rest stop near present-day Nashua, Pitts wandered into a glade of towering pines along the Little Cedar River and was spellbound by the spot's pastoral beauty. He envisioned it the perfect setting for a church.

So taken was he by this vision that when he returned to Wisconsin he wrote a hymn about a church and called it "The Little Brown Church in the Vale." The song was soon collecting dust in his desk drawer, while Pitts married and continued with his teaching career in Wisconsin.

Meanwhile, the members of the First Congregational Church of Bradford, unaware of Pitts' song, began construction of a little brown church right on the spot Pitts had visited. Because the Civil War was going on, they used brown paint rather than the traditional white paint because brown paint was cheaper.

Imagine Pitts' surprise when he returned to the area in 1863 and saw a little brown church being built on the exact spot he had so admired. He resurrected his song for the astonished congregation and on December 29, 1864, the day the church was dedicated, "The Little Brown Church in the Vale" was sung for the first time in public with its classic refrain, "Come to the church in the wildwood, / Oh come to the church in the vale./ No spot is so dear to my childhood / As the little brown church in the vale."

As dear as the story was to local churchgoers, it might never have left Chickasaw County if it were not for the Weatherwax Brothers, Lester, William, Asa, and Tom, a popular gospel quartet of the early 1900s. Natives of Iowa, the Weatherwax Brothers made "The Little Brown Church in the Vale" their theme song and sang it to audiences nationwide. Other gospel groups and church congregations used the song, and soon visitors began flocking to the little church with the romantic history.

Today, millions of people worldwide know the song, and up to 150,000 people visit the church each year. It still stands in a wooded field neighbored only by Old Bradford Pioneer Village—a collection of local historic buildings—and Bradford House Motel, which has its own honeymoon suite.

Lush pine trees shade the church. Their branches sway in the wind and send graceful shadows dancing through the church's tall paned windows. Heather bushes, a gift from an English couple who wed at the Little Brown Church, grow outside the entrance. Painted on the church steps is the saying, "Let me live by the side of the road and be a friend to man."

Pastors Bob and Linda Myren do live by the side of the road, right across the highway from the Little Brown Church, and are friends to the eighty-eight-member congregation and the steady stream of tourists who love anything "original" about the church: the original pews, the original bell in the tower, the original key, which lies in a glass case under the sign, "This key opened and closed the Little Brown Church for over 50 years."

A glass-enclosed copy of the original song manuscript hangs on the wall safely away from zealous Little Brown Church fans. "Visitors used to steal the hymnals or rip the song out of them," says Pastor Linda. "One pastor was forced to stamp 'Thou shalt not steal' on the page with the hymn. People don't do that so much anymore ever since we started giving away free copies of the hymn and selling copies of the hymnal. But even if people buy a hymnal, they'll still sometimes replace it with one from the pews that has been used during a service—we sing the hymn at every service."

Other souvenirs are on sale at the back of the church, including booklets such as "Songs and Poems of the Little Brown Church," "History of The Little Brown Church in Story and in Song," and "The Lighter Side of the Little Brown Church." These booklets are full of poems and songs composed in honor of the little church and its faithful fans.

Americans are not the only ones enamored of the Little Brown Church. "We get a lot of visitors from Japan," says Pastor

Linda. "The Japanese use the song to teach English. We also get a number of people from Australia who come here to renew their marriage vows. I think at one time an American gospel group toured Australia and the song became popular there."

It's the weddings that have attracted the most attention to the Little Brown Church. Every day of the week except Sunday, Pastor Linda or Bob will don the ministerial robe and wed couples in a church that has seen as many as twenty-eight weddings in one day. "People are attracted to the Little Brown Church because it's just a simple little church that sits here in the woods," says Pastor Linda. "We help couples make their ceremony personal and unique, but we still have some guidelines. I did turn down a couple's request to have the song 'Drop Kick Me Jesus, Through the Goal Post of Life' played during the ceremony. Our goal is still to have a respectful service. We're not a marriage mill. We're not Las Vegas."

The services are mostly short and simple. The officiating pastor quickly runs through the directions—where to stand, what documents to sign, and how long to kiss. "If you don't hold the kiss long enough to get pictures, I'll make you do it again," says Pastor Linda efficiently.

Juanita Goings, hostess at the Little Brown Church, sets the wedding march playing on the stereo, and down the aisle the couple goes. After the ceremony, she takes pictures as the newlyweds leave the church. All weddings end with a Little Brown Church tradition: Together, the couple pulls the rope of the bell while the pastor recites, "As you ring the bell may you remember that as a couple you need to pull together through all the ups and downs of life that face you." In about half an hour—the time generally allotted for the service, which runs from $120 to $240, depending on how long the couple uses the church—the couple is wedded and out the door.

One thing couples must do before they leave is sign the mailing list so that they can be invited to the annual wedding reunion. Every August since 1952, the church holds this reunion to welcome back couples who married there. After the renewal of vows, awards are given to the couple married the longest, the couple that traveled the farthest to get there, and the couple most recently married. So numerous are the attendees that seating inside the church is reserved for those married fifty years or more.

Appropriately enough, it was music that brought together John and Irene Marean of Scioto Mills, Illinois, who wed at the Little Brown Church on a lovely day in May. "We met at a weekly Sunday polka dance," reports Irene, a grandmother and machine operator at Microswitch.

"I learned to polka before I learned to walk," says John, a soft-spoken grandfather who farmed for thirty years before starting work in a cheese factory.

"Polka people are happy people," declares Irene. "In fact, if you play 'The Little Brown Church in the Vale' fast enough, you can pick up a polka step! I told them at our wedding that we could polka down the aisle!"

Their love of polka and each other is matched by their love for the Little Brown Church. "I knew about the Little Brown Church years ago," says Irene. "My late husband and I visited the church, and I always wanted to get married there. It's a lovely place, so quiet and peaceful and pretty. A plain simple farm girl, that's what I was. I don't need a lot of frills or expensive things. It's quiet, that's what I like. You can't help falling in love with it."

"I knew the song when I was growing up," adds John. "After I met Irene she took me to see the church and I liked it right away. I've always been from the country, so I liked the quaint outdoor setting. When we were there a tour bus stopped and they were singing an old fashioned hymn sing-along. It was just wonderful."

"After the bus left, we asked a couple who was about to get married if we could watch their service to see if it's what we wanted," says Irene. "After seeing their ceremony, I was 1,000 percent sure it was what I wanted. When I told my friends we were getting married there they said, 'Why do you want to go clear out there to get married?'—it's a two-hundred-mile drive from our house. But when they came to the wedding, they saw why. There was even a busload of tourists before the wedding, so everybody got to hear about the history."

John and Irene were married surrounded by their children and grandchildren, who walked them down the aisle to the strands of "The Little Brown Church in the Vale." Both John and Irene say that the presence of all their family is what made the day special, but Irene can't help adding, "I just love the Little Brown Church. I'm in love with it. Pastors Bob and Linda make you feel so happy and at home."

John and Irene attended their first wedding reunion a mere three months after their wedding and plan to celebrate many happy years together. "I was so down in the dumps before I met Irene," says John. "She's completely changed my life."

"I've never felt so loved in my life," responds Irene. "John is so loving and thoughtful and kind. I get told every day how much I'm loved."

Lester Weatherwax once wrote, "We predict that down through the years, white fleecy clouds of happiness will float over our little Shrine, and on these clouds will be Tom, Bill, Asa, and Les Weatherwax, singing at the top of our voices....'OH, COME TO THE CHURCH IN THE VALE.'"

If a couple like John and Irene, giddy with newly married bliss, looks up over the tops of the Little Brown Church's towering pines into clear blue Iowa skies and golden sunshine, this prediction might just prove true.

The Little Brown Church in the Vale
2730 Cheyenne Avenue, Nashua, Iowa 50658
515-435-2027

Precious Moments Chapel

CARTHAGE, MISSOURI

"When the chapel opened in 1989, this was just a dirt road," says wedding coordinator Joette Blades of the paved two-lane highway that leads through gently rolling farmland to the Precious Moments Chapel in Carthage, Missouri. "Now nearly one million people visit the chapel every year and hundreds of couples have come here to get married. I think that unless you've been to the chapel, you don't understand what Precious Moments are about."

To impassioned collectors, Precious Moments figurines—the teardrop-eyed cartoon children created by Sam Butcher—are more than just cute knickknacks to place on a shelf and dust once a year; they represent a philosophy, a way of life.

"Precious Moments figurines remind people of the truths of the Bible," says Blades. "They carry the message of love, caring, and sharing and remind people of a special person who helped them through a difficult time in their life."

Since Sam Butcher's first figurine debuted in 1978, he's designed more than a thousand different figurines, all emphasizing acts of compassion and caring. Marketed throughout the world, Precious Moments are the world's number one collectible.

But it's the Precious Moments Chapel that Butcher considers his most momentous achievement. Whether a fan of the figurines or not, it's hard not to be impressed by the integrity of Butcher's vision as realized in the chapel, its gardens, and the adjoining museum and gallery.

Long before the success of Precious Moments, Butcher raised seven children on a limited income. With the success of his porcelain ministry, he felt called to give glory back to God for all his blessings. One day he was traveling through the countryside outside Carthage when the beauty of the landscape overcame him. Many years before, he had visited the Sistine Chapel in Rome and dreamed of creating his own tribute to the Lord. On this land, he thought, was where his dream would take shape. He bought the land, began construction of the Precious Moments Chapel, and in 1989 opened it free of charge to his adoring fans.

Rows of bronze Precious Moments angels line the walkway

leading to the chapel, the terra-cotta tiled roof and beige exterior of which lend it a Mediterranean flavor. Large wooden doors carved with Precious Moments angels open onto the lofty marble sanctuary. Butcher's interpretation of heaven is definitely less intimidating than Michelangelo's. Fifty-two murals and thirty stained glass windows depict scenes from the Bible—all illustrated with Precious Moments characters. Meanwhile, on the sky-blue chapel ceiling, Precious Moments baby angels float through the clouds.

The focal point, Hallelujah Square, is a towering, ever-evolving mural at the front of the chapel. In the mural, Precious Moment angels greet new arrivals—all children—to heaven. Many of these children are re-creations—in Precious Moments form—of actual children who have been killed in car accidents or who have died of cancer and other diseases.

Side rooms of the chapel are also dedicated to people who have passed away. One room honors Butcher's son Philip, who was killed in a car accident. Another honors Blade's first husband, Tim, who died of cancer. Books are available in which visitors write about precious moments spent with their own lost loved ones. Boxes of tissues are plentiful.

There's even a Precious Moments headstone on display in the adjacent museum/gallery and information on how one can be ordered. What stops it all from becoming a bit oppressive is Butcher's devotion to his art, his belief in God's forgiveness and salvation, and his mission of bringing solace to grieving families.

The sense of loss that pervades the chapel did not stop Precious Moments fans from flocking there to marry. "The chapel was so popular for weddings we were booking them as late as 9:00 P.M. after the last tour," says Blades. Always eager to take on new artistic challenges, Butcher alleviated wedding congestion by creating Dusty's Honeymoon Island Wedding Chapel. Located on a 40-acre man-made island a short drive from the main chapel, Dusty's Honeymoon Island Wedding Chapel began welcoming couples in 1996.

A ninteenth-century country church found new life as the

Angie and Jason inside the Precious Moments Wedding Chapel on Dusty's Honeymoon Island

wedding chapel. Stained-glass windows show Precious Moments characters in wedding scenes, while a mural of Precious Moments angels floating through clouds takes shape on the front wall. The wooden floor and pews are pearled a soft white to warmly reflect incoming light.

Brides prepare in the newly built Bridal Cottage, while a restored Victorian mansion provides an elegant ballroom and honeymoon suites—all designed by Butcher. Photo opportunities can be had on Sammy's Sweetheart Island, a heart-shaped island in the middle of the lake. Timmy the Angel can even make wedding appearances. Wedding packages in Dusty's Honeymoon Island Wedding Chapel begin at $1,600, while weddings in the original Precious Moments, Chapel begin at $300.

"My whole family collects Precious Moments," says Angie Mietus of Palatine, Illinois, who wed Jason Mietus on Dusty's Honeymoon Island. "For every little turning point in my life I've gotten a Precious Moments figurine. There's a meaning behind every figurine that Mr. Butcher creates. They're very inspirational."

"When I met Angie, I didn't really know what Precious Moments were," admits Jason, a metal worker and student who met Angie, who works in accounting, on a blind date. "She showed me her collection, and for some reason I was drawn to them. I'd see a little boy on a stump fishing and I'd think, 'I did that when I was a boy!' and I'd want one for my desk. I even found myself buying a few."

"Since we both liked Precious Moments, we really didn't consider any other location," says Angie. "Also, I had a cousin who was killed in a car accident in 1995, so getting married at the chapel was a way to remember him."

"It's a beautiful setting," says Jason. "There's a lot to see and do, but there's not a lot of urbanism. You feel like you're in God's country."

So excited were Jason and Angie about their Precious Moments wedding that they made about eight trips to the chapel—a ten-hour drive from their home in Palatine—to make sure all the details were just right. One detail proved particularly challenging—finding a Catholic priest to marry them at the chapel. "Initially, the priest who agreed to marry us was hesitant," says Jason. "He had never been to the chapel and thought it would be a circus-type environment like a theme park with a Precious Moments roller coaster, a big Timmy Land. But when we showed him the figurines and the Precious Moments catalog, he found a spiritual connection with the place. He found it very respectful and Christian. He was surprised that there was such meaning there."

Jason and Angie also worked to convince family and friends that the experience would be worth the trip. "My mother only knew that Precious Moments were cute and were sold in Hallmark stores," reports Jason. "When I showed her some brochures, she was supportive, but a lot of people wondered why we wanted to go so far away. They wondered what was driving us, but after the wedding, they realized what the chapel meant."

"My father never really understood Precious Moments," says Angie. "In fact, when I lived at home, I kept my collection in boxes so he wouldn't know how many I had and think I was wasting my money. But after my wedding, he was so impressed. He said if he had five other daughters he would want them to get married there."

Jason and Angie's wedding was a formal affair. She wore a traditional white gown, and Jason wore a tuxedo. After the ceremony, they and their fifty guests made their way to Tiffany's, a restaurant in the Precious Moments complex. "We were married on July 5 because my cousin always liked fireworks," remembers Angie, "but because it was a holiday weekend, there was wall-to-wall people. Security had to clear a way for us through the crowds. Everyone was shouting, look! There's a bride and groom!' and taking pictures. We felt like a king and queen or celebrities!"

Butcher, himself a celebrity at the complex, made a special appearance at their reception. "I could tell my father was impressed by Mr. Butcher," says Angie, "because after he left, my father was running through the complex trying to find him so he would autograph a figurine. He talks about it all the time now.

"I actually met Mr. Butcher the day before the wedding in Joette's office. I couldn't believe it when he came up. He signed a figurine right in front of me. He gives you a very warm feeling. Later on that day I saw him again at the chapel. People were going nuts. Ladies were giving him their leather purses and eyeglass cases to sign. It was like he was a movie star."

Even after the wedding, couples needn't leave Precious Moments behind. Jason and Angie spent the night in the Precious Moments honeymoon suite at the Precious Moments–themed Best Western—designed by Butcher, who also designed a Precious Moments RV park.

"Our wedding was unique and special," says Angie. "If it had taken place at any other church I would've just said, 'Oh, I got married at St. Such and Such,' but when I tell people I got married at the Precious Moments Chapel, they go, 'Wow!'"

"Sometimes, the men who come here are resistant," says Blades. "They think it's a ladies thing, that it's a big gift shop for women. But it's always the men who say how glad they are they came."

"I don't care how much of a macho man you are, you'll definitely relate to them once you visit the chapel," agrees Jason.

"I even overheard this football-player-type guy talking about how he now saw Precious Moments in a whole new light.

"The curio cabinet I got Angie as a wedding present is almost full of figurines, She has about 250. I guess I consider myself a professional collector now too. They add such a comfort to the home."

No matter how many figurines Angie and Jason collect together, the moment they each said "I do" in the Precious Moments Wedding Chapel will always be the most precious moment of all.

Precious Moments Chapel
480 Chapel Road, Carthage, Mo. 64836
800-543-7975 / www.preciousmoments.com

Paradise Garden

SUMMERVILLE, GEORGIA

For couples wed by the Reverend Howard Finster in Paradise Garden in Summerville, Georgia, the service can take as many unconventional twists as the spiraling vine-entwined tower of bicycle and lawnmower parts that rises from the middle of the eighty-two-year-old Finster's most astonishing and most wondrous garden.

"When we showed the wedding video to our family, some of them didn't quite know how to take it," says David Hopkins, a graphic artist from Nashville who wed Kitty Hopkins, an insurance claims processor who he met through friends, at Paradise Garden. "My grandmother said, 'I would've told him, 'Let's get this thing over with!'"

But Finster, whose loquaciousness is as renowned as his garden, will not be hurried. A Baptist preacher with a sixth-grade education, this self-proclaimed "stranger from another world" has spent almost forty years converting a three-acre piece of swampy Georgia earth into a fantastical, bewildering "display case" for his collection of sacred folk art.

Inspired by a vision, Finster began the garden around 1961 in what was then his back yard. His purpose was to chronicle the mechanical "inventions of mankind" and thereby honor man's genius and creativity. Staffing with some tractors and appliances, Paradise Garden gradually grew to be a truly astounding mazelike collection of cement moldings and sculptures, hand-constructed buildings, paintings, and various other unusual sights, all focusing on the perils of sin and humanity's need for God's salvation.

The World's Folk Art Chapel on the grounds
of Paradise Garden

Finster used to preach in more conventional ways until one evening in 1965 when he discovered that no one in his congregation could remember what his sermon of that morning had been about. He immediately resigned from the ministry—he had preached for over thirty years—and devoted his days to cultivating his garden. Nearly ten thousand people from around the world visit the garden each year to marvel at the results of one man's visionary obsession.

Shimmering mosaic walkways wind from the small frame house, now an art gallery, throughout the garden. The World's Folk Art Chapel, a five-story tower rising like a giant tiered cake, looms over all. Other remarkable sights include the Bicycle Tower; a giant cement shoe with the message "Blessed are the feet of those that who spread the gospel of peace"; the Tomb of the Unknown Body—the reburied remains of a young girl's skeleton found underneath an old Civil War–era house that was being demolished; a white casket filled with slips of paper on which visitors have written messages to Finster; and large beehive-shaped cement moldings embedded with glimmering ceramic pieces and images of Christ and his mother.

Strewn throughout the garden are the rusting "mechanical inventions of mankind"—wagon wheels, appliances, old cars, bed frames, an old gas mask. Many of these objects are strewn with beads, sparkly doo-dads, glittering ornaments, and, naturally, the greenery that grows and sprawls and crawls amongst these rusty remains.

Yet the reputation of Finster and his garden rests with his paintings. One day in 1976, Finster saw a face speaking to him from a smudge of paint on his fingertip. "Paint sacred art," the vision instructed him, and so he did. Since that day, he has created thousands of paintings. Large and small, they fill the garden and the gallery. From grinning trumpet-blowing angels to dancing pitchfork-wielding devils to heavenly mansions to wide-eyed Santas and Elvises, Finster's sacred art is both whimsical and profound.

And always, always, there are the words. Every single piece of art contains a Bible verse—tightly spaced, insistent pleas to turn away from evil. Indeed, Bible verses can be found throughout the garden, not just on the paintings, but printed on plywood and hung from every surface, spelled out in ceramic tiles in the walkway, painted on the rusting remains of an old Cadillac. They sprout as profusely as the garden's greenery. Their presence overwhelms.

Finster's garden had already received national attention, but when people discovered his incredible paintings, his fame grew. His art now sells in galleries from Los Angeles to Venice. He's spoken to students in university art departments. He's designed album covers for R.E.M. and the Talking Heads, appeared on the "Tonight Show" with Johnny Carson, painted an egg for the annual White House Easter egg hunt and an eight-foot Coke bottle for the Atlanta Olympics. His work and personality never cease to dazzle and amaze.

"Paradise Garden is a place where people come to meditate and to be alone in the nooks and crannies," says Cynthia Wilson, one of Finster's in-laws, who works at the garden. "There's a lot of nooks and crannies. Lawyers, doctors, all kinds of people come here. There's a stressed-out businessman from Atlanta, very intense and intelligent, who comes to meditate in the garden regularly. He writes and reads Scriptures. He stays the whole day, and when he leaves he says, 'The gardens did their magic,' and he's more peaceful."

The garden has also proved a magical place for weddings, and Finster officiates at all of them, asking only a donation for his services. "People come here to get married because the preacher means what he says. He's lived what he's written," says Wilson. "We get all kinds of weddings from brides in full-blown wedding gowns to I guess what you'd call modern clothing, culture-shock people with their hair green and orange. There was this Lurch-like guy with dreadlocks and sewn-on leopard skin stripes on his clothes. He was wearing what evidently were once nice shoes, but he had cut holes in them. The girl wore pointy glasses and had a nose ring."

Kitty and David's attire was a bit more conventional. Kitty wore an off-white antique-style wedding gown; David wore a jacket and vest. "My sister was maid of honor, best man, flower

Kitty and David Hopkins with the Reverend Howard Finster

girl, and ring bearer," says Kitty. "Our only other guest was Brandy, my fifteen-year-old dog. When I was younger I wanted a big traditional wedding, but at forty, I'm a lot more practical. I can't see spending all that money, but I wanted to do something special."

"I'd been married before in a traditional wedding," says David, "so I also wanted to do something different. We thought about going out to Vegas and getting married by Elvis or getting married on a mountaintop. Then I heard from a friend that couples had gotten married at Paradise Garden. Folk art has always interested me, and I knew who Howard Finster was although I'd never been to the garden. Folk artists are untrained, but they just believe in their art. To me there's an honesty there that isn't in a lot of pieces done by so-called artists."

Kitty was not familiar with Finster's work, so she and David looked at some pictures of Paradise Garden at a bookstore. "We knew right then that that's what we wanted," says Kitty. "Throughout our search for the right place, I told David that all

I wanted was a holy ceremony. Getting married at Paradise Garden combined David's interest in art with someplace spiritual that was a little different. It was the perfect combination."

But once Kitty told some friends of their decision, she began to have doubts. "A friend at work had been to Howard's art shows. She almost scared me because she said, 'He's really wild. He's out there.'"

When David and Kitty made a prewedding trip to the garden, Kitty's doubts intensified. "It was early spring, and the place was kind of a mess," says Kitty. "No one had had time to do anything yet. The grounds were all grown up, and the grass was real long. I looked at David and said, 'I don't know. Are they going to cut the grass?' I kept asking them, 'Are you going to cut the grass?' And they kept saying, 'No, no, it's been raining and the guy who usually cuts it had a death in the family.' We also weren't able to meet with Howard, so I was seriously starting to think of other places."

"I tried to convince her it'd be okay," says David. "That at least it would be something to remember." But once they began walking around the garden, they became intrigued by Howard's vision. "It was so neat to look at everything that he had done," says David. "You stopped and asked yourself, What was going through his head? Then the sun came out in the mosaics area and was reflecting off all the pieces of mirror in the sidewalk. I thought, Wow! This would be a nice place to wed. So we decided we'd get married in that mosaics area."

Unfortunately, it was raining in Paradise on their wedding day, so the ceremony took place in the Paradise Suite, a bed-and-breakfast room right off the gallery. But it's Finster's presence that lends the ceremony character, no matter where it's held.

"When we walked in the door of the gallery on our wedding day, all we saw was a couple of legs sticking out from a doorway," reports David. "We saw bright bluish turquoise polyester pants, white socks, and black shoes, and we thought, Oh my gosh, is that him?"

"Then we saw him and he was wearing this canvas fishing hat," says Kitty, "and I thought, Oh my God. Did we make a mistake? We didn't know anything about him at that point."

Kitty and David soon learned, however, that they had made the perfect decision. "All my life, I knew I would just cry all throughout my wedding," says Kitty, "but Howard made it so I didn't shed a tear." She laughs. "He was so interesting. I was amazed just watching and listening to him. He would start with part of the ceremony then say, 'That reminds me of a story' and he'd start off on something and talk and talk and talk. Then he'd break into another part of the ceremony then stop to talk and talk and talk."

"He talked about commitment and wisdom and being true to each other even until death," says David, "but he also talked about some pretty bizarre things, things you never thought you'd hear at a wedding, like how the noise from airplanes was causing earthquakes in California and how you're supposed to bake cakes for neighbors who poison your dog!"

Howard Finster has said that he's never met a person he hasn't loved. People who visit Paradise Garden feel likewise toward him. "It was a special thing that everyone there had Howard in common," says Kitty. "He was bringing everyone together, and everyone was getting along. He also made us feel very special, like he really and truly believed we'd be together forever. That's a neat feeling to have someone tell you that on your wedding day."

On a painting titled *Cow Woman* Finster—who's been married to his wife, Pauline, for sixty-two years—wrote this about marriage: "Marriage is love. If you don't have that companionship then you don't have marriage. Licenses, ministers, county laws, sermons is not marriage for it is love between two people that's honest and true."

Companionship on common ground brings a couple together for life's journey, but it's their marriage on the Reverend Howard Finster's very uncommon ground that reveals to them how the pursuit of dreams can turn an otherwise ordinary trip into a journey of boundless delight.

Paradise Garden / Finster Folk Art, Inc.
P.O. Box 413, Summerville, Ga. 30747
800-FINSTER / www.finster.com

Blind River Chapel
GRAMERCY, LOUISIANA

"When I first saw the Blind River Chapel, I thought it was the most beautiful thing I had ever seen stuck out in the middle of nowhere," says Lisha Brady, a homemaker from Port Vincent, Louisiana, who wed Chad Brady in the chapel.

"It's hard to explain what you feel when you walk in and speak to Miss Martha, the woman who built it. She strikes you as a very spiritual person. She makes you believe in her visions, and you want to believe. It gives you hope. She brings out things in your mind that you don't think about all the time, that there really is a God and that things in the nineties aren't as bad as they could be."

"I believe some people like Martha do have spiritual visions," says Chad, a pipe welder, who met Lisha in a local restaurant and bar. "I don't thrive on it myself, but to some people, I believe there's ways things like that could happen."

For twenty years, sixty-eight-year-old chapel owner Martha Deroche has lived on Blind River, which winds through the swampy back-alley bayous of Gramercy, Louisiana. Although the murky river may be "blind," Martha's vision remains focused, sharp, and clear, and she has the paperwork to prove it: old suitcases stuffed with letters from admirers, paper bags bursting with correspondence, a box containing videotapes of news coverage she's received, scrapbooks full of magazine and newspaper stories about various religious events, and seventeen notebooks full of her carefully recorded visions.

"When my husband, Bobby, and I came to live on Blind River, we didn't know we were going to stay here permanently," says Martha, "but God was leading us, telling us that something very beautiful would come from this river."

The Blind River Chapel is that thing of beauty, a fourteen-by-twenty-four-foot cedar-shingled chapel built on the river's edge right next to the Deroches' home, both reachable only by boat. Its brown cedar shingles hang as shaggy as the moss that solemnly drapes from the surrounding oak, cypress, and tulip trees, their tapered bases flaring gracefully into the surrounding greenish-brown water. Beyond the chapel lies the dark Louisiana swamps with their dense and entangling collection of greenery and gators.

Martha's visions and inspirations, which gave rise to the chapel, are intensely felt experiences and are touched with that sense of mystical otherworldliness associated with Louisiana's Cajun country. They date from a time in her life when emotional turmoil caused her life's path to career chaotically through ways as murky and deep as the river she now lives on. She drank, suffered a nervous breakdown, attempted suicide.

It was a July Fourth evening in the early 1980s when she began to see through the abyss. "I could feel the walls closing in on me," she says. "I went into the house for a cool drink, and I began to pray the rosary. I put my hands on the picture of the Sacred Heart and prayed, 'Sacred Heart of Jesus please give me another chance.'"

It was then she saw beams of light streaming forth from Jesus' eyes, piercing her with their intensity. "His eyes were just coming toward me," she says, still in awe. "Their power was so intense I never had another drink after that night."

A short while later she had another vision. "I saw Jesus kneeling by a rock and then that saying came to my mind, 'Upon this rock you shall build a church.' I immediately asked Bobby, 'Do you want to build a church for me?' He didn't say anything at first, but

Martha Derouche inside her chapel

I showed him a picture from a St. Jude calendar of what I wanted and he built it."

It took Bobby Deroche and a crew of volunteers four and a half months to build the chapel, hauling the materials in by boat, persevering even when the first foundation got swept away in a flood. It was dedicated Our Lady of Blind River Chapel in 1983 before a crowd of three hundred people, all circling in boats around the chapel's deck.

Inside the chapel, a statue of Mary stands inside a large hollowed out oval of cypress tree. In either corner of the chapel smaller statues of Jesus and Joseph also stand in hollowed-out frames of cypress made from the same tree. An eclectic collection of religious paintings and sculptures hangs from the chapel's walls.

And then there's the photograph. According to Martha, a visitor took a picture of the statue of Mary inside the chapel, using a point-and-shoot camera. When he had the film developed, Mary's image appeared on the outside of the chapel above the sign that bears her name. Martha insists that the photograph was not tampered with and uses it as proof that many powerful blessings will be obtained for visitors who come in good faith to the chapel.

Over a hundred thousand people from around the world have visited the Blind River Chapel, and Martha greets each one with a blessing and a finger rosary. The local tourism office used to bring visitors to the chapel until Martha decided that they were not being respectful of it. "The tourism people wanted to put the emphasis on the architecture of the chapel," says Martha. "I wanted to put my emphasis on the spiritual things. I didn't want people to come here and admire the cypress tree, so they don't bring people out here anymore. The people who come now come for God and his mother. I've had people from Ireland, Yugoslavia, Germany, England, El Salvador, Korea, Africa."

Despite the universal appeal of the chapel, Martha has struggled with the local Catholic diocese over her devotion to her chapel. She says passionately, "They're saying I'm nuts. I'm not naive. I know what they think. Let me tell you, they are persecuting me, making a mockery of me. Just what they did to Jesus, they're doing to me. The devil getting to people wants to destroy this beautiful beautiful work of God."

It's her intense spirituality and her belief in God's blessings that makes the Blind River Chapel so intriguing, and it's what compels couples to marry there. When Lisha and Chad first visited the chapel together they had no plans to marry, but the chapel was one of the first places Lisha thought about when they did decide to wed.

"I said to Chad, 'I hope you're not going to laugh at me, but I just love that little chapel.' We're down-to-earth people. We didn't want a big blow-out wedding with a dress and tuxedo. The chapel was more us than some big fancy church. It's a very peaceful place. You enjoy going there every time you go. Also, Miss Martha started building the chapel on Easter Sunday. Chad and I met on Easter so we thought it'd be appropriate. In the end, we felt nothing else was for us."

"I'm from a very large family," says Chad. "It was overwhelming to think of planning a wedding with all those people. Getting married in the chapel on the river, we didn't have to worry about inviting everyone."

At first a lot of Chad's family was upset that there was no room in the chapel for them to attend. "At one point we almost changed our mind because of the family situation and how they all wanted to be there," says Lisha. "The stress was just eating us away, but in the end we did get married where we wanted to get married."

Once they decided on the chapel they had to meet several times with Martha so she could talk with them and make sure they were right for each other. "I burn a candle for everyone who comes to marry in the chapel," says Martha, who has been married fifty-three years herself and who asks only for a donation for use of the chapel. "People from all religions have been married here, and I pray to the Blessed Virgin Mary that if the wedding wasn't meant to be, to make something happen so it won't take place."

On the day of Chad and Lisha's wedding she also prayed that the threatening rains would hold off until after the ceremony. A bad storm could leave people stranded on the river. "My friends were worried when I told them where we were having the wedding," says Lisha. "They said, 'Lisha, you better pick a different place. It's going to rain and you're not going to be able to get there.' It did rain, but not until we got home that night. That will always stick in my head—how Miss Martha prayed it wouldn't rain and it didn't until we got home."

The Bradys' wedding was small, just Chad's parents and brother and Lisha's sister. Lisha and Chad met Bobby Deroche at the local boat club and he rode them in his boat to the chapel. Lisha wore a tea-length lace dress, and Chad wore blue jeans and a silk shirt. Chad's uncle, a judge, officiated. The only other guests were Martha and Bobby and perhaps an alligator peering up from the murky waters.

"Chad and I are real animal lovers," says Lisha. "We take any kind of animal under our wing, so it's fitting we got married in the swamp. And Chad always boats and hunts in the swamps. When you're the only one out there, it's breathtaking. It's so peaceful. Being as it was in the swamp, the chapel was a real special place to get married. After we did it, everyone thought it was real neat that we got married there. Miss Martha is a also a special person. She really wants you to be feel at peace in the chapel."

Before completion of the chapel, Martha and Bobby's life as the only permanent residents on the river was a quiet one. "It was like a paradise we were living in," says Martha. "We just enjoyed it so much."

"I always said, 'When I retire I'm going to live on the river,'" recalls Bobby. "People'd say, 'Bobby, what are you going to do on the river?' I said, 'I'll sit on the front porch and watch the trees grow.'"

Although Martha and Bobby Deroche's life on the river is still a tranquil one, the visitors to the Blind River Chapel and the couples who have married there—all seekers of a special kind of peace—have given Martha added reason to believe in the clarity and power of her unique way of seeing.

Blind River Chapel
P.O. Box 205, Gramercy, LA 70052
504-869-5780

The Orange Show

HOUSTON, TEXAS

Although Houston, Texas, postal worker Jeff McKissack never married, his life was not lacking an object of devotion. It's just that the object he devoted years of his life to might strike some people as just a little fruity: Jeff McKissack loved the orange. In fact, one could say that he adored oranges, idolized oranges, and revered oranges and still not come close to describing his passion for the fruit.

McKissack—who died in 1980 at age seventy-seven—devoted the last twenty-three years of his life to the orange and to the creation of the Orange Show, a dazzling mazelike monument to the fruit and to his belief that it was the source of ultimate happiness and health. He even wrote a book, *How You Can Live 100 Years...and Still be Spry,* in which he related longevity to good nutrition, hard work, and eating oranges.

To walk through the Orange Show in its working-class

Postcard of the Orange Show in Houston, Texas

residential Houston neighborhood is like discovering a crazed but whimsical combination of side show, sacred space, and fruit stand. Sitting on a mere tenth of an acre, this concrete, brick, and steel structure is adorned almost entirely with found or salvaged objects that McKissack collected: wind vanes, carriage wheels, mannequins, ceramic tiles, cast-iron tractor seats, statuettes.

Brightly painted red, orange, blue, green, yellow, and purple, the Orange Show with its museumlike exhibits also includes an oasis, a wishing well, a pond, a stage, a museum, a gift shop, and several flag-festooned upper decks for a bird's-eye view of the colorful spectacle.

Embedded within the Orange Show's white washed walls are colorful ceramic tiles spelling out proclamations such as "Love Oranges and Live!" "Go Orange" and "I Love Oranges."

As visitors wind their way through the structure's passageways, they quickly find that McKissack found a way to relate almost every item in the Orange Show to his favorite fruit. In one area of the Orange Show, old mannequins in rumpled clothing stare into space, but McKissack has provided visitors insight into their orangey musings. Beneath a cherubic looking mannequin in a faded velvet Santa suit—McKissack called him "Santa's Son"—a sign reads, "Santa's son said 'I love oranges. I'm going to McAllen, Texas and plant a big orange grove so everyone can have oranges for Xmas. Dad love oranges. Dad know best.'"

A red-haired mannequin in an old bride's dress stands in the corner next to Santa's Son. Above her dusty veil a sign draped with plastic orange blossoms reads, "PURITY. The orange is absolutely pure. It grows out of the bloom—protected by the rind."

No one's quite sure what inspired McKissack to create the Orange Show on his property. In 1954, he built and began operating a nursery on the lot, the exterior walls of which make up the Orange Show. Tiring of the nursery, he dreamed of running a beauty salon, but in 1964 he abandoned this idea, writing, "Had a permit to build a beauty salon at 2401 Munger. Beauty salons went out of style and many are closed down. Had a better idea. The Orange Show."

During the Depression he trucked oranges from Florida to Georgia and may have developed an affinity for the fruit then. He even met with Thomas Edison and dreamed of inventing the perfect orange juicer. He also told people that when he was standing across the street from the property, a voice came to him and said, "The Orange Show."

Whatever his inspiration, it took him twenty-three years and $40,000 to complete the Orange Show, which he opened to the public in 1979. Of the fruits of his labor, he wrote, "I started working on it in 1968 and I worked on it every day....For two years, I was completely lost, but I knew I had a good idea. Then it began to make a pattern and it grew and grew, until now, without fear or hesitation, I say it is the most beautiful show on earth, the most colorful show on earth and the most unique show on earth."

McKissack even sent out invitations to the grand opening.

"Dear Friend," he wrote, "Come to the Orange Show. It is as new as the moon. As new as the domed stadium."

He was certain more Americans would want to see the Orange Show than either Disney World or the Grand Canyon.

One hundred fifty people showed up on opening day. Their numbers, however, fell off in the following weeks and soon no one was coming to see his attraction. Eight months after the Orange Show opened, McKissack died, a death some attribute to his disappointment that the crowds he anticipated never materialized. His ashes were scattered over his beloved production.

Today, however, thanks to the Orange Show Foundation—a nonprofit arts organization devoted to the extraordinary artistic expressions of ordinary people such as McKissack—over thirty thousand people visit the Orange Show every year. Because of its colors, composition, and textures, scholars consider the Orange Show to be one of the finest examples of folk art in the United States.

Many couples have also considered it a fine place to get married. Nearly every year several couples pay anywhere from $125 to $500 to marry within its quirky confines, a fact that doesn't surprise Susanne Theis, director of the Orange Show Foundation. From her office, located in a small house across the street from the Orange Show, Theis collects information on everything from bottle gardens to beer-can houses—the remarkable structures that dot our landscape and that speak of the powerful human drive to create.

As she looks through her window at the flag-festooned structure that is the Orange Show she says, "It's so hard for any of us to truly follow our dreams. The Orange Show reverberates with the energy of people like Jeff who do follow their own path." She laughs. "I guess I've never asked or wondered why anyone would want to get married here. I've always thought, 'Of course you want to get married at the Orange Show!'"

Having herself married at another Houston oddity, the Beer Can House—a privately-owned home famous for the strips of shimmering beer cans that cover its exterior walls—Theis understands the intangible allure of structures such as the Orange Show. "There's something romantic about it," she reflects. "There's a serenity at the Orange Show that you can feel." This serenity undoubtedly comes from McKissack's unflagging devotion to his project coupled with his unconditional love of the orange.

It wasn't the love of oranges that compelled Marian Luntz and James Kanan to wed at the Orange Show, but it was their combined passion for artistic expression that led to their nuptials at 2401 Munger Street. "Since I was raised Jewish and James Catholic we were looking for a neutral territory in terms of religion to have the ceremony," says Marian, curator of film and video at Houston's Museum of Fine Arts, Houston. "Since art appeals to both of us, the Orange Show seemed like a good spot. The place says so much about the possibility of the imagination. It's the whirligigs and the colors and the funky quality of the place. It speaks of endless possibility."

"When I moved to Houston some friends took me to see the Orange Show," says James, who builds sets for motion pictures and who met Marian through a friend. "They prepped me that I should expect something really off the wall. When I saw it I fell completely in love with the whole thing. That an individual like Jeff had taken some idea he had about life and turned it into his own personal reality barring no expense or the judgment from neighbors. It's incredible!

"When Marian suggested we marry there, I fell right in with the idea. The Orange Show seems like a sacred space, and Jeff was a character who had deep beliefs. It's a miracle itself that the place still exists. I never thought it possible anything like that could last."

Most couples who wed at the Orange Show do so in the Side Show, a small amphitheater that seats 150 people. Large red hearts surrounded by colorful ceramic tiles line the back wall of the space, while terrazzo tile benches ring the stage like steps and provide seating.

"Many of our 150 guests were from out of town," says James, "so they came without any expectations about what the place would be like." If any of them expected the wedding to be at all traditional, their expectations were shaken up when they saw the car in which James and Marian rode to their wedding. While a treat for many couples is the limousine ride to the wedding site, James and Marian chose transportation more in keeping with the flavor of the Orange Show. "We rode to our wedding in the Fruitmobile." James laughs. "It was a station wagon that artist Jackie Harris had covered with all kinds of plastic fruit."

Once at the Orange Show juiced up and ready to go, James, clad in a sharkskin western-style suit and iridescent cowboy boots, and Marian, dressed in an off-white lace Victorian-style dress, made their way into the Side Show. While McKissack dreamed of constructing a turntable in the Side Show on which an organist would play and spin, Marian and James dreamed up something just as unexpected for their opening act. Instead of the stately strains of an organ, a sousaphone player stood on stage with her large tubalike instrument and belched out an unparalleled rendition of the classic wedding march.

But once past the offbeat introduction, their wedding was a serious affair. "We both have a lot of respect for our families," says Marian, "and we wanted to have aspects of the wedding that were ritualized. Even though we wrote our own vows, we did incorporate some traditional rituals like the Jewish custom of smashing the glass."

There was, however, one unplanned element of the wedding that had the affair go down in Orange Show wedding history. "We had planned to have a catered reception at the Orange Show," says James, "but during the receiving line we heard a huge explosion. It turned out that one of the propane tanks used to heat up the serving dishes exploded, and the serving dish went flying across the fence into a neighbor's yard! Then I heard someone yell, 'Fire! Fire! Women and children first!' and I saw a big fireball and I thought, Oh no! This is the nightmare I dreamed would happen! The caterer asked, 'Where's the fire extinguisher?' and Susanne, the director, asked, 'What fire extinguisher?' People were really scared. But when you think about it, there was really nothing there to burn. The place is all concrete and steel!"

In the end, however, it was McKissack's beloved and humble orange that saved the day. "We had big vats of orange juice that we were going to serve at the reception," says Marian, "but our friends ended up dousing the fire with it!"

The heated event forced James and Marian to reboard the Fruitmobile so they could celebrate the remainder of the evening at a hall they had rented in case of rain. "Although our guests would have had more time to roam around and explore the Orange Show if the fire had never happened, they all seemed to like the place," says James. "No one got up and ran off during the ceremony!"

Jeff McKissack once said, "The main purpose of the Orange Show is to encourage people to eat oranges, drink oranges, and to be highly amused." While Marian and James' hot-tempered guest consumed all of McKissack's favorite drink, there's no doubt that their invited guests were nothing but delighted with the final outcome of the happy couple's amusing and fruitful union.

The Orange Show Foundation
2402 Munger Street, Houston, Tex. 77023
713-926-6368

7

Love on the Rocks

Some women measure their lover's affection by the size of the rock he presents as an engagement ring. Marriage counselors would say that such alliances are truly off to a rocky start. But for many couples, rocks symbolize strength and stability—thus the desire to wed in their presence.

Couples from as far away as Japan have wed on the observation platform before the stony granite stares of the formidable Mount Rushmore quartet in the Black Hills of South Dakota.

America's Stonehenge in New Salem, New Hampshire, remains a mysterious collection of stone chambers, walls, and large standing stones believed by some researchers to have been created over four thousand years ago to plot solar and lunar events. Couples with a New Age bent wed amid this giant megalithic astronomical complex that used to be known, less scientifically, as Mystery Hill.

New Age couples on the West Coast strap on their hiking boots and head for the rocky red hills of Sedona, Arizona. Sedona's vortexes—swirling centers of subtle energy coming out from the surface of the earth—are world renowned, and couples marrying on them are in for a truly uplifting experience. Cathedral Rock and Bell Rock are two of the most popular wedding spots.

Sentinel Dome in California's Yosemite National Park has been the site of ceremonies with a view arranged by John Paris of Your Wedding in Yosemite. A rounded lunar-like expanse of granite at an elevation of 8,122 feet, Sentinel Dome offers a 360-degree view of Yosemite's majestic valleys and waterfalls. The last two hundred yards of the one-mile trail to the dome are considered strenuous, so wedding attire is generally casual on this rocky pinnacle. One bride, however, did pack her wedding dress in her backpack and changed once atop the dome.

Couples with an eternally smoldering passion wed in Hawaii Volcanoes National Park on the island of Hawaii. Craters, cinder cones, and hardened rivers of lava make up some of the landscape in this park, home to two active volcanoes. Popular wedding sites include the overlook above the still-steaming Kilauea Caldera crater—said to be home to Madame Pele, goddess of volcanoes—or the overlook over the one-mile wide Kilauea Iki crater.

Back in 1898, gold miners set up shop at the Crow Creek Mine in Girdwood, Alaska, forty miles south of Anchorage. Now a National Historic Site, this century-old mining camp with original buildings such as a barn and blacksmith shop is also a rustic wedding site—there's no electricity, running water, or telephones. The lack of modern amenities, however, doesn't stop couples from wedding here. Perhaps that's because after the ceremony they head down to the creek, where they start prospecting for more than golden memories of the big day.

But no matter the location, rocky sites provide solid ground on which to build the foundation of a strong relationship.

Chimney Rock Park

CHIMNEY ROCK, NORTH CAROLINA

Briana Roths of Keller, Texas, grew up in Iowa. Her husband, Monty, grew up in Kansas. To such longtime residents of the Midwest, the expansive view over a sea of mountain greenery can create a giddy, drunken joy, a feeling of limitless

View of Chimney Rock Park

possibility—even when glimpsed from a glossy travel brochure. So it was when Briana showed Monty a brochure from North Carolina, pointed to the 315-foot-tall towering column of granite known as Chimney Rock in the Blue Ridge Mountains, and, half kiddingly, said, "Let's get married on top of this rock."

Monty didn't even blink. "I thought it was a great idea," he says. "Although at the time we had no idea whether a preacher would go up there."

The idea of getting married one thousand miles away atop a 535-million-year-old monolith would have remained a joke for many couples. An outdoor wedding can be risky enough even when it's staged in your own backyard, much less four states away atop a windswept promontory 2,280 feet above sea level with the unpredictable mountain weather as a backdrop.

What might seem highly impractical and stressful to more tradition-bound couples, however, was a sort of liberation for the Rothses. "Let's just say that when opportunity gives us the chance to go against the grain, we do," says Monty, who met Briana through their jobs with a company that makes railcars. "Especially with four kids between us—opportunity doesn't give us the chance to explore all that often. I knew I didn't want a traditional wedding. Growing up in Kansas, I played in a band, so I was in church all the time singing for every one of my classmates' weddings. I felt I had already been in so many traditional weddings I wanted mine to be different."

"In a traditional wedding, the bride does a lot of the thinking and planning," says Briana. "That can be very stressful. One of our mottoes was 'No stress.' Life is too short to be all stressed out."

Although it appears that getting to the top of Chimney Rock would be a rather strenuous affair, it's actually rather easy thanks to modern engineering. In 1949 an elevator was blasted into the mountainside, sparing visitors the grueling four hundred-step climb to the top of the rock. It took eight tons of dynamite and eighteen months to complete the elevator which visitors reach through a pedestrian tunnel. In a mere forty-two seconds visitors ascend twenty-six stories to the base of the summit and the Sky Lounge—a gift shop and snack bar with a view. From there it's a forty-step climb to the top of the rock.

There, a lone wind-bent tree stands alongside an American flag among rock platforms that sprout like rough-edged mushrooms on the surface. The view extends as far as seventy-five miles over the Hickory Nut Gorge, Lake Lure, and the Blue Ridge Mountains. The ease in reaching this spectacular view has made the top of the rock a popular wedding spot—about twelve weddings take place there each year.

But even in pre-elevator days, Chimney Rock was popular with couples. "There have been weddings at the park ever since it opened," says Mary Ritter, public relations director for the privately owned park twenty miles east of Asheville. Although the park was first opened in 1885, it wasn't until Dr. Lucius Morse and his brothers bought the sixty-four-acre tract of land that contains Chimney Rock in 1902 that the park became a major tourist attraction. An advertising slogan used during the park's early days declared it the "most widely known, the most stupendously interesting, and the most universally enjoyed scenic objective in the South."

It was Dr. Morse's dream that the astounding views be as accessible as possible without sacrificing the rugged natural beauty of the area. He had a bridge built across the Rocky Broad River at the base of the mountain and created a winding dirt road leading up three miles to the base of the rock.

Morse also developed the park's trail system, which includes some complicated stairways. Perhaps the trickiest is the Needle's Eye. This narrow 176-step stairway threads straight up between massive rocks and is the first challenge awaiting hikers who bypass the ease of the elevator and take the Skyline–Cliff Trail from the parking lot to the chimney.

Other trails lead to the 404-foot Hickory Nut Falls, one of the tallest falls in eastern America. So dramatic is the scenery that film crews have frequently shot movies in the park, most recently "The Last of the Mohicans."

Although some couples marry at the base of Hickory Nut Falls or in the grassy Meadow, most couples choose to wed atop Chimney Rock. "We're pretty open to working with couples and try to meet their expectations," says Ritter. "We've had everything from brides in long gowns and trains to a preacher in hiking boots and a flower dog."

The bride and groom get in to the park free. Other guests pay regular park admission—$9.50 for adults and $5.00 for children. Group rates are also available.

The Roths planned a 6:15 A.M. sunrise wedding in June, an idea that was a bit unsettling to some of their guests. "I'm a morning person," says Monty, "but my aunt said, 'I ought to hit you over the head for making me get up that early!'"

"In the morning, Monty takes his coffee outside in the silence when no one's awake," reports Briana. "The birds are singing and the sun comes up. I love that time now too. It's such a quiet moment, especially when you have kids."

The location of the wedding also brought some concern. "My sister is a city person and lives in Chicago," says Briana. "She literally had nightmares that her three-month-old baby would fall off the mountain."

The mountain experience was far more positive for Monty and Briana. "The closer we got into the beautiful country and all those winding mountain roads, I felt like a kid in a candy store," Briana recalls. "Maybe it's because we don't see the mountains all that often. They're just awesome."

"It was an ultimate experience," agrees Monty. "I haven't been to the Grand Canyon, but I imagine it as a similar feeling. Driving on mountain roads, you forget all about the city."

The Rothses arrived in North Carolina the evening before the wedding. Even though they didn't have a chance to visit the park before their wedding, Chimney Rock still made its presence known. "That night, we sat on the porch of our cabin looking at the rock," says Briana. "It was lit up and it was like looking at a star. I thought, That's where we're going to get married. I couldn't wait till the morning."

It wasn't nerves that kept Monty and Briana awake that night, though. It was some of Mother Nature's rowdy uninvited guests: rain, thunder, lightning, and wind. "The thunder was booming, and it was pouring, pouring, pouring," says Briana. "I've never seen a storm like it."

Monty adds, still in awe, "The thunder roared and the lightning would just trade mountains. It'd hit one mountain and then trade with the other."

They were up past midnight waiting for their invited guests, who were delayed by the storm. When they awoke for the day at 3:30 A.M. it was still raining. But the Rothses had not come all that way to have their wedding inside or to postpone it to the prosaic hours of the afternoon. They got ready just as if there were sunshine and blue skies and made their way to the park.

Dressed in a full-length white dress and veil, Briana clutched her bouquet while her sister fought the winds with an umbrella as they dashed from their car into the tunnel leading to the elevator. Once in the office of the Sky Lounge, Briana waited with the preacher, scanning the skies, looking for relief.

Meanwhile, Monty in his white tuxedo stood huddled with their guests under umbrellas on the gusty mountaintop. "My grandmother had to have someone hold on to her in the wind because she's so tiny," says Monty, "but she wanted to climb up there. She said, 'I braved that elevator for you, I can make the stairs.'"

Miraculously, relief came. When the pouring rain diminished to sprinkles, the preacher looked at Briana and said, "I'm game if you are," and Briana said, "Let's go!"

Monty and Briana come down from the rock

She gleefully recalls: "My train was blowing all over and dipping in the puddles. Everyone was mad at my sister because the maid of honor is supposed to look after the dress, but my sister said, 'Heh! I was holding onto her arm so she wouldn't blow over! It was either her or the train.' Once I set the train down it just blew on out. I also thought my veil was going to blow off. Then I was trying to figure out where to go because there's no aisle and we had no rehearsal. That's when I got the giggles. There was no formality. I just saw Monty and headed toward him."

"There were puddles of water all over the rock," says Monty. "Everyone had to watch where they stood. The preacher went and stepped in one puddle I think so no one else would. He even took a couple steps backward sometimes because of the wind."

Despite the wind, Briana and Monty were able to hear each other recite their vows, but Briana laughs, "Every time I said my vows, the wind picked up. I felt a little picked on!" They had a traditional ceremony that included a taped version of themselves singing Elvis' "I Can't Help Falling in Love With You." The clanging of the flagpole in the wind also provided some unexpected accompaniment.

Despite the natural distractions, Monty and Briana were thrilled with the location and their wedding. "There's a lot of freedom on top of the mountain," says Briana. "It gives you a wonderful, glorious feeling. Even though we'd never been there, we'd knew that's how it would be."

After the ceremony, they had a breakfast reception in the Sky Lounge. By the time they had eaten, the day had cleared and park visitors were making their way to the top. "Everyone was excited, "says Briana. "They said, 'Oh my goodness! Did you just get married here?' and they stood by and let us pass. It was fun to have all those strangers. We had the privacy of the park for the wedding then the crowds afterward. I had bustled up my train but the fringe and lace at the bottom of my dress were all brown, but everyone said, 'You're so beautiful!' We just ate up all that attention."

The following week, the Rothses explored the park, going hiking, white water rafting, and canoeing. But they also enjoyed just sitting. "We spent a lot of time watching and listening to the water running over the rocks in the river," says Briana, "not spending a penny and yet having a blast."

Novelist Thomas Wolfe grew up in Asheville and brought attention to the North Carolina mountains with *Look Homeward, Angel,* a novel that speaks of the desire to find a home place, a resting place, for the spirit. For Briana and Monty, that home place seems to be the Blue Ridge Mountains of North Carolina, and they talk eagerly of wanting to relocate within their rolling embrace. Whether or not they do, their windswept wedding on Chimney Rock will always remain a heavenly memory.

Chimney Rock Park
P.O. Box 39, Chimney Rock, N.C. 28720
800-277-9611 / www.chimneyrockpark.com

Big Brutus
WEST MINERAL, KANSAS

People do not often equate coal mining with romance—not, that is, until they meet Big Brutus in West Mineral, Kansas. Sixteen stories tall and weighing 11 million pounds, Big Brutus is the second largest electric shovel in the world. Although now retired, Big Brutus still has the same magnetic personality he had when he removed tons of dirt and rock covering seams of rich coal in southeastern Kansas. Every year, thirty thousand people visit Big Brutus, eager to get inside and climb around the heart of the machine.

When Big Brutus was being assembled in 1962, an observer remarked, "That's a brute of a machine," and the name stuck. Indeed, so large and so powerful is the shovel that locals bestowed upon it a benevolent, almost protective, personality so as not to feel eclipsed and threatened by its awesome might.

"Big Brutus put the oooohs and aahs in the backyard of the Heartlands!!!" reads the shovel's brochure. "Standing beside it makes one aware of how fragile he or she is. The men who worked in, with and round this giant had a feeling for it. A lasting bond was formed between the men and machine. The feeling was so strong it lives on today not only in men who worked Mine 19, but also remains with their wives, children, and grandchildren. Indeed it is infectious! There are people of the region as well as many visitors who walk through Big Brutus and feel there is something akin to a bit of soul left behind in the resounding, echoing steel hulk."

Photo of Big Brutus

Considering the role this soulful towering giant of the plains has in the community—it's almost as if he were a member of the family—it should come as no surprise that weddings have taken place in his powerful embrace. "There have been a handful of weddings at Big Brutus," says Betty Becker, manager of Big Brutus and the adjacent mining museum. "Most weddings took place on the grounds, but there was a couple who got married at the top of the boom. She had on a long formal dress, so it was very tricky climbing the steep stairs to get up there."

Terri and Kenny Burkhart's wedding was a little more accessible. They got married in Big Brutus' glass-enclosed operator's cabin. "My friends and family couldn't believe I was getting married at Big Brutus," says Terri, a cable TV account executive from Dodge City. "They said, 'Why would anyone want to get married on a giant shovel?'"

"People don't look at machinery," says Kenny, a heavy equipment operator who met Terri at a Christmas party. "They see a truck on the highway and they don't think anything about it, but if you really get into it and know what it's about, what it took to put it together, it's amazing."

It took 150 railroad cars to deliver the pieces of Big Brutus to West Mineral. Fifty-two employees of the Pittsburg and Midway Coal Mining Company worked twenty-four-hour days for eleven months to assemble the eleven-million-pound shovel, which went into operation in 1963 and worked nonstop until 1974, when rising costs silenced its roar. In its lifetime, it removed overburden from nine million tons of coal.

Aware of Big Brutus' powerful personality, neighbors were loath to see him sit idle and rust. According to his brochure, "Community leaders were well aware people were compelled to cross forbidden boundaries just to get closer to this 160 foot giant—to touch it—to climb it." Their answer was to form Big Brutus, Inc., and in 1985 Big Brutus, sixteen acres of surrounding land, and the mining museum opened to the public. Since then, Big Brutus has been the guest of honor at family reunions, school field trips, picnics, and weddings.

The massive black and orange shovel sits on the bank of a strip pit, "like an old ship resting in its harbor" says the brochure. Brown, twisted hoist cabling lines the pathway to Big Brutus. This cable was used to lift Big Brutus' bucket, which held 150 tons of material. Even though each foot of cable weighed twenty-five pounds, it would still break every six months with the heavy loads Big Brutus carried as it lumbered at a top speed of 0.22 miles per hour through the pits.

To get inside the machine, visitors walk alongside Big Brutus' "feet"—its four seven-foot-tall crawlers, each weighing 2,008 pounds. Once inside the belly of the beast, there's a lot more technical information to take in, all about crowd gears and ballast tanks and hydraulic jacks and synchronous motor controls, but most people are content simply to stare in wonder at the size and power of Big Brutus' internal organs.

Brave climbers ascend the narrow, steep stairway 160 feet to the top of the boom. The climb is dizzying, and no one under the age of thirteen is allowed to attempt it. The view sixteen stories above the earth looks out over a sea of crops and the fifteen thousand acres of the Mined Land Wildlife Areas.

Back inside the visitor's center, poems, letters, and reports from local students and residents attest to the allure of Brutus. One student triumphantly declares that Big Brutus is more impressive than the Eiffel Tower. Another proudly proclaims that Big Brutus is twice as tall as the Mount Rushmore faces and is wider than Route 66. Another instills Big Brutus with the sentiment of the Tin Man and says that when news reached Brutus of his forced retirement, "he nearly burst into tears."

Although Big Brutus is well known in southeastern Kansas, his reputation was not as strong in the southwestern portion of the state. "I didn't know a lot about Big Brutus until one day a guy was admiring the asphalt eater I was working on and he went and showed me a brochure," says Kenny. "When I showed the brochure to Terri, we read where people had gotten married there and that's when we thought it'd be a neat idea. We really didn't consider any other place."

"We're all brought up and conditioned to do the old traditional wedding where everyone just thinks, 'Oh, I have to go to this wedding. I have to go get a dress. I have to go get a present,'" says Terri. "Getting married at Big Brutus was more relaxing. It gave our guests the opportunity to have a good time and learn something about machinery."

The machinery is what impressed Terri and Kenny when they met Big Brutus the day before their wedding. "We were quite a ways away, but, boy, you could see the boom sticking up into the sky miles away," says Terri. "All the statistics are what impressed me, how tall it was, how much things weighed, that it ran twenty-four hours a day."

"The swing gears on the piece of equipment I operate are a couple feet wide," says Kenny. "You look at Big Brutus and the gears are fifteen to twenty feet apart. When I sat in the cab, which is hundreds, maybe thousands of times bigger than anything I've been in, it was amazing."

Kenny and Terri had ten guests at their wedding, which made

for a tight fit in the operator's cabin. "It was pretty close," says Terri. "We had people standing in the doorway. We didn't really consider getting married at the top of the boom. We had some older relatives at the wedding, and they weren't fit to climb something like that."

Although they wed on a gray, misty March day, it could've been the Fourth of July based on their wedding attire. Terri wore a blue western-style skirt and jacket with white silk tassel trim and white boots. Kenny wore blue jeans and a red, white, and blue shirt complete with stars and stripes. "Those are just the colors we like," says Terri. "Kenny's grandmother even wore red, white, and blue bell bottoms that she got back in 1976."

A local minister officiated the ceremony. "He's rather elderly," says Terri. "When we asked him to marry us at Big Brutus, he only said, 'I hope you don't want me to go clear to the top of that thing.'"

Following their wedding, Kenny and Terri were on the top of the world and set out north toward Kansas City to celebrate. But it wasn't toward a fancy hotel with a heart-shaped Jacuzzi that they steered their camper. So excited were they by Big Brutus that they braved the pouring rain, endured a wedding dinner of McDonald's hamburgers, and spent the night in a Wal-Mart parking lot—all in hopes of visiting a large crane that a visitor at Big Brutus had told them about.

Getting married high above a strip pit surrounded by the levers and dials of a monstrous rock-moving shovel seems distinctly unromantic and cold as stone to many people, but for the Burkharts, the incomparable fiery might of Big Brutus lent the setting a unique elegance.

"To me, that machine is beautiful," says Terri. "My dad was a foreman of a construction company, so I grew up around construction equipment. If someone's father wore a suit and tie, I don't know if deep down they could appreciate Big Brutus. Some people just aren't going to see the beauty in a big shovel."

"If a person is mechanically minded," says Kenny, "Big Brutus is like a piece of gold."

The rocky history of Big Brutus will always be a moving one, and, like the world's most treasured element, he will forever remain a cherished adornment to the West Mineral landscape.

Big Brutus, Inc.
P.O. Box 25, West Mineral, Kans. 66782
316-827-6177

Glacier Weddings

JUNEAU, ALASKA

Even though they got married in the dog days of August, Glenn and Jean Tonge of Wallingford, Connecticut, literally had cold feet on their wedding day. While many couples prefer to tie the knot on a warm sandy beach surrounded by the resplendent reds and glittering golds of a dramatic sunset, Glenn and Jean boarded a helicopter in perpetually damp Juneau, Alaska, flew to the slick surface of Herbert Glacier, and wed on a frosty field surrounded by gray granite peaks and incredibly blue yet distinctly chilly glacial ice.

"The color of the ice was absolutely incredible," says Glenn, an auto mechanic who met Jean at a party. "It was royal blue like the color of the blue liqueur curacao."

"There were so many different shades of blue. Pictures can never do it justice," says Jean, who works in the computer center at Quinnipiac College. "The water pockets in the crevices of the ice were full of this deep blue water. It was amazing."

The ever-varying colors of nature's chilly chapel are one of the reasons Juneau marriage commissioner Russ Hansen remains eager to perform wedding ceremonies on Herbert Glacier, the 8.5-mile-long icy bridal aisle twenty miles northwest of Juneau, reachable only by helicopter. "The blues can be beyond description, like something from *National Geographic*," says Hansen, who officiates at approximately a dozen glacier weddings each summer in packages that run from $700 to

Glen and Jean Tonge on Herbert Glacier

$1,000. "The colors range from very very very light blue to deep azure blue, like the deep blue of those poly tarps, but even deeper than that."

Describing the deep yet luminous blue of glacier ice is challenging, but Glenn and Jean found it just as challenging to explain to East Coast family and friends why they wanted to journey to the Alaskan coast and marry atop a glacier where daytime summer temperatures average between 50 and 60 degrees—on a warm day. "Some of my friends weren't sure what a glacier was," says Glenn. "They pictured us getting married on top of one big ice cube."

Jean laughs, "Everyone was kind of shocked. They were worried I was going to fall off the edge of it."

Glenn and Jean weren't quite sure what to expect either; neither of them had ever been to Alaska. They were sure, however, that they did not want a traditional wedding. "You get pulled in too many directions with a traditional wedding," says

Jean. "Everyone gets so caught up in a show. Most people have their wedding in a church they don't even attend. It's too much of a hypocrisy. We wanted our wedding to be for us."

Glenn agrees. "A big wedding is too much of a strain on the bride and groom. By the time we figured out how much we'd spend on everything we wouldn't have had any money left over."

"We decided to get married in Alaska because pictures of it always look so beautiful," says Jean, "so we booked a cruise along Alaska's inside passage and began investigating wedding sites. A lady at the Juneau visitor's center said she had heard that someone had gotten married on a glacier. I immediately liked the idea. We figured we'd want to see a glacier anyway so why not get married on one?"

"I thought it would be great to get married on top of the world," says Glenn. "It would go along with the whole feeling of being married." He laughs. "But once we decided on the location we found it funny because Jean is always cold! If it's one hundred degrees outside, she's cold."

Cold notwithstanding, every couple Hansen has married on the glacier has had no regrets. "They've all been in awe of what they see and do," says Hansen. "Some are fearful at first. They're afraid of the helicopter flight or they're afraid of being on an ice field, but once we take off there is so much to see they forget all about their fears. I had one couple who brought their father along on the flight. He was terrified of heights, but he was so in awe of everything that when we flew back to Juneau he asked if he could sit by the window."

A glacier is much more than a towering ice cube. Ever moving and changing, glaciers are vast fields of ice formed from compacted snow. So dense is glacier ice that the higher frequencies of light can't escape or penetrate it, thus the intense blue color. Covering twenty thousand square miles in Alaska, glaciers are a definite presence in the frozen north.

Of Juneau's thirty-six major glaciers, Mendenhall Glacier is the most popular because it's only eleven miles from downtown—a veritable suburban glacier—but Hansen prefers the solitude of isolated Herbert Glacier. Most of the couples he marries each summer are on a cruise, so when their ship docks in Juneau, Hansen, clad in suit and hiking boots, meets the couple at the dock. Together they drive to the airport in his Alaskan limousine—a Toyota 4Runner—and board the helicopter for the thirty-minute trip to the glacier.

"At first I was more worried about the helicopter," remembers Jean, who arrived for the day in tea-length white dress and heels. "I'm petrified of heights. When the pilot shut the door, he showed us the lock and said, 'This is locked and this is open.' I was sitting right next to that window terrified the door would come unlocked, but the minute we got up in the air, I forgot all about it. The scenery was so spectacular. Big waterfalls appearing out of nowhere from the mountainsides, lakes and pine trees as far as you could see, sheer faces of rock, and snow-capped mountains. It was gorgeous."

"When we landed, we were awe-stricken," says Glenn, who dressed in suit and tie. "It was massive, like we were in a big horseshoe, a big room with walls of mountains rising around us and fog for the ceiling. It was spectacular. And then the blues. It was just incredible."

Spreading outward like a field of frozen cotton balls, the undulating and ever-changing surface of the glacier has the icy granular consistency of a snow cone, so navigating the bridal path can be tricky, especially if the bride is wearing heels. This is where Hansen's supply of moon boots comes in handy. "The ice can be pretty slick," he says. "Most of the brides wear some type of wedding gown, and it's hard to walk on the glacier with heels, so we encourage them to wear the moon boots. We just try to take pictures so their feet won't show."

Although cloudy weather intensifies the blue colors in the ice, it can also bring Juneau's other famous element—rain. "It started to rain as soon as we got out of the helicopter," says Jean. "It was very light rain, like a fine steady mist. You couldn't really see it, but it made it very cold, like in the forties. We were freezing during the ceremony."

"The rain was God's way of cleansing us." Glenn laughs. "It was holy water."

"The ice was really slick so I pretty much had to wear the moon boots," says Jean. But that's where she drew the line. "Russ' wife was our witness and she handed me this big purple coat to wear, but I decided not to wear it. I didn't want to look all bundled up."

Hansen performs the brief ceremony—one benefit of the cold is that the wedding rings slip right onto chilly fingers—and then it's time for pictures. "At most traditional wedding places you have just one background," says Glenn. "Here, you have five or six different backgrounds for pictures, and they're all incredible. A glacier is one of earth's last pure places, untouched by man. We live close to New York City where everything's been touched and retouched and mangled and touched again. Everything is purity on a glacier."

"I tell couples that the footprints they're making in that ice will never be there again," says Hansen. "The glacier is always moving and changing. That moment in time is theirs."

And there's very little chance that anyone will crash the ceremony. The only uninvited guest would be a mountain goat, and they very rarely venture down from the surrounding peaks. "We never saw or heard a soul," says Jean. "We wanted to be alone on our wedding day, and we were completely alone."

That evening Glenn and Jean were back on their cruise ship, surrounded by hundreds of other tourists heading farther into the frozen north.

Far from being a giant ice cube floating treacherously in a frigid sea, Herbert Glacier was for Glenn and Jean a vast and luminous place of great beauty and emotional warmth. And even though they were head over heels in love with each other, they never fell off the edge.

Russ Hansen—Marriage Commissioner
P.O. Box 34199, Juneau, AK 99803
907-789-7811

The House on the Rock

SPRING GREEN, WISCONSIN

"A rock and a whole lot more."

At one time, this was the line the marketing department used to lure visitors to the House on the Rock near Spring Green, Wisconsin. When describing this architectural curiosity, sometimes the fewer words said the better. Words barely do justice to a house that is usually described as "indescribable."

And when Amanda and Ed Pala of Wisconsin Rapids said they married at the House on the Rock because it was the "only interesting place in Wisconsin," they certainly got the "interesting" part right.

"Most people are overwhelmed when they first visit," says Melissa Lease, marketing assistant at the House on the Rock. "They want to tell other people about it, but they have no words to do so. It's more than they ever expected. Couples who marry here have definitely found someplace different."

The "rock" part is easy to describe. It's a sixty-foot-tall

Outside view of the House on the Rock

limestone chimney rock that towers over the rolling hills of the Wyoming Valley in southwest Wisconsin.

The "house" part is hard. Alex Jordan, the legendary genius behind the House on the Rock, began constructing this mesmerizing, mystifying structure in the 1940s. What began as a fourteen-room weekend home sculpted atop the rock gradually evolved into a two hundred-acre complex housing Jordan's extraordinary and whimsical collections.

Legend has it that Jordan carried work materials up to the rock in wicker baskets strapped to his back and that he built as he went without a plan. When curious locals began coming by, Jordan charged them fifty cents, thinking it would keep them away. Intrigued even more, they kept on coming until Jordan officially opened the House on the Rock to the public in 1960. Today, over five hundred thousand people visit the House on the Rock every year to marvel at the work of this amazing man, who worked continuously on his dream home up until his death in 1989 at the age of seventy-five.

Visitors know they're in for something a little bizarre as they pass the giant flower pots that line the winding road leading to the house. Large lizardlike creatures cling to the sides of the pots, staring and grimacing at passing motorists.

But these mysterious pot crawlers seem tame in comparison to what's inside the House on the Rock. Jordan collected everything from suits of armor to dollhouses to music machines, and in each room, each wing, each building of the structure he displayed his collections in almost dreamlike, surrealistic settings.

In a way, Jordan's House on the Rock is rather like a monumental junior high school project combining art, music, history, and science. It's the fantastic project kids dream of creating at an age when they're old enough to understand the intellectual principles of the project, but still young enough, enthusiastic enough, crazy and goofy enough to be impressed with number, size, and spectacle as they work to amuse themselves but also to stupefy and sometimes even dupe and annoy the adults.

For instance, in the Heritage of the Sea Building, over two hundred model ships are displayed alongside a wide collection of maritime information and memorabilia, but it's all dwarfed by the two hundred-foot-long snarling fiberglass sea creature fighting tenaciously with an enormous bulging-eyed octopus. It's said Jordan wanted the creature to be longer than the Statue of Liberty is tall and had workers continuously tear its eye out until it looked more and more vicious. At Christmas, when the House on the Rock is decorated with over six thousand Santas, a Santa in shorts rides a surfboard on the fiberglass waves generated from the tempest.

In the room housing the World's Largest Carousel, a herd of valuable antique wooden horses line the walls, but attention immediately goes to the bevy of scantily clad, bare-breasted winged mannequins flying from the ceiling, violins strapped to some of their chins. Like the winged unicorns who share the ceiling with them, these department store angels hover and float in a red-toned room ablaze from the twenty thousand lights that cover the carousel. Sea serpents, boars, frogs, zebras, rabbits, walruses, elephants, unicorns—these are the some of the 269 handcrafted creatures that prance and dance round and round and not one of them is a horse.

Indeed, music plays an integral part in the House on the Rock. Automated self-playing musical instruments are incorporated into many exhibits. Sometimes, whole rooms are wired for sound as in the Blue Room. Under crystal chandeliers, mechanically operated self playing musical instruments— violins, cellos, violas—"lounge" about on the elegant French Provincial furniture until a visitor deposits a token and they come eerily to life and break into a raucous symphony, like guests who've had too much to drink.

Other exhibits include a three-level merry-go-round with hundreds of bisque dolls; a million-piece miniature circus displayed alongside a pyramid of life-size elephants that itself is overwhelmed by a colossal circus wagon; 250 dollhouses; and the World's Largest Doll Castle.

Then there's the Infinity Room, a long, thin glass room projecting like an airplane wing 218 feet over the Wyoming Valley. Its 3,264 windows offer an unparalleled view, while a glass cocktail table in the floor allows a look into the treetops 156 feet below. It's almost like walking on air. Of this room, Jordan said, "Ah-h-h, that's a great one! That's the most beautiful idea I've ever had. It's given to very few to do a thing like that."

When the Infinity Room opened in 1985, the public was awed but leery. On windy days, the room would bounce and give, just like an airplane wing in the wind, but once its sturdiness was proved, it became a truly inspirational airy hangout.

The glassy aisle of the Infinity Room has proved the most popular place to wed at the House on the Rock, and it's where Ed and Amanda married—other favorite spots include alongside the blazing carousel and in the outdoor gardens.

"I liked the idea of being together for infinity," says Ed, a paper mill worker who met Amanda, who works in a photo lab, at a gym. "And since the room is also shaped like an aisle, we thought it'd be the best place. Even though I can really get the room to bouncing if I'm the only one in it, we weren't worried that our guests might get shaken up during the wedding."

Despite the apparent fragility of the glass room, it's actually quite a sturdy spot to tie the knot—approximately fifty to seventy-five people can fit into the crystal corridor.

"I knew I didn't want to deal with the same old wedding that's been done a million times," Ed continues. "I wanted to be completely different. My grandmother always told me to go see the House on the Rock, but I always thought it was just a house. When Amanda and I went there several years ago, I knew as soon as we entered the driveway that it was going to be something different, and then when we saw all the rooms, it was amazing."

In keeping with the drama of the house, Ed and Amanda married on Halloween in a medieval-themed ceremony. "Halloween has always been the funnest holiday for me," says Amanda, "and I've always liked the medieval period—the castles and the adventure."

"I like the medieval era too," agrees Ed, "I think knights are cool."

Even before their wedding, Ed got into the knightly mood. "When Ed proposed to me he knelt at my feet with a decorative sword, one with a shiny gold hilt and a lion's head with red eyes—like Richard the Lion Hearted—and asked, 'Will you be my queen for today if I can be your king?'" says Amanda. "At first I wasn't quite sure what he was talking about! He had to repeat it a couple times!"

Ed and Amanda had to repeat a couple times to their families why they wanted to travel several hours to wed at the House on the Rock. "Some of our families thought it was too far away," says Amanda, "or they complained about having to come in costume. But it's what we wanted to do."

On their wedding day, Ed and Amanda had a lot of practice navigating the narrow mazelike hallways and passageways that wind through the House on the Rock—they spent the morning carrying chairs for their forty-five guests to the Infinity Room. Ed laughs, "It was a lot of work, so we saw a lot of each other before the wedding!"

There was plenty of time, however, for Ed to change into a knight in shining armor—or at least a knight—for the ceremony. He wore black pants and boots and a medieval-style blue tunic, while Amanda wore a long blue velvet gown and rhinestone crown. They had six guards at their wedding, all dressed in red tunics with a black dragon outlined on the chest.

While music by Enya played, the guards marched into the Infinity Room, and Ed and Amanda followed behind. As they approached the peak of the room, the guards made an arch of raised swords for Amanda and Ed to walk through. The short ceremony was conducted by a black-robed justice of the peace who, with a touch of his sword, conferred the title of husband and wife upon the kneeling couple. The colorful ceremony was matched only by the brilliant reds and golds of the autumn trees spread out beneath their feet.

"The wedding was great," says Ed. "We felt we were

suspended out there in space. It made for a very pretty start of our life together."

Almost any portion of the House on the Rock is available for receptions. Ed and Amanda shared their castle-shaped cake in the House on the Rock's Transportation Room, where the mood was distinctly postmedieval. "We chose the room because it has a cobblestone floor, so it felt kind of medieval," says Amanda, "and the staff brought down round wooden tables to make it feel even more so, but we were still surrounded by a car covered with ceramic tiles and a collection of Burma Shave signs."

When Alex Jordan drew up plans for the Infinity Room, critics doubted that the room could ever be built, and if it could be built, then they wouldn't risk their lives and go out into it. But Jordan found a way to support his glass room on a platform of rock and send it soaring gracefully into space. Couples wedding in the Infinity Room at the House on the Rock make a similar leap of faith, trusting that the solid foundation they're starting their life on will lead them in infinite and stunning directions.

The House on the Rock
5754 Highway 23, Spring Green, Wis. 53588
608-935-3639

8

Swing Your Partner:
Weddings With Western Flair

The rugged good looks of the Marlboro man leave many women swooning. Now any man can be cowboy for a day if he and his "pardner" get hitched at a western-theme town or ranch. Although life was a little rough in the wild and wooly West, western weddings nowadays combine the rugged romanticism of frontier life with the finest of modern conveniences for a celebration that would stop Jesse James in his tracks.

Couples in love not only with the starry skies of the west but the stars who shone in television and movie westerns stage their western wedding at a site related to the silver screen. Paramount Ranch in Agoura Hills, California, was Hollywood's backyard for many years, and luminaries such as Gary Cooper and Mae West filmed here. Today, the National Park Service directs the action of couples who select these western sets for their wedding backdrop.

Ponderosa Ranch, home of the Cartwrights on the television show "Bonanza," opens its gates to love in Incline Village, Nevada. After the wedding in the Church of the Ponderosa, an authentic 1870 country church, everyone enjoys the activities of "Bonanzas'" western town—daily gun fights, pony rides, and action at The Moonshine Shootin' Gallery—before moseying over for a tour of Cartwright Ranch House where they can view film clips from Bonanza.

Kanab, Utah, calls itself Little Hollywood because over 150 movies and television shows have used the surrounding dramatic red cliffs as backdrops. The folks at Frontier Movie Town have rounded up movie sets used by stars such as James Garner and Clint Eastwood and assembled them into a western town. A wedding here will make any couple's day.

There's also a full roundup of western towns made famous by real people, such as Nebraska native Harold Warp. Many pioneers were forced to discard items as they made the arduous journey west. If they did, chances are they can be found at Harold Warp's Pioneer Village in Minden, Nebraska, the only "Museum of Progress" in the United States. Warp collected over fifty thousand items from "every field of human endeavor"— everything from horse-drawn rigs to bathtubs—to cut glass to historic flying machines and arranged them chronologically in their respective order of development in twenty-six buildings arranged clockwise around a village green. Every summer, couples marry in the village's country church, built in 1884.

In 1947, John Quigley chose the top of MacDonald Pass outside Helena, Montana, to singlehandedly build Frontier Town. It took him thirty-three years to create this log-and-rock Old West–theme fort. Locals predicted his crazy dream would come crashing down the mountainside in the rain and snow, but it hasn't—so far. The Frontier Town Chapel, made of massive logs, straddles the Continental Divide for weddings on a grand scale. Following the wedding, guests can belly up to the bar— one huge Douglas fir log—on stools made of saddles.

Theme parks have also gotten into the western wedding business. At Silver Dollar City in Branson, Missouri, couples wed in the Wilderness Church, a little log chapel set amid an 1890s mining town. At Knott's Berry Farm in Buena Park, California, couples marry in the 120-year-old Church of the Reflections, head for photo opportunities with the Knott's Old West

Gunslingers, then gather in the authentic 1880s Wilderness Dance Hall for a boot-stomping good time.

Couples without the duds need never despair. Although mail-order brides are a thing of the past, couples can still mail-order authentic western wedding attire and accessories from Bonham Western Wedding in Cheyenne, Wyoming.

So, no matter what direction couples come from for their western wedding or where they head for the ceremony, they're always guaranteed to ride off into the sunset.

Apacheland Movie Ranch

GOLD CANYON, ARIZONA

At weddings, a moment of polite silence usually follows the officiant's routine question, "Does anyone here present object to the marriage about to take place?" At Sherri and Kris Cruser's wedding, there was a moment of silence. It just took a little longer than usual to come.

Right after the justice of the peace asked the question of their guests, a gruff, dirty cowboy with an unkempt beard burst into the back of the small Arizona desert chapel. "I met this little filly this morning," he growled as he eyed Sherri in her white dress at the altar, "and I aim to take her back to Montana with me."

But before the love-struck cowboy could make his way into the crowded chapel and grab his object of desire, Kris, spurred by fear and outrage, pulled a pistol from out of his black western-cut tuxedo jacket and fired several shots at the deranged desert Romeo.

Wedding guests cried in horror as white gun smoke filled the air, temporarily obscuring the results of Kris' marksmanship. When the smoke cleared, the old cowboy lay at the back of the chapel, dead. Only then did the moment of silence come as the Crusers' family and friends, stunned and speechless, stared at the crumpled body of the uninvited guest.

Quickly, however, the silence was broken. Once again, the chapel doors flew open, ushering in swirls of desert dust. Two other cowboys materialized, looked impassively at the dead man at their feet, then dragged him out the door without saying a word. Kris stood next to his quivering bride-to-be. Looking into the eyes of the shocked guests, he brandished his pistol and asked, "Anyone else?" But instead of reacting with wild panic, Kris and Sherri's guests let out rounds of hearty laughter. The justice of the peace called for order, and the wedding went on without a hitch.

No, the guests at the Crusers' wedding weren't callous to the murder of a confused old cowboy. Rather, they discovered that they had become part of the show at Apacheland Movie Ranch, a world-famous replica of an 1880s western town in the Superstition Mountains east of Phoenix, Arizona.

"We had a choice of other skits too," says Sherri, a salesperson from Chandler, Arizona, who met Kris, a roofer, when she was selling him roofing supplies. "I could've been kidnapped and Kris would've had to go around to our guests and collect money for my ransom, or Kris could've gotten thrown in jail and I'd have to go around and collect money for bail. Those skits would've been fun too, but we didn't want to beg people for money, so we decided to kill someone instead."

Apacheland Movie Ranch has a long history of dramatic happenings. Created in 1957 on eighty-five acres of pristine Sonoran desert, the ranch with its nearly thirty buildings has been the site of hundreds of films, television shows, and commercials. Giant saguaro and ocotillo cacti dot the thousands of acres of state and federal land that surround Apacheland. With the Superstition mountains rising in the background, Apacheland Movie Ranch provides filmmakers with the perfect wild and woolly western environment.

Ronald Reagan was one of the first stars to walk the wide, dusty streets of the town. From 1959 to 1968, he hosted "Death Valley Days," a popular television series filmed at the ranch. "Maverick," starring James Garner and "Wanted Dead or Alive," with Steve McQueen were also filmed at Apacheland.

Films shot at Apacheland have starred John Wayne, Dean

Martin, Jerry Lewis, James Garner, Henry Fonda, Kenny Rogers, Clint Eastwood, and Armand Assante, to name just a few. Even Elvis Presley strapped a gun belt around his hips and walked the wooden boardwalks in his 1969 movie *Charro!* It was Elvis as Jess Wade who saved Apacheland's church from destruction by a group of Mexican outlaws.

"He was the best looking man I've ever seen," says Sue Birmingham, who owns and runs Apacheland with her husband, Ed. When her father took over Apacheland in 1959, she worked as an extra in many of the films, including *Charro!* "Elvis was slim and trim and could do all the gun twirls," she says.

But Elvis didn't just leave footprints in the Apacheland dust. Following *Charro!* Apacheland's little white church was named the Elvis Presley Chapel. After his death, it became the Elvis Presley Memorial Chapel. Although an Elvis impersonator in Stetson and spurs has yet to marry or serenade a couple in the desert chapel bearing his name, that could change. For the past several years, Apacheland has been the site of Elvis Lives, an Elvis impersonator contest that drew close to a thousand people in 1997.

Given the rough and tough flavor of Apacheland, it's not surprising that couples seek it out for western weddings. The entire set is available for weddings, starting at $5,625 for up to fifty guests. This includes practically every detail from invitations to the gourmet buffet dinner.

"We didn't get married at Apacheland because of Elvis," says Sherri. "It was just a perk that he filmed there. We did know that we wanted a western wedding. We like country music, and that's just us. Everyone in the wedding dressed western. The girls wore broomstick skirts and black granny boots, and the guys wore black western-cut tuxedo jackets and black cowboy hats."

Brides at Apacheland prepare in the feed and grain store, but they're surrounded by more than wheat and rye. "Victoria Principal used the feed and grain store as a dressing room when she filmed *River Wild* at Apacheland," says Birmingham, "so it's fixed up kind of funky elegant. It's got a red velvet couch, brocade curtains, and a lighted mirror."

Ready for action, Sherri and Kris rode in an antique horse-drawn surrey with the fringe on top from the feed and grain store down the wide main street to the Elvis Presley Memorial Chapel. Their 150 guests filled the eighty-five-seat white wooden church to overflowing. Even though some guests had to stand outside and look in through the windows' lace curtains, Sherri and Kris knew they had picked the perfect location when the bullets started to fly. "Everyone loved it," says Sherri. "Even though one little girl was crying, that's all anybody talked about."

"Except for the ring bearer, we didn't tell anyone that was going to happen," says Kris. "We wanted to do something fun to lighten up the ceremony."

The fun continued after the wedding when everyone sauntered over to the Paladin Hotel—home of Richard Boone for his television series "Paladin"—for some great country music and steak grilled over Arizona oak and pecan. After dinner, Kris and Sherri danced the wedding waltz where Linda Evans danced for Kenny Rogers in *The Gambler* and where Juliet Prowse danced with Brian Keith in *2nd Chance*.

The western atmosphere was contagious. "I had a friend at the wedding who never liked country music," says Kris. "But after the wedding, he started listening to it. He still wears the cowboy hat he wore to the wedding, and he still listens to country music."

Kris and Sherri both agree that their action-packed wedding ceremony, the surrey ride, the sun setting over the desert cactus, the western figure silhouettes glowing from Apacheland's buildings, and the howl of coyotes from the Superstition Mountains made them feel like stars in one of the best and most memorable westerns ever made.

Apacheland Movie Ranch
4369 South Kings Ranch Road, Gold Canyon, Ariz. 85219
602-288-0957

Boot Hill Musuem
KANSAS

Dedicated to the memory of Unice and Janet Stigall.

When Dodge City, Kansas, was founded in 1872 it had a lot going for it. Its location on the Santa Fe Trail—the great prairie highway—meant that thousands of buffalo hunters, railroad workers, soldiers, cowboys, drifters, and travelers would be passing through. It was destined to be a major trade and social center, an oasis of civilization in the vast ocean of prairie.

There was one thing, however, that early Dodge City lacked: law enforcement. And there was one thing it had in abundance: saloons. At one time sixteen saloons lined the town's two blocks. Fueled by alcohol, men with independent and powerful personalities settled their differences in shoot-outs in the streets. Lawlessness reigned. Dodge City became known as "The Wickedest Little City in America," "The Bibulous Babylon," and "A Den of Thieves and Cutthroats." Troublemakers and penniless drifters were not afforded a proper burial in nearby Fort Dodge, so they were buried with their boots on in a windswept spot of cactus-covered prairie that came to be known as Boot Hill Cemetery.

Although law enforcement eventually came to Dodge through famed peacemakers such as Wyatt Earp and Bat Masterson, the town continues to conjure up images of rough-and-tumble lawlessness. Even today, when people want to flee a bad situation they say "Let's get the hell out of Dodge." The television series "Gunsmoke" also helped solidify Dodge City's reputation as the quintessential western town.

Today, the Boot Hill Museum allows visitors a kinder, gentler, safer taste of the old west. Located on the edge of downtown Dodge City, the Boot Hill Museum re-creates the businesses along old Dodge City's Front Street, many of which burned to the ground in 1885. There's the Long Branch Saloon, made famous in "Gunsmoke," Collards Dry Goods, a blacksmith shop, and a tonsorial parlor, to name a few.

The only people falling dead in this Dodge City are the actors who hit the dusty streets during the daily staged reenactments of gunfights. "We Welcome Your Boots on Our Hill," a brochure proclaims. Indeed, more than a hundred thousand people from around the world trod through the town each year.

It might seem illogical to marry in a place associated with death and discord, but it's the spirit of down-to-earth adventure that draws couples to wed at the Boot Hill Museum. "Couples can have everything from gunfighters to can can dancers at their wedding," says Bonnie Jernigan, Boot Hill Museum's entertainment director, who also plays Miss Kitty from "Gunsmoke" in the daily variety show.

"We have complete costume rental, everything from can can dresses, ball gowns, and prairie dresses for the women, to drover's outfits with cowboy boots and gun belts for the men. Couples usually get married on the stage in the Long Branch, but we even arranged for one couple to get married alongside the ruts from the Santa Fe Trail out on the prairie west of town." Weddings at Boot Hill start with a $50 rental fee of the facility.

Paula Stigall, a medical technologist from Ozark, Missouri, grew up in Dodge City and is well aware of its cowboy reputation. "When I was in high school our band went to Washington, D.C.," she remembers. "When the band members got back, they said that people had actually asked them if we still rode horses in Dodge City!" But when it came time to marry, she and her husband, Jim, a surgical technician whom she met at work, were only too happy to make the town's history a backdrop for their own historic event.

"I'm kind of a cowgirl," says Paula. "I've always worn western clothes and listened to country music. My grandparents had a farm, and that's the way I grew up. I've always wanted a western wedding. I'm not the type to dress up in a little white frilly dress. When my mother told me about weddings at the museum, I thought it'd be the perfect place."

"At first I thought we should get married in a church," says Jim, who grew up on a farm in Missouri. "But then I realized a wedding didn't have to be in a church to be meaningful. A lot of times when you have a church it's all elaborate, but it's also all set up, so it's kind of fake. A wedding at the Boot Hill Museum was more down to earth and more fun."

"We already knew we were going to be nervous about getting married," says Paula, "so why be uncomfortable where we were? At the Boot Hill Museum we were in clothes we loved and in a place that was cute to us. It took the nervousness off."

The clothes they loved were, naturally, western. Paula wore a white tea-length hand-crocheted dress and white boots. Jim and his groomsmen wore black jeans, white tuxedoshirts, and black vests. Just in case some roaming outlaw might happen through town, the men also carried replicas of Colt 45's at their sides.

Boot Hill is not on the black limo line, so Paula, her mother, and her maid of honor climbed aboard the bright red stagecoach of the Boot Hill Stage Line to ride from the bridal dressing area in the Long Branch Saloon to the wedding site. "Some of the tourists were taking pictures of me getting in the stagecoach," says Paula. "I thought, Hold on! This is for real! I told them I wasn't part of the act, but they didn't care."

Chilly weather had Jim and Paula moving their outdoor wedding into the Occident, a restaurant where framed photos of "Gunsmoke" stars line the walls—occasionally, people who have visited Boot Hill have been disappointed to find that the "Gunsmoke" characters were fictional. The judge who performed the traditional ceremony also wore western attire as did many of their fifty guests. Jim and Paula chose country tunes by George Strait and Tracy Byrd for the ceremony, while Jernigan as Miss Kitty provided period piano music.

After the ceremony, Jim and Paula rode off in the stagecoach heading for the reception at the Long Branch Saloon. Their guests, however, could not immediately follow as they were held up by a holdup. As soon as the stagecoach rumbled out of sight, a band of rowdy undesirables from the wrong side of the tracks stormed into the Occident and put a stop to any further celebration.

Jim and Paula Stigall stand in front of the stagecoach

Their voices muffled by the bandannas hiding their faces, the outlaws yelled, "Everybody out!" as they rounded up the guests like so many startled cattle and herded them into the green. Shooting their pistols into the air, the desperados demanded money and valuables while the guests looked anxiously around them for their possessions. When the judge protested their uncivil behavior, one unsavory fellow grabbed him, stuck a gun to his throat, and snarled, "Shut up or I'll shoot you.'"

Meanwhile, Jim and Paula, far from being terrified by the wedding day shoot-out, were stifling rounds of laughter. "As soon as Jim and I pulled away in the stagecoach we heard the gunfire and started cracking up!" says Paula. "We didn't tell anyone the raid was going to happen. People had their hands up or were looking for their purses and wallets. On the video you can see that my grandmother was a little worried. She was like, 'Oh my God!'"

Peace was restored when the sheriff showed up, confronted the outlaws, and drove the disgruntled crew out of town. "My little nephews just ate it up," says Paula. "They got so riled up, someone had to walk them around a bit to calm them down."

Calm, however, was relatively short-lived. Once everyone had gathered in the Long Branch for the reception, several of the gunmen had the audacity to slip back into town and belly up to the bar for a few beers and a handful of wedding mints. It wasn't long before a fight broke out.

"These two guys at the bar just started pushing and shoving each other," says Jim. "It started out as one of those 'I said, you said' fights. Then one guy got real mad and knocked the other down. All our guests got real quiet, but then all of a sudden the two guys got over it and went right back to drinking their beers. It was just like those fights you see in old TV movies where the piano player starts up again and it all goes back to normal."

"I just looked over to the bar and saw them fighting," says Paula, "so at first I was a little concerned too. Jim and I didn't really know they were going to do that. My grandmother got all worried again. I had to convince her that they were just pretending."

Although there were no can can dancers at the reception—"I wanted to be the pretty girl," declares Paula, laughing—there was cake and champagne and plenty of dancing to Jim and Paula's favorite country tunes. If couples choose to serve food, they can have anything from buffalo burgers to chuck wagon dinners with barbequed roast beef, trail beans, and cornbread.

Nobody at Jim and Paula's wedding had to do any acting when they said they loved the ceremony. "Everyone was wishing they had done something like that at their wedding," says Jim.

While a couple looking for peace and stability might have fled Dodge City in the wicked days of its youth, there's no reason now that couples beginning a stable relationship shouldn't scoot a boot to Dodge City and the Boot Hill Museum for a western wedding worth kicking up their heels about.

Boot Hill Museum, Inc,
Front Street, Dodge City, Kans. 67801
316-227-8188

Old Trail Town

CODY, WYOMING

It appears a forgotten ghost town on a sagebrush prairie, its empty buildings brown and gray and weather-beaten as they stand outlined against the Absaroka Mountains west of Cody, Wyoming.

But far from being neglected and crumbling relics of the frontier, the buildings that make up Old Trail Town are some of the most cherished in the West. If it weren't for Bob Edgar, many of these nineteenth-century structures would have reached the end of their respective trails long ago. Abandoned throughout the vast Wyoming countryside, some would have just fallen in or been destroyed by grazing cattle. Others would have been sawed up for firewood.

In 1967, Edgar, a Wyoming native, historian, archeaologist, and artist, began collecting endangered historic buildings throughout northwestern Wyoming and moving them to a five-acre plot of land west of Cody, the site of the original "Cody City" in 1895. Some buildings were brought to Trail Town in one piece. Others Edgar meticulously took apart and reassembled at the site.

Determined to preserve the legendary West he loved, Edgar and his wife, Terry, poured all their money into the project and lived for several years in a one-room log cabin on the site, hauling water and using a wood stove.

Over time, their pioneer endurance paid off. Trail Town now consists of twenty-six buildings dating from 1869 to 1901, one hundred horse-drawn vehicles, and various artifacts and memorabilia from the Wyoming frontier. The buildings—including saloons, homestead cabins, and stores—stand on either side of a set of old wagon wheel ruts still visible in the grass.

Two of Trail Town's most historic buildings are Curley's Cabin, home of the Crow Indian scout who was the only one of

Postcard of Old Trial Town

General Custer's command to escape from the Battle of the Little Bighorn in 1876, and the Outlaw's Cabin, a rendezvous spot for Butch Cassidy, the Sundance Kid, and other outlaws in Wyoming's formidable Hole-in-the-Wall country.

Edgar also worked to get grave sites of mountain-loving men and women relocated to the Trail Town Cemetery. In 1974 over two thousand people, including Robert Redford, attended the reburial of Jeremiah "Liver Eating" Johnston, the colorful (and renamed) trapper Redford portrayed in the movie *Jeremiah Johnson.*

For couples enamored of the unbridled spirit of the Wild Wyoming West, a wedding among the time-worn buildings at Trail Town is as close as they'll get to experiencing the tenacious vitality of men and women who made a colorful living in unsettled times. For the $150 rental fee, most couples wed in the 1890 livery barn or in the 1888 Rivers Saloon, reveling in the authentic Old West atmosphere of this uncommercialized tribute to frontier fortitude.

Few couples could better represent the spirit of Trail Town than Chris and Clay Gibbons of Worland, Wyoming, who got hitched at the hitching rail on the boardwalk outside the Rivers Saloon.

Wyoming natives and lovers of history, they met on the Outlaw Trail Ride, a hundred-mile guided horseback adventure through the mountains of Wyoming. Chris was a trail guide, while Clay, a well-versed storyteller and historian, entertained the riders with nightly history talks around the crackling fire. Together, they run a farm and implement store in Worland.

They both grew up in Wyoming and feel a strong connection with its open spaces, independent spirit, and colorful history. "My great grandparents rode over the Teton Pass in a buckboard," says Chris, a native of Jackson. "My grandfather, John Wort, was a great cattleman and is in the Cowboy Hall of Fame in Colorado Springs. He was a real western cowboy and my idol. That's how I got my love of horses."

For her to leave the West is unimaginable. "At one point in my life, I was about to move, but one evening I was out with my brother, who was a real estate agent. I began looking through some photos of the area in a coffee-table book at one of the houses. Suddenly I realized, 'I know all these people and these ranches.' I realized how much I loved the area and the way of life, how much I didn't want to give up on its history—my history. I never moved."

"Besides the store, my life is history," says Clay who grew up in Worland. "My dad used to drive me around the countryside when I was growing up and talk about the outlaws, the Indians, the settlers, and mountain men who made history here. I got such pleasure trying to understand what life was like back then. When I got older I became friends with Bob through our work on various history projects. We have a real passion for history."

Like Edgar, Clay has not just read and talked about history.

He was instrumental in getting a state historical marker placed at the site of the Spring Creek Raid, the last battle in the range wars between the cattlemen and the sheepmen that took place south of Ten Sleep, Wyoming, in 1909.

When it came time to wed, there was no other place Chris and Clay thought of that so perfectly reflected their spirits and lifestyle. "We were born 120 years too late," says Chris. "But being at Trail Town is the closest thing you can get to actually being in the Old West. A lot of times I've done things that weren't me. This wedding was definitely me. Since we'd both been married before, we didn't think it appropriate to have a big church wedding. Neither of us are twenty years old anymore. Also, people get to acting like robots in a traditional wedding. It didn't surprise anyone that we were getting married at Trail Town. It's what they expected."

"The first time I got married, I had nothing to say about it," adds Clay. "I just felt like a fixture. When I made a suggestion to the priest at the wedding rehearsal, he said, 'I don't tell you how to sell tractors, and you don't tell me how to do a wedding.' This time I thought, I'm going to do what I want to do. Being at Trail Town surrounded by all that history is really moving, just to stand in Butch Cassidy's cabin or on the old worn floors of the saloon. The first wedding wasn't me at all. This was me."

The Rivers Saloon, where Chris and Clay wed, is the oldest saloon in northwestern Wyoming. "It was still in good shape when it was moved from nearby Meeteetse," says Clay. "The wooden threshold shows wear from all the boots coming over it. Butch Cassidy signed a petition in front of the saloon to get a bridge built over the Greybull River. Inside, it still has the original wood floors and wainscoting, and right at eye level there's a number of original bullet holes in the door."

There was no cause for a fracas at Chris and Clay's wedding. If anything, storyteller Clay had the fifty guests in tears as he talked about the support he and Chris felt they received for their new life together. With the fresh winds of May blowing in from the mountains and across the Trail Town grass, Chris, wearing a short ivory dress, and Clay, wearing black jeans, a black frock coat and string tie, and a black felt hat, stood on the boardwalk of the Rivers Saloon, underneath a bleached rack of deer antlers, and pledged to be partners along life's trail.

After the short ceremony, officiated by a local minister, everyone moseyed over to the livery barn for the reception with some live country music. While many Old West towns stage gun battles to startle the guests, Chris and Clay's guests were genuinely alarmed by a real shoot-out when Edgar commenced to extinguish Chris and Clay's flame of passion.

"Chris and I lit two candles, made an inverted **V** with their joined flames, then stood in front of a wooden post," says Chris. "Then Bob took a .45 pistol, aimed at the flame, then shot it right out. When we told people what he was about to do, they said, 'He's going to do what?! You just got married, now he's going to kill you!' But Bob is an excellent marksman. One time, he shot something out of the Prince of Monaco's mouth when he was visiting Cody."

Chris and Clay agree that their Trail Town wedding was a truly western affair. "At the end of the day, we were watching the sun go down behind the canyon while the band was singing about the bend in the river and the prairie light," says Clay. "People in the city can have their bright lights. This was the perfect way to end our day."

But the spirit of the Old West followed Chris and Clay even after they left Trail Town. "We stopped into a nightclub in Cody for a drink when all of a sudden we heard all this noise," says Chris. "Here, this guy comes riding right through the bar on a horse! It was amazing! But instead of being really shocked, all I could think was, 'That's a pretty cool horse!'"

"Will Rogers once said, 'There's nothing better for the inside of a man as the outside of a horse,'" says Clay. "Nothing draws Chris and I closer together than a horse, so we felt pretty good about it all!"

Chris and Clay with Bob Edgar,
creator of Old Trail Town

While Chris and Clay dream of the time they can devote their life to nothing but history and horses, they have many fond memories of how their meeting on the Outlaw Trail happily led to their legal union on the boot-trodden wooden aisle of Old Trail Town.

Old Trail Town
Cody, Wyo. 82414
307-587-5302

9

Love Me Tender:
Marriage With the King

The unifying power of Christ the King is the focal point at many couples' weddings, but for some couples, the King of Rock and Roll, Elvis Presley, makes the King of Kings take a back pew for the day.

Whether performing or witnessing the ceremony, Elvis lives on in the wedding industry. While a couple vows to stick with each other till death do they part, fans of Elvis have remained true to their musical messiah even after his death and have summoned him to sing at every conceivable wedding setting. His resurrected presence lends just the right "sacred" touch to an otherwise secular affair.

It's not known whether Elvis sang at his own wedding—he married Priscilla in 1967 at the Aladdin Hotel in Las Vegas—but since Elvis has become synonymous with Vegas, thousands of couples have walked down the town's neon aisles each year while a man in a jumpsuit croons "Love Me Tender."

But the Strip does not have a monopoly on Elvis-related weddings. Numerous sites throughout the United States attract couples merely because they're associated with the King.

Each year thousands of faithful Elvis fans make the pilgrimage to Tupelo, Mississippi, to visit the humble two-room cottage of his birth. The adjacent Elvis Presley Memorial Chapel, complete with pews and stained-glass windows, allows couples to wed in a sacred setting close to the hallowed birth site. Newlyweds often stop into Tupelo's Elvis-themed McDonald's, which displays an amazingly extensive and thoughtful collection of Elvis memorabilia.

Worlds away from Tupelo, the Fern Grotto in Kauai, Hawaii, welcomes couples into its misty embrace. Elvis filmed parts of *Blue Hawaii* on the Wailua River outside the Fern Grotto, and this large misty cave beneath fern-covered rocks has become Kauai's busiest tourist attraction and a favorite wedding spot. Couples marrying here never lack for musical accompaniment. Lei-bedecked tourists in glass-bottomed boats are encouraged to belt out the "Hawaiian Wedding Song," just like Elvis.

Elvis and Priscilla spent their wedding night in the Alexander Estate in Palm Springs, California, now known as the Honeymoon Hideaway. Available for rental, this coral-colored stucco home also houses some Elvis memorabilia, including a replica of the newlyweds' bed where Lisa Marie was supposedly conceived. Plans even include making Elvis' honeymoon an annual celebration.

While Elvis has become the topic of academic conferences and scholarly dissertations, the real love he inspires in his fans—like the ineluctable chemistry of attraction between a couple—can never be wholly or rationally explained. Whether the King of Kitsch or the most revered example of the American Dream, as untouchable as the flag or the crucifix, Elvis lives on.

What's he doing at so many weddings? Perhaps the unconditional love his fans have for both the man and the myth provides a good example of the undying love a marriage requires.

Graceland Wedding Chapel
LAS VEGAS, NEVADA

"I know about forty-five or fifty Elvises," says Bill Salton, wedding coordinator at the Graceland Wedding Chapel in Las

Vern and Kathy McMurray and Elvis

Vegas, "but only about ten of them are good enough to make a living at it."

Norm Jones is one of the chosen few. Five days a week, he arrives at Graceland, dons one of his jumpsuits, grooms his sideburns, and waits for couples to stop by. His wait in the wings is never long. Every week, about ninety couples come to Graceland to marry or renew their vows, and over half of them want to do so in the presence of the king. Although Elvis doesn't officiate Graceland weddings, he'll sing the bride down the aisle, give her away, and perform a mini-concert after the ceremony.

Having impersonated Elvis thousands of times, Jones, whose large frame has him playing the seventies Elvis, remains adamant that his personal life remain separate from that of his "boss." "Some Elvis impersonators get into the business, see some success, and end up taking it off stage as well," he says.

"Their ego takes them over. If I can make people happy, that's what's worthwhile."

Jones' association with the Mighty One goes back beyond the wild lights of Vegas to the Wild West. "I played in a band throughout Montana and Utah," he says, "and I kept getting requests to do Elvis. I've worn sideburns since I was seventeen and I guess people thought I looked like Elvis. I never minded doing Elvis. I appreciated him and respected his music, but I never studied him a lot. I fell into the voice pretty naturally. It's just a feeling I have."

Couples marrying at Graceland also have a feeling. "Many times, the couples who marry here are dyed-in-the-wool Elvis fans," says Salton. "They come here because the ceremony is meaningful and we take it seriously. There was even a lady from England who came in just to see the chapel. Elvis' marriage license is on display here, and when we gave her a copy of it, she broke down crying. She just bawled her eyes out. Her husband had to apologize for her. He said she was a big fan. But people also have fun with the ceremony. We've had grooms that show up dressed like Elvis. Bon Jovi got married here and ordered five other professional Elvises to be here too."

Although named for Elvis's outrageously opulent Memphis home, Graceland Wedding Chapel appeals to the lover of a subtler Elvis. From the outside, it resembles a small white country church with a steeple and stained-glass windows accented with mother-of-pearl. White picket fencing lines the walkways, which have been named Priscilla Drive and Elvis Avenue.

Inside, there's no shag carpeting or fur-covered lampshades. The thirty-five-seat chapel is decorated a tasteful antique white and maroon, and a crystal chandelier hangs from the ceiling. A small podium at the front of the chapel stands before a stained glass window of roses and doves. Besides its name, the only indication of the chapel's association with Elvis is the Wall of Fame, an entire wall in the chapel lobby covered with photographs of couples who have wed with the King.

Graceland Wedding Chapel has actually been a Vegas landmark for close to sixty years. Originally called the Gretna Green, its owner was a friend of Elvis'. At one time, he had asked Elvis if he could rename the chapel in his honor, and Elvis gave him his blessing. Shortly after Elvis' death, the chapel was renamed Graceland and its association with the King began.

In 1988 it hired a full-time Elvis, one of the first chapels to do so. Since then, Elvis impersonators have become as commonplace in Vegas as slot machines, but true lovers of the King still head for the Graceland Wedding Chapel, where wedding packages run from $55 to $220; Elvis is an additional $120.

There was no doubt that Kathy and Vern McMurray of Cedar Rapids, Iowa, loved each other; they'd been living together twenty-five years when they decided to get married. "After being together so long, we certainly didn't want a traditional wedding," says Kathy, a seamstress. "Several years ago we were in Vegas and saw a couple renew their vows at Graceland. It was really nice. I'm a big Elvis fan. When our son moved out, I turned his bedroom into the Elvis room. I have a plate collection, clocks, guitars, mirrors, pictures. Anytime any of the girls I play pool with buys me a gift, they buy me something with Elvis. I've always liked his music. I even got to see him perform in Ames, Iowa, in 1974 even though I was nine months pregnant. Vern and I knew we wanted to go to Vegas to get married. To go there and not do Elvis would've been silly for us. All my friends would've asked, 'Why didn't you do Elvis?'"

"I'm not really an Elvis fan," says Vern, a printing press operator, "but I was willing to do whatever Kathy wanted. We originally thought we'd just go out there ourselves, but when we told our friends we were getting married, they started buying tickets to go out too. I guess they wanted to see whether we'd really go through with it. We had about twenty-five guests."

Although Kathy felt it would have been silly to go to Vegas and not get married with Elvis, she also admits she felt a little hesitant to walk down the aisle on his arm. She laughs. "I didn't know I'd have to walk down the aisle with him. I did feel a little bit silly! I mean, he is an impersonator. Although I like Elvis' music, I'm not one of those women you see crying over his grave."

Despite her professed embarrassment, she carried off the walk with aplomb. Wearing a cream-colored dress, she took the arm of Elvis in his beaded black jumpsuit and cheerfully began the short walk to the podium. Meanwhile, Elvis played his guitar and sang "Love Me Tender."

After the short ceremony, Elvis sang several more songs before finishing his act with the classic "Viva Las Vegas" and tossing Kathy the famed Elvis scarf to throw over her shoulders. Happily wed, Kathy and Vern posed for some pictures, then went off to celebrate their once-in-a-lifetime Elvis wedding. Meanwhile, Jones took a glass of water and prepared once again to impersonate the king for another star-struck couple.

Graceland Elvises get a bit more involved with vow renewals, actually performing the ceremony. When Donna and Richard Wallock of Tinley Park, Illinois, renewed their vows at Graceland, Brendan Paul, Graceland's part-time Elvis, happily officiated.

"I suggested we go to Vegas and renew our vows," says Richard, a controller. "Donna added the Elvis. I'm not a big fan, but Elvis is synonymous with Vegas, so that was all right with me."

"My mother was a big Elvis fan," says Donna, a hotel worker. "When I was in sixth grade we went to Graceland, and my mom jumped onto a stone wall and climbed a hill to pick some leaves off a tree in Elvis' yard. She still has the leaves. Even though I grew up knowing all Elvis' music, I'm not a fanatic. I don't have the velvet Elvis painting on the wall, but I think everyone is a little bit of an Elvis fan.

"Since Richard and I had a traditional wedding ten years ago, we wanted to do something a little crazy. We called the Graceland Chapel, thinking if Elvis wasn't there he wouldn't be anywhere. I also wanted to pick our Elvis. I didn't want an Army Elvis or a Hawaiian Elvis. I wanted the jumpsuit Elvis. That's the whole thing for me. I wanted the fringe and beads."

Their Elvis did not disappoint. Decked out in white jumpsuit, he was exactly what she was looking for—Paul's Elvis wardrobe also includes a sports jacket for the fifties Elvis and black leather for the sixties Elvis. "The ceremony was lighthearted," says Donna. "He sang 'It's Now or Never,' then told us it was our last chance to back out. During the vows we had to promise to love each other tender and not treat each other like a hound dog, not to step on each other's blue suede shoes. Afterward he sang 'Viva Las Vegas,' and we both just started dancing and singing along. We were getting a little crazy!"

"I was surprised," admits Richard. "I didn't expect as much of a show, the caliber of the performance and the attention to detail. He was really good. He looked better than Elvis! And even though he's not a reverend or a pastor or a priest, the ceremony was still meaningful in its own way."

Judging by the thousands of couples who wed or renew their vows at Graceland each year, Elvis' ability to stir passion and invite romantic, even spiritual, reflection appears to be growing stronger with the passing years. "He's a legend," says Donna. "Until the day everyone's not on the earth, he'll still be as strong."

Graceland Wedding Chapel
619 Las Vegas Boulevard, Las Vegas, Nev. 89101
800-824-5732 / www.gracelandchapel.com

24-Hour Church of Elvis

PORTLAND, OREGON

Elvis hasn't knocked Christ off his throne quite yet, but he's nudged him over a bit and forced him to share the seat. Be the intention reverent or irreverent, the widespread adoration of the King of Rock and Roll has taken on a distinctly religious flavor.

But while countless cathedrals, chapels, and churches have been built in Christ's honor, devotees of Elvis have had few churches in which to gather and praise their king. That is, until

Stephanie Pierce—Georgetown law graduate and artist—founded the 24-Hour Church of Elvis in Portland, Oregon, in 1985.

That the Church of Elvis is also a coin-operated art gallery and wedding chapel should tell potential "members" that Pierce's is an irreverent homage to the King—Pierce says she doesn't even like Elvis—but in its own kitschy way, the 24-Hour Church of Elvis honors the spirit of the man who has simply refused to die.

Pierce's "church" is actually several rooms above a Thai restaurant in downtown Portland. Its creed: "What we can't get rid of we might as well worship." The items in her "Where's the Art!!" gallery provide a foundation for some distinctly different devotions. From a life-size cutout of Pamela Anderson to the Bionic Beauty Salon to Church of Elvis chalices—a.k.a. coffee mugs—and two dollar bits of cloth from the D-Luxe Shroud of Elvis, Pierce pays tribute to the many popular manifestations of our obsession with fame, fortune, fashion, and faith. "Our Holy Trinity is plastic, Styrofoam, and Elvis," she says.

Weddings began at the Church of Elvis when the coin-operated Miracle of the Spinning Elvises occupied the church's storefront in its first location. Photos of Elvis inside big prize buttons wildly rotated when patrons deposited a quarter, while a computer-generated voice offered confessions, catechism, and "cheap but not legal" weddings with multiple-choice vows.

Soon, couples requested cheap but legal weddings at the Church of Elvis, and Pierce, an ordained minister in the Universal Life Church, complied. From grooms in plaid flannel bathrobes to brides in full traditional attire, hundreds of couples have wed over the years at the Church of Elvis in ceremonies that run from $25 to $40.

Couples willing to spend an extra $25 can have Elvis impersonator John Schroder sing at the wedding. Couples looking for a slick Vegas-style Elvis with jumpsuit and sideburns, however, have come to the wrong place. "We're more into reinterpreting the reinterpretation of Elvis," says Pierce. "Our

Elvis doesn't look like Elvis. He doesn't wear Elvis clothes or sound like Elvis. He doesn't always sing Elvis songs. It's more a Zen thing. It's Elvis as if he were a Church of Elvis Elvis."

Schroder, a cult figure of sorts in Portland for the playing of his cardboard guitar at the popular Saturday Market, is a bearded and bespectacled thirty-five-year-old performer whose idiosyncratic impersonation of the King earned him the title "Best Elvis Impersonator" by Portland's weekly alternative newspaper. Several years ago, he began visiting the church, befriended Pierce, and soon found himself called into service.

"I started doing Elvis when I was in high school," says Schroder. "It started out as a joke. My friends would ask me to go outside at lunch and sing. I try to get as close to Elvis' voice as possible. I've watched some of his concerts to get the feel of how he walks, how he moves. I enjoy singing. I enjoy the smiles I get from people."

That Schroder neither looked like Elvis nor sounded like Elvis did not stop Kerry Krueger and Tom Hohn of McDonald, Pennsylvania, from having him perform at their wedding. "Neither of us wanted to do anything remotely traditional," says Kerry, a web page designer. "I am totally not a white dress person. We both think a traditional wedding is such a gross waste of money. We wanted something fun that would get us legally married. Our original idea was to go to Vegas and get married by the biggest, ugliest, fattest, greasiest Elvis we could find. We wanted something completely irreverent."

"But then we thought, 'Nah, a lot of people do that,'" says Tom, a software consultant who met Kerry following a performance of his band, the Cynics. "It's become almost a cliché."

"I'm from Portland," explains Kerry, "so I knew about Stephanie and the Church of Elvis. She's just awesome, a ball of energy. When I suggested it to Tom he thought it was a good idea. He'd been to Stephanie's store when it was in another location, so he kind of knew what to expect."

There is no altar at the Church of Elvis, no pews, no stained glass windows. Weddings take place in a room crammed full of "art." "There was stuff just sitting around everywhere," says Tom. "You had to think creatively to recognize it as art. There were some naked mannequins and collages. It was really crowded. If there had been five more people, there would not have been room to move."

Kerry and Tom had about twenty guests at the wedding, including five tourists who happened into the gallery and asked if they could stay for the ceremony. Since many of the guests had never been to the Church of Elvis, the first sight of the church was a shocker, especially to Kerry's mother.

"The look on her face was priceless." Kerry laughs. "She looked like she was going to pass out. Her face turned ash colored and she said, 'You're getting married here? Where's the church? Where's the wedding supposed to be?' We had a heck of a time finding chairs for her and my father to sit in."

Once everyone was settled and accustomed to the surroundings, the ceremony began. Like any church wedding, ceremonies at the Church of Elvis incorporate ritual. "Stephanie takes the traditional ceremony and turns it sideways," says Kerry, "but it's really a lot of fun." First, there's the wedding march of the bridal party to the tune of "Pomp and Circumstance."

At the Church of Elvis, guests don't have to worry about finding discrete ways to check out everyone's wedding finery. Once assembled in the church, everyone, including guests, spins around during the Fashion Twirl to show off their outfits while Brenda Lee's "It's a Marshmallow World" plays in the background.

Kerry wore an ankle-length mocha-colored satin slip dress and carried a bouquet of plastic flowers. "I didn't bring a bouquet," says Kerry, "so Stephanie pulled out this dusty, musty bouquet of tacky-looking plastic flowers for me to carry. What's funny is that everyone who looks at our wedding pictures says, 'Oh, what a lovely bouquet.'"

Tom wore black jeans, black shirt, and a plaid jacket.

Although the bride's attire usually takes center stage at a

wedding, at the Church of Elvis, it's Pierce's ministerial garb that demands attention. In her pink satin ruffled dress with multicolored sequins and trim, yellow stockings, and red shoes, she seems more fairy godmother than minister. For extra power she carries a pink feather duster/magic wand.

And then there's Elvis. For Kerry and Tom's wedding, Schroder wore a red T-shirt and a greenish-colored jacket and pants.

Although guests may depart into the Portland night confused as to why a couple chose to marry at the Church of Elvis, they'll never leave confused about why the couple chose to marry. During Testimonial Time, Pierce invites the guests to talk about the couple and offer reasons why they believe the couple should be married. This is followed by the Inspirational Message where the couple explains why they want to marry each other. Pierce then plays the section from the movie *It's a Wonderful Life* where Jimmy Stewart, realizing the importance of his family, begs to be returned to his wife and children.

Next comes the Touching Legalization of the Vows where, with a touch of the magic wand, Pierce has couples exchange rings and pronounces them "spouse and spouse." "I didn't have a ring for Tom because he doesn't like rings," says Kerry, "so during the ring exchange, Stephanie gave me a plastic spider ring to put on Tom's finger. It was one of the best parts of the ceremony."

Finally, Elvis gets a chance to perform a mini-concert for the newlyweds. During the Big Kiss and First Dance, he sings "Love Me Tender," but then it's anyone's guess as to what he'll do next. "The Church of Elvis Elvis doesn't impersonate Elvis," says Tom. "He channels Elvis, and Elvis tells him what's appropriate to sing. He knows the words to hundreds of songs, but most of the songs he sings aren't even Elvis songs. At our wedding he sang things like 'The Candy Man Can.'"

"But he's very warm and friendly," says Kerry. "He asked me if I had any special requests, but he did do one unusual thing. When he found out that my father's name is Fred Krueger, he kept channeling Freddy Krueger from *Friday the 13th* to the ceremony. He'd move his fingers around like he had razor blades on the ends of them. My father didn't get it at the time. He was already overcome by emotion and crying, so he wasn't quite connected with what was going on."

Anyone in the neighborhood of the Church of Elvis certainly knows what's going on when the Traditional Sidewalk Parade makes its way down the street. Grabbing her "Applause" sign, Pierce leads the wedding party to Powell's Bookstore, a popular Portland hangout. "Kerry's sister carried a 'Just Married' sign," says Tom, "while our other guests dragged tin cans on the sidewalk. Even the tourists who were at our wedding joined in. Stephanie was waving and shoving the Applause sign at cars. They all honked. Then we paraded into Powell's Bookstore. It was Saturday night and really crowded. We got a huge ovation. Then we marched back to the store where we hung out and talked to Elvis for a while."

It was quite a night for guests used to the white gown and black tux affair. "Tom and I loved the ceremony, but some of our guests were a bit horrified," says Kerry. She laughs. "Everyone who couldn't think of something to say about the ceremony kept telling me how beautiful I looked!"

"When my parents saw our wedding pictures, they just laughed and said, 'Oh boy!'" says Tom. "They know me by now and know that I have untraditional tastes. Nothing surprises them. But my ninety-year old grandmother asked, 'Who's this woman in the pink Cinderella outfit, and what's that thing she's holding?' She was kind of surprised when I told her it was the minister with her magic wand.

"When I showed the pictures to friends they either thought the wedding looked like a great time or they didn't get it. They'd be looking for an Elvis that actually looked like an Elvis. Some people asked, 'Why would you want to do this? A wedding is a sacred ceremony. Why would you want to treat it like that?' But the wedding reflects our alternative mind-set. Even though we're both really successful in our careers, we do things our own way."

"Segments of our life are sort of immature," Kerry says, laughing, "but we're responsible human beings. We own a house and drive normal automobiles. We just happen to have bizarre interests, but I think the ceremony was very meaningful."

While the 24-Hour Church of Elvis may seem blasphemous to those Elvis fans who keep candlelit shrines in their homes to their king of kings, it's a place of creative delight to anyone able to laugh at our outrageous round-the-clock obsession with the posthumous career of this man-turned-myth.

24-Hour Church of Elvis
720 SW Ankeny, Portland, Oreg. 97205
503-226-3671 / www.churchofelvis.com

Viva Las Vegas Wedding Chapel's
Viva Las Vegas Wedding

LAS VEGAS, NEVADA

When Elvis began his run of 837 consecutive sold-out shows at the Las Vegas International in 1969, he was well on his way to becoming the sun around which all the other stars in this brightly lit city paled in comparison.

His effect on his fans was dazzling. Blinded by love, women brawled over props and rushed the stage for a sweaty kiss. In a city that encouraged excess, the incomparable allure of Elvis became an excuse to let it all hang out even more. Given the license the king gave people to let their emotions rule, it's not surprising that he's been summoned back so often.

"When I'm behind those glasses, I can get away with almost anything," says Ron DeCar who, as Elvis, presides over themed weddings at his Viva Las Vegas Wedding Chapel. "When people on the street see me as Elvis, they start screaming, 'Elvis! Elvis! We saw Elvis!' They just go crazy!"

With an estimated three thousand Elvis impersonators nationwide, DeCar has a lot of company when it comes to

Dave and Peggy Underhill and the cast of characters
at their wedding

stirring up excitement. "I started doing Elvis when I performed
on a cruise ship," he says. "There was a blond singer and me, so
since I have dark hair I got asked to be Elvis. I never thought
about doing him myself."

But when DeCar left his job with the cruise ship and moved to
Las Vegas, Elvis followed. "I sang at weddings and people would
ask, 'Do you do Elvis?' Since I had done him so many times, I just
started doing him again."

DeCar's chance stumbling into the role of the King eventually led to his calculated decision to open the Viva Las Vegas Wedding Chapel. Although he offers everything from Camelot to Beach Party weddings at prices ranging from $490 to $650, it's still Elvis that about 70 percent of his couples invite to their big show. And while his Blue Hawaii Elvis Wedding comes complete with coconut trees and hula dancers—a Priscilla impersonator can even stand by her man—it's his Viva Las Vegas Wedding with its show girls, roulette wheel, craps game, and, of course, Elvis, that proves a show stopper.

"Our wedding video definitely draws crowds," says Dave Underhill, an attorney from Roseville, Michigan, who wed Peggy Underhill, an office manager, in a Viva Las Vegas ceremony. "We think we'll put it on sale for $19.95."

The odds are high that those who'd buy would not be disappointed. "We thought if we started out laughing, we'd stay laughing," says Peggy, who met Dave at a gym. "I've never witnessed a big traditional wedding where the couple wasn't ready to kill each other afterward. We weren't willing to do that over a ceremony that's over so quickly."

"Planning a traditional wedding is like a job that you spend twenty grand on," says Dave. He laughs. "We thought we'd go to Vegas and lose the money on gambling and not on a wedding. Since we got engaged at sunset on an island in Aruba, we'd already done the 'cute romantic' thing, and if anyone's going to marry you, why not Elvis? We thought about the Graceland chapel, but we wanted something a little flashier. A Viva Las Vegas wedding was more in tune with the surroundings. There's enough seriousness in life as it is.

"We're not Elvis flunkies in that we dream of going to Memphis," says Peggy, "but I personally admire a performer whose music lives on. Actually, my ten-year-old son Teddy was the real fan! He went through this phase where he dressed up like Elvis and had Elvis stuff all over his room and collected his tapes. We had no choice but to listen to Elvis, so I knew he would like the wedding. But since Dave did most of the planning, no one, not even me, knew quite what to expect."

Come "opening day" in Vegas, Elvis had a little help in keeping the ceremony from becoming too serious or sentimental. "We've always liked Pee-Wee Herman," says Dave, "so I arranged to have him walk Peggy down the aisle. If you want to keep it light, you have to have Pee-Wee!"

There was certainly enough light from the popping flashbulbs of their fans as Dave and Peggy arrived for the event in a 1956 pink Cadillac. There was nothing understated or demure about their wedding attire. Peggy wore a long red-and-gold sequined evening dress, and Dave wore a tuxedo with a gold-sequined bow tie and cummerbund.

If Dave and Peggy were at all overdressed for their ceremony—at least by traditional standards—the two Vegas show girls who mingled with their guests were definitely underdressed. Both show stoppers wore silver-sequined bikinis adorned with blue feather boas, towering blue and silver feathered headdresses, and elbow-length blue gloves.

"If not necessarily risqué, the chapel decorations were definitely risky." Large playing cards lined the aisle leading to the front of the chapel where the outline of a craps game lay on the floor. Front and center stood a roulette wheel under a photograph of Elvis, while a twirling disco ball provided glittery and dramatic lighting. The only thing white at this wedding was the theatrical fog that billowed down the aisle.

When show time arrived, Elvis in his spangled jumpsuit stood center stage crooning "Love Me Tender," while Pee-Wee escorted Peggy down the aisle. Rather, Pee-Wee walked beside her down the aisle as he was wringing his hands together in typical high-strung Pee-Wee fashion and couldn't take hold of her arm.

As official master of ceremonies, Elvis led Dave and Peggy through some distinctly Vegas prenuptial rituals. Since every couple will argue down the road over who does what chore, Dave and Peggy took steps to prevent these future altercations by spinning the roulette wheel of obligations. "We each had two turns to spin the wheel," says Peggy. "I got 'Do the dishes' twice! Dave got vacuuming, but he also got that he had to give me a kiss."

Since marriage remains somewhat of a gamble, a game of craps played with large oversized dice seemed appropriate. "We each rolled to see who'd be the first to say their vows," says Peggy. "I rolled a seven and Dave rolled an eleven so I guess that made us a winning couple!"

After the opening act, Elvis led Peggy and Dave into the main number, but Pee-Wee apparently hadn't had enough of the warmup. When Elvis asked if anyone objected to the marriage about to take place, Pee-Wee yelled out "Keno!" much to the delight of the audience. But despite Pee-Wee's crowd-pleasing antics, Elvis decided he would not be upstaged and continued with the ceremony.

Dave and Peggy promised to love each other tender, not to step on each other's blue suede shows, never to check into the Heartbreak Hotel. As they gazed lovingly into each other's eyes, however, the showgirls decided that things were getting too serious and that it was time for a brief intermission.

"Right in the middle of our vows, the showgirls started walking around with trays of drinks calling, 'Cocktails! Cocktails!'" says Peggy. "Everyone had to stop and have a drink even though it was only water."

Once everyone was loosened up again, Act II began, culminating in the jackpot—the successful marriage of Peggy and Dave. Elvis brought down the house with "Viva Las Vegas," while Dave and Peggy received a standing ovation when they danced down the aisle with Pee-Wee to his trademark song "Tequila."

"It was a lot of fun," says Peggy. "Everyone was laughing and had a good time, although they probably thought the ceremony was going to be a little more serious. It was definitely very light. No one was crying."

"My mom thinks she got the wrong kid" Dave laughs. "She

kept saying, 'I can't believe what I'm seeing.' Mostly she wanted to know if it was legal."

"Throughout the ceremony, my dad just sat there like, 'What is going on?'" says Peggy. "But we're old enough to pick our own wedding. It wasn't romantic in the traditional sense, but it was romantic to us because it was memorable. We'll always have fond memories of it."

"The more secure you are the more you can steer away from tradition," says Dave. "Life is short! Play hard!

While Dave and Peggy returned to their professional careers in Michigan, their free-for-all attitude, as represented by Elvis, spread to their family. "Back home, Dave's mother had a reception for us at a fire hall," says Peggy, "and who comes walking in the door but Elvis!"

In his 1964 movie *Viva Las Vegas,* Elvis sang that the bright light city set his soul on fire. For couples burning to do something out of control for their wedding, there's no better place than Las Vegas to feed their flames of passion and no better spot than the Viva Las Vegas Wedding Chapel to extinguish any notion of traditional restraint. Here, for a $690 Viva Las Vegas Wedding, couples get a healthy dose of Elvis' hunka-hunka-burning love.

A Viva Las Vegas Wedding Chapel
1605 Franklin Ave., Las Vegas, Nev. 89104
800-574-4450 / www.vivalasvegasweddings.com

Acknowledgments

Thanks to the many couples who shared their wedding stories with me. May your lives together be as wondrous and as full of beauty and surprise as the singular sites at which you wed.